GIVING IS GOD

GIVING IS GOD

A Practical Guide to Giving

CLAUDETTE GUNTER

Giving Is God: A Practical Guide to Giving

Copyright © 2017 by Claudette Gunter
7600 W. Roosevelt Rd
Lower Level, Suite 11
Forest Park, IL 60130

Second Edition. All rights reserved.
Published in the United States of America.

All Scripture quotations in Giving Is God is taken from the King James Version of the Bible, unless otherwise noted are the following:

Scripture quotations marked (KJV) are taken from the Holy Bible, King James Version, Cambridge, 1769. Used by permission. All rights reserved.

Scripture quotations marked (AMPC®) are taken from the Amplified Bible, Classic Edition ® Copyright © 1954, 1958, 1962, 1964, 1965, 1987 by The Lockman Foundation. Used by permission

Scripture taken from the New King James Version® (NKJV®), Copyright © 1982 by Thomas Nelson. Used by permission. All rights reserved.

Scripture quotations marked (MSG) are taken from The Message. Copyright © 1993, 1994, 1995, 1996, 2000, 2001, 2002. Used by permission of NavPress Publishing Group.

Scripture quotations taken from the New American Standard Bible® (NASB), Copyright © 1960, 1962, 1963, 1968, 1971, 1972, 1973, 1975, 1977, 1995 by The Lockman Foundation Used by permission. www.Lockman.org

Scripture quotations marked (NIV®) are taken from the Holy Bible, New International Version ®, NIV ® Copyright © 1973, 1978, 1984, 2011 by Biblica, Inc. ® Used by permission. All rights reserved worldwide.

Scripture quotations are taken from the Holy Bible, New Living Translation, copyright ©1996, 2004, 2007, 2013, 2015 by Tyndale House Foundation. Used by permission of Tyndale House Publishers, Inc., Carol Stream, Illinois 60188. All rights reserved.

Published by Claudette Gunter
Thoughts expressed by author. All rights reserved.
Author's website at www.kingdomofGodflag.com®.

Cover design by Katecovers, a Fiverr Cover Designer

No part of this publication may be reproduced, stored in a retrieval system or transmitted in any way by any means, electronic, mechanical, photocopy, recording or otherwise without the prior permission of the author except as provided by USA copyright law.

Library of Congress Control Number: 2017908733
ISBN: 978-0-9990833-0-7

TO ALL GOD HATH PLACED IN MY PATH

Acknowledgment

I look back on my life and realize how I wouldn't be here if someone had not given to me [life]. First and foremost, I must honor my Father God for giving me life by creating me. I thank Jesus Christ for dying on the cross to create the opportunity for me to accept and to receive Him as my personal Lord and Savior, He gave me eternal life. I thank my Holy Spirit for leading and guiding me and giving to me by showing me all things in life. I thank my parent; John W. (1928-2015) and Earnestine Anderson for giving me natural life. I thank God for my loving husband, Aaron Gunter, our two children Cynthia and Aaron III and family, relatives, and loved ones, name by name, for giving into my life. I thank God for all the men and women of God He have placed in my path, especially my pastor; Dr. William S. Winston of Living Word Christian Center in Forest Park, Illinois, who opened my spiritual eyes to inspired me to thrive to be all God has called me to be. The Holy Spirit said this book is a tribute to God and His people. It is to let His people know that their labor is not in vain (Isaiah 65:23) so faint not (Galatians 6:9) for what you are saying is working (Mark 11:23). This book is the beginning to show them how grateful and appreciative I am and to show them for the remaining of my one hundred and twenty years (Genesis 6:3), in case Jesus tarries.

CONTENTS

Introduction 17
Action 27
Allow 29
Angels 33
Anoint / Anointed / Anointing 37
Avenge 49
Believe 51
Better World 55
Bless / Blessed / Blessing 63
Care 69
Cause 73
Character 79
Choices 83
Commission 87
Commitment 91
Communion 93
Compassion 95
Continual 97
Covenant / Promise / Vow 103
Creating Value 109
Our Daily Living 113

Deliverance	115
Diligence	117
Direction	121
Discern / Discernment	123
Do / Doer / Doing	129
Dominion	131
Dying / Eternity	135
Eradicating Poverty	139
Faith	143
Family	153
Favor	159
Fear of the Lord	163
Fearless	167
Focus	171
Forgiving	177
Freedom	179
Fruit of the Spirit	181
Fulfilling a Need	183
Gentleness	185
Gifts	187
Giving What Is Due	191
God, the Father	195
God's Way	215

God's Will 221

God's Word 225

Good / Goodness 229

Good Success 233

Grace 237

Healing / Health 241

Holiness / Holy 245

Holy Spirit 247

Honor / Respect .... .253

Hope 255

Image / Identity / Sons of God
/ Body of Christ / the Church 259

Increase / Receiving 271

Influence 277

Integrity / Trust 281

Giving Is Jesus Christ 285

Joy 291

Justice 295

Kindness 299

Kingdom of God / Kingdom of Heaven 303

Knowledge 309

Letting Go 313

Life / Salvation 315

Light 333

Love 337

Mercy 341

Giving Is Never Lacking 345

Obey / Obedience 351

Opportunity 355

Patience 357

Peace 361

Power / Reigning 365

Praise and Worship 369

Pray / Prayer / Praying 373

Prepare / Preparing 381

His Presence 385

Protection / Safety 387

Purpose 393

Reconcile 397

Redemption 401

Relationship(s) 405

Remember / Remembrance 415

Repent 419

His Rest 423

Restoration 427

Right / Righteousness 431

Sacrifice	437
Self-Control	441
Selflessness	443
Serving	445
Souls	449
Sow / Sower / Sowed / Sowing	459
Spiritual Warfare	463
Surrender	469
Testimony	473
Thankful / Thanksgiving	477
Tithe and Offerings	481
Transformation	485
Trinity	491
True / Truth	493
Understanding	501
Unity	507
Victorious	511
Voice	515
Wealth	523
Wisdom / Wise	527
Work(s)	537
Yielding Good Fruit	541

Introduction

Giving Is God was written to show how much the Bible talks about *giving* and the different ways to give. Yes, it talks about money a lot, which is how the earth operates. God gave us this provision in the Beginning (Genesis 2:10-14, KJV). Money is needed for everything; especially to get the Word of God to all the world (Mark 16:15, NKJV). This book will give a certain *giving* word and back it up with scripture(s).

There is an abundant [number] of ways to give, to make someone's life better, such as a smile; eye contact; give your time to show that we care by listening; a thank-you; and/or giving food, clothing, shelter, resources, etc. The main point of *Giving Is God* is that we are to give wherever it is needed. God is not a respecter of persons (Acts 10:34, KJV), so why are we trying to be different? God made us in His image and after His likeness (Genesis 1:27, KJV). It is true that we are not assigned to give to everyone, but we have to be sensitive to the Holy Spirit, when He tells us to do something; we must do it. We will certainly miss a blessing for being disobedient (Hebrews 4:6, AMPC). God is so good to us, if we will open our eyes and see. Yes, look with our natural eyes, but also see with our spiritual eyes, from the inside.

With our natural eyes, we will see a lot of bad things, but if we would focus on Jesus, we will see the good in that situation and He will help us through it all (John 16:33 AMPC) *Giving Is God* is this and more. Just imagine the world, when each person gives something to someone every day, it doesn't necessary have to be money, even though that helps (Ecclesiastes 10:19, KJV). An encouraging word has enough power to wake a person out of darkness (Proverbs 15:4, AMPC).

All scripture in *Giving Is God* is regarding God, for it is impossible to find a scripture that has us doing or giving anything without God. Most importantly, "having" anything, without God (John 1:1–3, KJV) is impossible. God has given us free will, so it is totally up to us to decide to give His way.

The Bible says that when we give, we can receive more in return (Luke 6:38, KJV). There will be less angry people in the world, for that mentality is nothing but fear. It is fear of not being able to provide for their families, because of not enough money (such as a sufficient job or possibly no job), or illiteracy or arrest records, or even because of no clothing to be presentable to be hired for a job.

Giving Is God is about giving a person the opportunity to better themselves, to imagine being in a better life. When we can imagine ourselves owning a home, running a business, or writing a book, it can be done (Proverbs 29:18, AMPC) when we stay focused on that end result. We will have what we say, when we believe we receive, when we pray (Mark 11:24, KJV). God will cause people to come across our path to give us that opportunity (Galatians 6:10, AMPC). When the opportunity arrives, recognize it and go for it. Mankind has been given the ability to do all things, we imagine to do (Genesis 11:6, KJV). God blessed us and told us to be fruitful, multiply, and replenish the earth, and subdue it and take dominion (Genesis 1:28, KJV). Not over people, but take dominion over any injustice in the world (Ephesians 6:12, NLT). So it is our responsibility to put good things in the world, so that the good multiplies. We are able copy and multiply what we see, so how about it? Let us help the poor in spirit, the fatherless, the orphans, the widows, and the elderly (Psalm 82, KJV).

Also, do you know that the silver and gold and all good things are still in the earth as it was in the Garden of Eden? The wealth and resources has multiplied, it has not diminished. This hidden treasure as the Bible refers to (Isaiah 45:2-3, KJV) is in the wrong hands; those who are not doing things God's way; such as giving it where giving is due.

We have been given another opportunity to imagine as one, now as the body of Christ. Let us do it God's way (Matthew 6:33, AMPC). We will produce a happier, peaceful, and better life for all mankind.

Giving is a way of life; it is how we all live on earth, as it is in Heaven.

We have the freewill to decide whom we allow to control us, and no matter what you say or think, it is the truth anyway. We are all led by a spirit, mine is the Holy Spirit of God. Who is leading you? Oh, the other spirit is Satan (2 Corinthians 4:3–5, NLT). Let us manifest the sons of God (Romans 8:19, KJV), which is to help people in need, through the Blood of Jesus, in Jesus' name. Amen! The scriptures used in this book are Spirit-led, and Jesus is the source of my strength. God's word is the seed that has been planted in me, now by the Grace of God, this book is the fruit.

Genesis 2:10–14 (KJV) [10] And a river went out of Eden to water the garden; and from thence it was parted, and became into four heads. [11] The name of the first is Pison: that is it which compasseth the whole land of Havilah, where there is gold; [12] And the gold of that land is good: there is bdellium and the onyx stone. [13] And the name of the second river is Gihon: the same is it that compasseth the whole land of Ethiopia. [14] And the name of the third river is Hiddekel: that is it which goeth toward the east of Assyria. And the fourth river is Euphrates.

Mark 16:15 (NKJV) [15] And He said to them, "Go into all the world and preach the gospel to every creature.

Acts 10:34 (KJV) [34] Then Peter opened his mouth,

and said, Of a truth I perceive that God is no respecter of persons:

Genesis 1:27 (KJV) [27] So God created man in his own image, in the image of God created he him; male and female created he them.

Hebrews 4:6 (AMPC) [6] Seeing then that the promise remains over [from past times] for some to enter that rest, and that those who formerly were given the good news about it and the opportunity, failed to appropriate it and did not enter because of disobedience,

John 16:33 (AMPC) [33] I have told you these things, so that in Me you may have [perfect] peace and confidence. In the world you have tribulation and trials and distress and frustration; but be of good cheer [take courage; be confident, certain, undaunted]! For I have overcome the world. [I have deprived it of power to harm you and have conquered it for you.]

Ecclesiastes 10:19 (KJV) [19]... but money answereth all things.

Proverbs 15:4 (AMPC) [4] A gentle tongue [with its healing power] is a tree of life, but willful contrariness in it breaks down the spirit.

John 1:1-3 (KJV) [1] In the beginning was the Word, and the Word was with God, and the Word was God. [2] The same was in the beginning with God. [3] All things were made by him; and without him was not any thing made that was made.

Luke 6:38 (KJV) [38] Give, and it shall be given unto you; good measure, pressed down, and shaken together, and running over, shall men give into your bosom. For with the same measure that ye mete withal it shall be measured to you again.

Proverbs 29:18 (AMPC) [18] Where there is no vision [no redemptive revelation of God], the people perish; but he who keeps the law [of God, which includes that of man]—blessed (happy, fortunate, and enviable) is he.

Mark 11:24 (KJV) [24] Therefore I say unto you, What things soever ye desire, when ye pray, believe that ye receive them, and ye shall have them.

Galatians 6:10 (AMPC) [10] So then, as occasion *and* opportunity open up to us, let us do good [morally] to all people [not only being useful or profitable to them, but also doing what is for their spiritual good and advantage]. Be mindful to be a blessing, especially to those of the household of faith [those who belong to God's family with you, the believers].

Genesis 11:6 (KJV) [6] And the Lord said, Behold, the people is one, and they have all one language; and this they begin to do: and now nothing will be restrained from them, which they have imagined to do.

Genesis 1:28 (KJV) [28] And God blessed them, and

God said unto them, Be fruitful, and multiply, and replenish the earth, and subdue it: and have dominion over the fish of the sea, and over the fowl of the air, and over every living thing that moveth upon the earth.

Ephesians 6:12 (NLT) 12 For we are not fighting against flesh-and-blood enemies, but against evil rulers and authorities of the unseen world, against mighty powers in this dark world, and against evil spirits in the heavenly places.

Psalm 82:1-8 (KJV) 1 God standeth in the congregation of the mighty; He judgeth among the gods. 2 How long will ye judge unjustly, and accept the persons of the wicked? Selah. 3 Defend the poor and fatherless: do justice to the afflicted and needy. 4 Deliver the poor and needy: rid them out of the hand of the wicked. 5 They know not, neither will they understand; they walk on in darkness: all the foundations of the earth are out of course. 6 I have said, Ye are gods; and all of you are children of the most High. 7 But ye shall die like men, and fall like one of the princes. 8 Arise, O God, judge the earth: for thou shalt inherit all nations.

Isaiah 45:2-3 (KJV) 2 I will go before thee, and make the crooked places straight: I will break in pieces the gates of brass, and cut in sunder the bars of iron: 3 And I will give thee the treasures of darkness, and hidden riches of secret places, that thou mayest know that I, the LORD, which call thee by thy name, am the God of Israel.

Matthew 6:33 (AMPC) ³³ But seek (aim at and strive after) first of all His kingdom and His righteousness (His way of doing and being right), and then all these things taken together will be given you besides.

2 Corinthians 4:3-5 (NLT) ³ If the Good News we preach is hidden behind a veil, it is hidden only from people who are perishing. ⁴ Satan, who is the god of this world, has blinded the minds of those who don't believe. They are unable to see the glorious light of the Good News. They don't understand this message about the glory of Christ, who is the exact likeness of God. ⁵ You see, we don't go around preaching about ourselves. We preach that Jesus Christ is Lord, and we ourselves are your servants for Jesus' sake.

Romans 8:19 (KJV) ¹⁹ For the earnest expectation of the creature waiteth for the manifestation of the sons of God.

Disclaimer & Disclosure: Be free to search the Bible for yourselves, for I am not a bible scholar, but I am a son of God. I know I can't get all of God's Word in this book, if so what would be the use for this book, when we all can go directly to our own Bibles. My hope is to release a desire in you to search the scriptures, so that the Holy Spirit can teach you about the things that you seek. ~ Claudette

Giving Is...

I've discovered that giving is addictive. I have to give something; it makes me happy.

Knowing that I have made someone else happy makes me continue and never stop giving.

Action

Action is a response. Action means to do something. When we say something, it is an action. When we do something, it is an action. Even when we believe in something or someone, this is an action. There is nothing we can say, do, see, hear, smell, taste, or believe that doesn't require an action. God has given us the ability to take this action in our giving. If you are in Christ, we have the choice to be in sync with Him. **A definition for *"Action"* is to do something toward a goal in order to achieve a purpose.**

You can find many "action" scriptures throughout this book. See the *Contents* page for a specific topic: "Believe" is one that is listed.

† **1 Samuel 2:3 (AMPC)** Talk no more so very proudly; let not arrogance go forth from your mouth, for the Lord is a God of knowledge, and by Him actions are weighed.

† **Isaiah 42:20 (NLT)** You see and recognize what is right but refuse to act on it. You hear with your ears, but you don't really listen."

† **Psalm 48:9-10 (MSG)** We pondered your love-in-action, God, waiting in your temple: Your name, God, evokes a train of Hallelujahs wherever It is spoken,

near and far; your arms are heaped with goodness-in-action.

† **Matthew 7:24 (AMPC)** So everyone who hears these words of Mine and acts upon them [obeying them] will be like a sensible (prudent, practical, wise) man who built his house upon the rock.

† **John 14:26 (AMPC)** But the Comforter (Counselor, Helper, Intercessor, Advocate, Strengthener, Standby), the Holy Spirit, Whom the Father will send in My name [in My place, to represent Me and act on My behalf], He will teach you all things. And He will cause you to recall (will remind you of, bring to your remembrance) everything I have told you.

† **Philippians 1:6 (KJV)** Being confident of this very thing, that he which hath begun a good work in you will perform it until the day of Jesus Christ:

† **James 2:18 (KJV)** Yea, a man may say, Thou hast faith, and I have works: shew me thy faith without thy works, and I will shew thee my faith by my works.

Allow

When we allow the mighty work of God, He will manifest Himself. When we believe that Jesus is our healer, we shall be healed. When we trust in His faithfulness and His great love for us, He will make a way for us. God hath completed everything before the foundation of the world; all we have to do is Believe Him! (Hebrews 4:2–4, see here)

† **John 9:1-3, 10-11 (AMPC)** As He passed along, He noticed a man blind from his birth. His disciples asked Him, Rabbi, who sinned, this man or his parents, that he should be born blind? Jesus answered, It was not that this man or his parents sinned, but he was born blind in order that the workings of God should be manifested (displayed and illustrated) in him. So they said to him, How were your eyes opened? He replied, The Man called Jesus made mud and smeared it on my eyes and said to me, Go to Siloam and wash. So I went and washed, and I obtained my sight!

† **Romans 1:23–25 (NLT)** And instead of worshiping the glorious, ever-living God, they worshiped idols made to look like mere people and birds and animals and reptiles. So God abandoned them to do whatever shameful things their hearts desired. As a result, they

did vile and degrading things with each other's bodies. They traded the truth about God for a lie. So they worshiped and served the things God created instead of the Creator Himself, who is worthy of eternal praise! Amen.

† **1 Corinthians 10:13 (NLT)** The temptations in your life are no different from what others experience. And God is faithful. He will not allow the temptation to be more than you can stand. When you are tempted, he will show you a way out so that you can endure.

† **Hebrews 4:2–4 (KJV)** For unto us was the gospel preached, as well as unto them: but the word preached did not profit them, not being mixed with faith in them that heard it. For we which have believed do enter into rest, as he said, As I have sworn in my wrath, if they shall enter into my rest: although the works were finished from the foundation of the world. For he spake in a certain place of the seventh day on this wise, And God did rest the seventh day from all his works.

† **Hebrews 4:2-4 (AMPC)** [2] For indeed we have had the glad tidings [Gospel of God] proclaimed to us just as truly as they [the Israelites of old did when the good news of deliverance from bondage came to them]; but the message they heard did not benefit them, because it was not mixed with faith (with the leaning of the entire personality on God in absolute trust and confidence in His power, wisdom, and goodness) by

those who heard it; *neither were they united in faith with the ones [Joshua and Caleb] who heard (did believe).* ³ For we who have believed (adhered to and trusted in and relied on God) do enter that rest, in accordance with His declaration that those [who did not believe] should not enter when He said, As I swore in My wrath, They shall not enter My rest; and this He said although [His] works had been completed *and* prepared [and waiting for all who would believe] from the foundation of the world. ⁴ For in a certain place He has said this about the seventh day: And God rested on the seventh day from all His works.

Angels

I believe everyone of us has had encounters with angels, whether we realize it or not. We may not have seen them, but we have wondered why and how something has happened. For instance, there are many occasions that I have been saved from harm. I didn't realize it, until after the incidents, that I was indeed protected.

My angel(s) find things for me all the time, when I didn't have a clue where they could be. I would say, "Angels, please find such and such, in Jesus' name, thank you," and then there it is. It was like it had always been there, but it wasn't there. I thank God for my angel(s).

† **Exodus 23:20 (KJV)** Behold, I send an Angel before thee, to keep thee in the way, and to bring thee into the place which I have prepared.

† **Exodus 23:20-21 (MSG)** "Now get yourselves ready. I'm sending my Angel ahead of you to guard you in your travels, to lead you to the place that I've prepared. Pay close attention to him. Obey him. Don't go against him. He won't put up with your rebellions because he's acting on my authority. But if you obey him and do everything I tell you, I'll be an enemy to your enemies, I'll fight those who fight you.

- † **Psalm 34:7 (KJV)** The angel of the Lord encampeth round about them that fear Him, and delivereth them.

- † **Psalm 91:11 (KJV)** For He shall give His angels charge over thee, to keep thee in all thy ways.

- † **Psalm 103:20–21 (KJV)** Bless the Lord, ye His angels, that excel in strength, that do His commandments, hearkening unto the voice of His word. Bless ye the Lord, all ye His hosts; ye ministers of His, that do His pleasure.

- † **Daniel 10:11, 13 (AMPC)** And [the angel] said to me, O Daniel, you greatly beloved man, understand the words that I speak to you and stand upright, for to you I am now sent. And while he was saying this word to me, I stood up trembling. But the prince of the kingdom of Persia withstood me for twenty- one days. Then Michael, one of the chief [of the celestial] princes, came to help me, for I remained there with the kings of Persia.

- † **Luke 1:19 (KJV)** And the angel answering said unto him, I am Gabriel, that stand in the presence of God; and am sent to speak unto thee, and to shew thee these glad tidings.

- † **Hebrews 1:14 (AMPC)** Are not the angels all ministering spirits (servants) sent out in the service [of God for the assistance] of those who are to inherit salvation?

- † **Hebrews 13:2 (AMPC)** Do not forget or neglect or

refuse to extend hospitality to strangers [in the brotherhood—being friendly, cordial, and gracious, sharing the comforts of your home and doing your part generously], for through it some have entertained angels without knowing it.

† **1 Peter 1:12 (AMPC)** It was then disclosed to them that the services they were rendering were not meant for themselves and their period of time, but for you. [It is these very] things which have now already been made known plainly to you by those who preached the good news (the Gospel) to you by the [same] Holy Spirit sent from heaven. Into these things [the very] angels long to look!

† **Revelation 19:9–10 (NLT)** And the angel said to me, "Write this: Blessed are those who are invited to the wedding feast of the Lamb." And he added, "These are true words that come from God." Then I fell down at his feet to worship him, but he said, "No, don't worship me. I am a servant of God, just like you and your brothers and sisters who testify about their faith in Jesus. Worship only God. For the essence of prophecy is to give a clear witness for Jesus."

Anoint / Anointed / Anointing

The Anointing is actually the Spirit of God. We can never separate His power; the anointing from Him, but we can quench or frustrate Him in a way that His power/anointing will not work in our lives. We may be able to do some physical things, but that's nothing, because our ability without Him is limited. With God's anointing on the inside of a born again believer, and when His Spirit comes upon us, we can do all things, according to His will. Our Father, Who is in Heaven does the work in us through Jesus, Who is inside of us. Christ in you, the hope of Glory (Colossians 1:27).

We, the body of Christ have this same anointing, because Jesus prayed to the Father to send the Holy Spirit to live within us, so that we can do greater works, then even He did. We indeed have the power to do all good things.

God commanded us to be His mouth to speak His Word, our hands to heal & help the needy, our feet to go and take Him with us to all the world. Jesus was God's willing vessel when He walked the earth, now that Jesus is in Heaven, we are His ambassadors.

The Anointed One is Jesus Christ; the Messiah and we, the sons of God is His anointed ones. Let the world see God's power in demonstration as we follow the leading of the Holy Spirit !!!

† **Psalm 20:6 (AMPC)** Now I know that the Lord saves His anointed; He will answer him from His holy heaven with the saving strength of His right hand.

† **Psalm 110:1-3 (AMPC)** The Lord (God) says to my Lord (the Messiah), Sit at My right hand, until I make Your adversaries Your footstool. The Lord will send forth from Zion the scepter of Your strength; rule, then, in the midst of Your foes. Your people will offer themselves willingly in the day of Your power, in the beauty of holiness *and* in holy array out of the womb of the morning; to You [will spring forth] Your young men, who are as the dew.

† **Psalm 133 (KJV)** Behold, how good and how pleasant it is for brethren to dwell together in unity! It is like the precious ointment upon the head, that ran down upon the beard, even Aaron's beard: that went down to the skirts of his garments; As the dew of Hermon, and as the dew that descended upon the mountains of Zion: for there the LORD commanded the blessing, even life for evermore.

† **Isaiah 10:27 (KJV)** And it shall come to pass in that day, that his burden shall be taken away from off thy shoulder, and his yoke from off thy neck, and the yoke

shall be destroyed because of the anointing.

† **Isaiah 11:1-3 (AMPC)** And there shall come forth a Shoot out of the stock of Jesse [David's father], and a Branch out of his roots shall grow *and* bear fruit. And the Spirit of the Lord shall rest upon Him—the Spirit of wisdom and understanding, the Spirit of counsel and might, the Spirit of knowledge and of the reverential *and* obedient fear of the Lord— And shall make Him of quick understanding, *and* His delight shall be in the reverential *and* obedient fear of the Lord. And He shall not judge by the sight of His eyes, neither decide by the hearing of His ears;

† **Isaiah 45:1-3 (AMPC)** Thus says the Lord to His anointed, to Cyrus, whose right hand I have held to subdue nations before him, and I will unarm *and* ungird the loins of kings to open doors before him, so that gates will not be shut. I will go before you and level the mountains [to make the crooked places straight]; I will break in pieces the doors of bronze and cut asunder the bars of iron. And I will give you the treasures of darkness and hidden riches of secret places, that you may know that it is I, the Lord, the God of Israel, Who calls you by your name.

† **Isaiah 61:1-3 (AMPC)** The Spirit of the Lord God is upon me, because the Lord has anointed *and* qualified me to preach the Gospel *of* good tidings to the meek, the poor, *and* afflicted; He has sent me to bind up *and* heal the brokenhearted, to proclaim liberty to the

[physical and spiritual] captives and the opening of the prison *and* of the eyes to those who are bound, To proclaim the acceptable year of the Lord [the year of His favor] and the day of vengeance of our God, to comfort all who mourn, To grant [consolation and joy] to those who mourn in Zion—to give them an ornament (a garland or diadem) of beauty instead of ashes, the oil of joy instead of mourning, the garment [expressive] of praise instead of a heavy, burdened, *and* failing spirit—that they may be called oaks of righteousness [lofty, strong, and magnificent, distinguished for uprightness, justice, and right standing with God], the planting of the Lord, that He may be glorified.

† **Job 32:6-10 (AMPC)** ⁶Then Elihu son of Barachel the Buzite said, I am young, and you are aged; for that reason I was timid *and* restrained and dared not declare my opinion to you. ⁷I said, Age should speak, and a multitude of years should teach wisdom [so let it be heard]. ⁸But there is [a vital force] a spirit [of intelligence] in man, and the breath of the Almighty gives men understanding. ⁹It is not the great [necessarily] who are wise, nor [always] the aged who understand justice. ¹⁰So I say, Listen to me; I also will give you my opinion [about Job's situation] *and* my knowledge.

† **Joel 2:28 (AMPC)** And afterward I will pour out My Spirit upon all flesh; and your sons and your daughters

shall prophesy, your old men shall dream dreams, your young men shall see visions.

† **Mark 5:30 (KJV)** And Jesus, immediately knowing in himself that virtue had gone out of him, turned him about in the press, and said, Who touched my clothes?

† **Luke 4:18-19 (KJV)** The Spirit of the Lord is upon me, because he hath anointed me to preach the gospel to the poor; he hath sent me to heal the brokenhearted, to preach deliverance to the captives, and recovering of sight to the blind, to set at liberty them that are bruised, To preach the acceptable year of the Lord.

† **Luke 4:18-19 (AMPC)** The Spirit of the Lord [is] upon Me, because He has anointed Me [the Anointed One, the Messiah] to preach the good news (the Gospel) to the poor; He has sent Me to announce release to the captives and recovery of sight to the blind, to send forth as delivered those who are oppressed [who are downtrodden, bruised, crushed, and broken down by calamity], To proclaim the accepted *and* acceptable year of the Lord [the day when salvation and the free favors of God profusely abound].

† **John 4:25 (KJV)** The woman saith unto him, I know that Messias cometh, which is called Christ: when he is come, he will tell us all things.

† **John 4:24-26 (AMPC)** God is a Spirit (a spiritual Being) and those who worship Him must worship *Him*

in spirit and in truth (reality). The woman said to Him, I know that Messiah is coming, He Who is called the Christ (the Anointed One); and when He arrives, He will tell us everything we need to know *and* make it clear to us. Jesus said to her, I Who now speak with you am He.

† **John 9:10-11 (KJV)** Therefore said they unto him, How were thine eyes opened? He answered and said, A man that is called Jesus made clay, and anointed mine eyes, and said unto me, Go to the pool of Siloam, and wash: and I went and washed, and I received sight.

† **John 14:10-12 (KJV)** Believest thou not that I am in the Father, and the Father in me? the words that I speak unto you I speak not of myself: but the Father that dwelleth in me, he doeth the works. Believe me that I am in the Father, and the Father in me: or else believe me for the very works' sake. Verily, verily, I say unto you, He that believeth on me, the works that I do shall he do also; and greater works than these shall he do; because I go unto my Father.

† **Acts 1:8 (NKJV)** But you shall receive power when the Holy Spirit has come upon you; and you shall be witnesses to Me in Jerusalem, and in all Judea and Samaria, and to the end of the earth."

† **Acts 1:4-5 (NKJV)** [The Holy Spirit Promised] And being assembled together with *them* He commanded them not to depart from Jerusalem, but to wait for the

Promise of the Father, "which," *He said,* "you have heard from Me; for John truly baptized with water, but you shall be baptized with the Holy Spirit not many days from now."

† **Acts 2:1-12 (NKJV)** [Coming of the Holy Spirit] ¹ When the Day of Pentecost had fully come, they were all with one accord in one place. ² And suddenly there came a sound from heaven, as of a rushing mighty wind, and it filled the whole house where they were sitting. ³ Then there appeared to them divided tongues, as of fire, and *one* sat upon each of them. ⁴ And they were all filled with the Holy Spirit and began to speak with other tongues, as the Spirit gave them utterance. [The Crowd's Response] ⁵ And there were dwelling in Jerusalem Jews, devout men, from every nation under heaven. ⁶ And when this sound occurred, the multitude came together, and were confused, because everyone heard them speak in his own language. ⁷ Then they were all amazed and marveled, saying to one another, "Look, are not all these who speak Galileans? ⁸ And how *is it that* we hear, each in our own language in which we were born? ⁹ Parthians and Medes and Elamites, those dwelling in Mesopotamia, Judea and Cappadocia, Pontus and Asia, ¹⁰ Phrygia and Pamphylia, Egypt and the parts of Libya adjoining Cyrene, visitors from Rome, both Jews and proselytes, ¹¹ Cretans and Arabs—we hear them speaking in our own tongues the wonderful works of God." ¹² So they were all amazed

and perplexed, saying to one another, "Whatever could this mean?"

† **Acts 2:16-21 (KJV)** ^{16} But this is that which was spoken by the prophet Joel; ^{17} And it shall come to pass in the last days, saith God, I will pour out of my Spirit upon all flesh: and your sons and your daughters shall prophesy, and your young men shall see visions, and your old men shall dream dreams: ^{18} And on my servants and on my handmaidens I will pour out in those days of my Spirit; and they shall prophesy: ^{19} And I will shew wonders in heaven above, and signs in the earth beneath; blood, and fire, and vapour of smoke: ^{20} The sun shall be turned into darkness, and the moon into blood, before the great and notable day of the Lord come: ^{21} And it shall come to pass, that whosoever shall call on the name of the Lord shall be saved.

† **Ephesians 3:20-21 (KJV)** Now unto him that is able to do exceeding abundantly above all that we ask or think, according to the power that worketh in us, Unto him be glory in the church by Christ Jesus throughout all ages, world without end. Amen.

† **Galatians 2:21 (KJV)** I do not frustrate the grace of God:

† **Philippians 2:13 (KJV)** For it is God which worketh in you both to will and to do of his good pleasure.

† **Philippians 4:13 (KJV)** I can do all things through

Christ which strengtheneth me.

† **Philippians 1:6-7 (KJV)** Being confident of this very thing, that he which hath begun a good work in you will perform it until the day of Jesus Christ: Even as it is meet for me to think this of you all, because I have you in my heart; inasmuch as both in my bonds, and in the defence and confirmation of the gospel, ye all are partakers of my grace.

† **Colossians 1:27 (KJV)** To whom God would make known what is the riches of the glory of this mystery among the Gentiles; which is Christ in you, the hope of glory:

† **1 Thessalonians 2:13 (AMPC)** And we also [especially] thank God continually for this, that when you received the message of God [which you heard] from us, you welcomed it not as the word of [mere] men, but as it truly is, the Word of God, which is effectually at work in you who believe [exercising its superhuman power in those who adhere to and trust in and rely on it].

† **1 Thessalonians 5:19 (AMPC)** Do not quench (suppress or subdue) the [Holy] Spirit;

† **James 5:14 (AMPC)** Is anyone among you sick? He should call in the church elders (the spiritual guides). And they should pray over him, anointing him with oil in the Lord's name.

† **1 John 2:20 (KJV)** But ye have an unction from the

Holy One, and ye know all things.

† **1 John 2:27 (KJV)** But the anointing which ye have received of him abideth in you, and ye need not that any man teach you: but as the same anointing teacheth you of all things, and is truth, and is no lie, and even as it hath taught you, ye shall abide in him.

† **1 John 2:19-21 (NKJV)** They went out from us, but they were not of us; for if they had been of us, they would have continued with us; but *they went out* that they might be made manifest, that none of them were of us. But you have an anointing from the Holy One, and you know all things. I have not written to you because you do not know the truth, but because you know it, and that no lie is of the truth.

† **1 John 2:26-28 (NKJV)** These things I have written to you concerning those who *try to* deceive you. But the anointing which you have received from Him abides in you, and you do not need that anyone teach you; but as the same anointing teaches you concerning all things, and is true, and is not a lie, and just as it has taught you, you will abide in Him. [The Children of God] And now, little children, abide in Him, that when He appears, we may have confidence and not be ashamed before Him at His coming.

† **1 John 2:27 (AMPC)** But as for you, the anointing (the sacred appointment, the unction) which you received from Him abides [permanently] in you; [so] then you have no need that anyone should instruct

you. But just as His anointing teaches you concerning everything and is true and is no falsehood, so you must abide in (live in, never depart from) Him [being rooted in Him, knit to Him], just as [His anointing] has taught you [to do].

Avenge

Being in Christ, it is a comfort to know that God fights my battles. I know that I don't fight people, so all I need to do is pray and decree a thing (see Job 22:28 under Better World). By faith, I know that everything is all right. My God avenges me.

† **2 Chronicles 20:15 (AMPC)** He said, Hearken, all Judah, you inhabitants of Jerusalem, and you King Jehoshaphat. The Lord says this to you: Be not afraid or dismayed at this great multitude; for the battle is not yours, but God's.

† **Psalm 24:7-9 (AMPC)** Lift up your heads, O you gates; and be lifted up, you age-abiding doors, that the King of glory may come in. Who is the King of glory? The Lord strong and mighty, the Lord mighty in battle. Lift up your heads, O you gates; yes, lift them up, you age-abiding doors, that the King of glory may come in.

† **Isaiah 34:8 (AMPC)** For the Lord has a day of vengeance, a year of recompense, for the cause of Zion.

† **Luke 18:7-8 (KJV)** And shall not God avenge His own elect, which cry day and night unto Him, though He bear long with them? I tell you that He will avenge them speedily. Nevertheless when the Son of man

cometh, shall He find faith on the earth?

† **Deuteronomy 3:21-22 (KJV)** And I commanded Joshua at that time, saying, Thine eyes have seen all that the LORD your God hath done unto these two kings: so shall the LORD do unto all the kingdoms whither thou passest. Ye shall not fear them: for the LORD your God he shall fight for you.

† **Deuteronomy 3:22 (AMPC)** You shall not fear them, for the Lord your God shall fight for you.

† **Romans 12:19 (KJV)** Dearly beloved, avenge not yourselves, but rather give place unto wrath: for it is written, Vengeance is mine; I will repay, saith the Lord.

Believe

What do you believe? There are so many things in this world to believe and within it is so much confusion. How can we possibly sort out the truth? For me, to believe is to have faith in someone or something. I believe in God, because in Him is where I belong, and also where I desire to be and to stay.

The Word of God (the Bible) is the way to know God, and to discover what to believe. God's Word is Truth, so the Bible will tell us where we were, where we are and where we will be. Whether we believe in God or not will manifest in our life (see Matthew 12:34 under Voice).

Our belief system is so powerful. What we say out of our mouths is what we believe; it is what we believe in our hearts. It is rooted deep inside of us. We should continuously watch what we hear and see, because all things can influence us (read and believe Romans 12:2 under "Letting Go"). Our beliefs will be seen by all, we may be able to hide for a while, but it will be seen. Let God be seen in your life, Amen !!!

† **2 Chronicles 20:20 (KJV)** Believe in the Lord your God, so shall ye be established; believe His prophets, so shall ye prosper.

† **Proverbs 23:7 (KJV)** For as he thinketh in his heart, so is he:

† **Matthew 9:28 (KJV)** And when He was come into the house, the blind men came to Him: and Jesus saith unto them, Believe ye that I am able to do this? They said unto Him, Yea, Lord.

† **Mark 9:23 (KJV)** Jesus said unto him, If thou canst believe, all things are possible to him that believeth.

† **Luke 6:45 (KJV)** A good man out of the good treasure of his heart bringeth forth that which is good; and an evil man out of the evil treasure of his heart bringeth forth that which is evil: for of the abundance of the heart his mouth speaketh.

† **Luke 8:50 (KJV)** But when Jesus heard it, He answered him, saying, Fear not: believe only, and she shall be made whole.

† **Romans 4:3 (KJV)** For what saith the scripture? Abraham believed God, and it was counted unto him for righteousness.

† **Romans 4:20–22 (KJV)** He staggered not at the promise of God through unbelief; but was strong in faith, giving glory to God; And being fully persuaded that, what he had promised, he was able also to perform. And therefore it was imputed to him for righteousness.

† **Romans 10:14–15 (AMPC)** But how are people to call upon Him Whom they have not believed [in

Whom they have no faith, on Whom they have no reliance]? And how are they to believe in Him [adhere to, trust in, and rely upon Him] of Whom they have never heard? And how are they to hear without a preacher? And how can men [be expected to] preach unless they are sent? As it is written, How beautiful are the feet of those who bring glad tidings! [How welcome is the coming of those who preach the good news of His good things!]

† **Romans 15:13 (KJV)** Now the God of hope fill you with all joy And peace in believing, that ye may abound in hope, through the power of the Holy Ghost.

† **2 Corinthians 4:17–18 (KJV)** For our light affliction, which is but for a moment, worketh for us a far more exceeding and eternal weight of glory; While we look not at the things which are seen, but at the things which are not seen: for the things which are seen are temporal; but the things which are not seen are eternal.

† **2 Thessalonians 2:13 (KJV)** But we are bound to give thanks always to God for you, brethren beloved of the Lord, because God hath from the beginning chosen you to salvation through sanctification of the Spirit and belief of the truth:

† **Hebrews 11:3 (AMPC)** By faith we understand that the worlds [during the successive ages] were framed (fashioned, put in order, and equipped for their intended purpose) by the word of God, so that what we see was not made out of things which are visible.

† **1 Peter 1:21–23 (AMPC)** Through Him you believe in (adhere to, rely on) God, Who raised Him up from the dead and gave Him honor and glory, so that your faith and hope are [centered and rest] in God. Since by your obedience to the Truth through the [Holy] Spirit you have purified your hearts for the sincere affection of the brethren, [see that you] love one another fervently from a pure heart. You have been regenerated (born again), not from a mortal origin (seed, sperm), but from one that is immortal by the ever living and lasting Word of God.

Better World

I remember having to write a paper for one of my social work classes. I had just recently been born-again, at least as an adult. I was explaining to a classmate of my desire for a better world. I don't remember him saying anything; I just remember him looking at me. I don't know if it was a look of amazement of my naivety, or he was happy that I believe we can have a better world. (I looked up definition for naïve; naïve is having or showing an extremely or excessively simple and trusting view of the world and human nature, often as a result of youth and inexperience.) But now I know by reading God's word, a better world is possible. Heaven on earth! *Definition found in Encarta Dictionary: English (North America) Online.*

† **Exodus 36:5 (NLT)** They went to Moses and reported, "The people have given more than enough materials to complete the job the Lord has commanded us to do!"

† **Job 22:28 (KJV)** Thou shalt also decree a thing, and it shall be established unto thee: and the light shall shine upon thy ways.

† **Ecclesiastes 10:19 (KJV)** A feast is made for laughter, and wine maketh merry: but money

answereth all things.

† **Matthew 6:10 (AMPC)** Your kingdom come, Your will be done on earth as it is in heaven.

† **Isaiah 51:3 (KJV)** For the Lord shall comfort Zion: He will comfort all her waste places; and He will make her wilderness like Eden, and her desert like the garden of the Lord; joy and gladness shall be found therein, thanksgiving, and the voice of melody.

† **Isaiah 61:1-11 (AMPC)** ¹The Spirit of the Lord God is upon me, because the Lord has anointed *and* qualified me to preach the Gospel *of* good tidings to the meek, the poor, *and* afflicted; He has sent me to bind up *and* heal the brokenhearted, to proclaim liberty to the [physical and spiritual] captives and the opening of the prison *and* of the eyes to those who are bound, ² To proclaim the acceptable year of the Lord [the year of His favor] and the day of vengeance of our God, to comfort all who mourn, ³ To grant [consolation and joy] to those who mourn in Zion—to give them an ornament (a garland or diadem) of beauty instead of ashes, the oil of joy instead of mourning, the garment [expressive] of praise instead of a heavy, burdened, *and* failing spirit—that they may be called oaks of righteousness [lofty, strong, and magnificent, distinguished for uprightness, justice, and right standing with God], the planting of the Lord, that He may be glorified. ⁴ And they shall rebuild the ancient ruins; they shall raise up the former

desolations and renew the ruined cities, the devastations of many generations. ⁵ Aliens shall stand [ready] and feed your flocks, and foreigners shall be your plowmen and your vinedressers. ⁶ But you shall be called the priests of the Lord; people will speak of you as the ministers of our God. You shall eat the wealth of the nations, and the glory [once that of your captors] shall be yours. ⁷ Instead of your [former] shame you shall have a twofold recompense; instead of dishonor *and* reproach [your people] shall rejoice in their portion. Therefore in their land they shall possess double [what they had forfeited]; everlasting joy shall be theirs. ⁸ For I the Lord love justice; I hate robbery *and* wrong with violence *or* a burnt offering. And I will faithfully give them their recompense in truth, and I will make an everlasting covenant *or* league with them. ⁹ And their offspring shall be known among the nations and their descendants among the peoples. All who see them [in their prosperity] will recognize *and* acknowledge that they are the people whom the Lord has blessed. ¹⁰ I will greatly rejoice in the Lord, my soul will exult in my God; for He has clothed me with the garments of salvation, He has covered me with the robe of righteousness, as a bridegroom decks himself with a garland, and as a bride adorns herself with her jewels. ¹¹ For as [surely as] the earth brings forth its shoots, and as a garden causes what is sown in it to spring forth, so [surely] the Lord God will cause rightness *and* justice and praise to spring forth before all the nations [through the self-fulfilling power of His word].

† **Isaiah 51:3 (KJV)** For the Lord shall comfort Zion: He will comfort all her waste places; and He will make her wilderness like Eden, and her desert like the garden of the Lord; joy and gladness shall be found therein, thanksgiving, and the voice of melody.

† **Jeremiah 33:9 (KJV)** And it shall be to me a name of joy, a praise and an honour before all the nations of the earth, which shall hear all the good that I do unto them: and they shall fear and tremble for all the goodness and for all the prosperity that I procure unto it.

† **Revelation 21:1-27 (KJV)** ^{1} And I saw a new heaven and a new earth: for the first heaven and the first earth were passed away; and there was no more sea. ^{2} And I John saw the holy city, new Jerusalem, coming down from God out of heaven, prepared as a bride adorned for her husband. ^{3} And I heard a great voice out of heaven saying, Behold, the tabernacle of God is with men, and he will dwell with them, and they shall be his people, and God himself shall be with them, and be their God. ^{4} And God shall wipe away all tears from their eyes; and there shall be no more death, neither sorrow, nor crying, neither shall there be any more pain: for the former things are passed away. ^{5} And he that sat upon the throne said, Behold, I make all things new. And he said unto me, Write: for these words are

true and faithful. ⁶ And he said unto me, It is done. I am Alpha and Omega, the beginning and the end. I will give unto him that is athirst of the fountain of the water of life freely. ⁷ He that overcometh shall inherit all things; and I will be his God, and he shall be my son. ⁸ But the fearful, and unbelieving, and the abominable, and murderers, and whoremongers, and sorcerers, and idolaters, and all liars, shall have their part in the lake which burneth with fire and brimstone: which is the second death. ⁹ And there came unto me one of the seven angels which had the seven vials full of the seven last plagues, and talked with me, saying, Come hither, I will shew thee the bride, the Lamb's wife. ¹⁰ And he carried me away in the spirit to a great and high mountain, and shewed me that great city, the holy Jerusalem, descending out of heaven from God, ¹¹ Having the glory of God: and her light was like unto a stone most precious, even like a jasper stone, clear as crystal; ¹² And had a wall great and high, and had twelve gates, and at the gates twelve angels, and names written thereon, which are the names of the twelve tribes of the children of Israel: ¹³ On the east three gates; on the north three gates; on the south three gates; and on the west three gates. ¹⁴ And the wall of the city had twelve foundations, and in them the names of the twelve apostles of the Lamb. ¹⁵ And he that talked with me had a golden reed to measure the city, and the gates thereof, and the wall thereof. ¹⁶ And the city lieth foursquare, and the length is as large as the breadth: and he measured the city with the reed, twelve thousand furlongs. The length and the breadth and the height of it are equal. [17] And he measured the wall thereof, an hundred and forty and four cubits, according to the measure of a man, that is, of the angel. [18] And the building of the wall of it was of jasper: and the city was pure gold, like unto clear glass. [19] And the foundations of the wall of the city were garnished with all manner of precious stones. The first foundation was jasper; the second, sapphire; the third, a chalcedony; the fourth, an emerald; [20] The fifth, sardonyx; the sixth, sardius; the seventh, chrysolyte; the eighth, beryl; the ninth, a topaz; the tenth, a chrysoprasus; the eleventh, a jacinth; the twelfth, an amethyst. [21] And the twelve gates were twelve pearls: every several gate was of one pearl: and the street of the city was pure gold, as it were transparent glass. [22] And I saw no temple therein: for the Lord God Almighty and the Lamb are the temple of it. [23] And the city had no need of the sun, neither of the moon, to shine in it: for the glory of God did lighten it, and the Lamb is the light thereof. [24] And the nations of them which are saved shall walk in the light of it: and the kings of the earth do bring their glory and honour into it. [25] And the gates of it shall not be shut at all by day: for there shall be no night there. [26] And they shall bring the glory and honour of the nations into it. [27] And there shall in no wise enter into it any thing that defileth, neither whatsoever worketh abomination, or maketh a lie: but they which are written in the Lamb's book of life.

GIVING IS GOD

Bless / Blessed / Blessing

We as children of God are Blessed to be a Blessing to all the world, as told to our father of faith; Abraham (Romans 4:16 see here).

We might not see it or even feel it, because of the situation(s) we may be in. When we hold on by faith, stay in faith in God's word, Jesus will strengthen us. No matter what is going on in our life, know that we are Blessed and the Blessings will manifest in the natural. Only believe by faith, which is the confidence and trust, we have in God !!!

The initial Blessing of God given to man is also found in Genesis 1:26–28 see under "Image ..."

† **Genesis 12:2-3 (KJV)** And I will make of thee a great nation, and I will bless thee, and make thy name great; and thou shalt be a blessing: And I will bless them that bless thee, and curse him that curseth thee: and in thee shall all families of the earth be blessed.

† **Genesis 12:2-3 (AMPC)** And I will make of you a great nation, and I will bless you [with abundant increase of favors] and make your name famous *and* distinguished, and you will be a blessing [dispensing good to others]. And I will bless those who bless you [who confer prosperity or happiness upon you] and

curse him who curses *or* uses insolent language toward you; in you will all the families *and* kindred of the earth be blessed [and by you they will bless themselves].

† **Genesis 24:35 (KJV)** And the Lord hath blessed my master greatly; and he is become great: and he hath given him flocks, and herds, and silver, and gold, and menservants, and maidservants, and camels, and asses.

† **Deuteronomy 28:1–13 (KJV)** ^{1}And it shall come to pass, if thou shalt hearken diligently unto the voice of the Lord thy God, to observe and to do all his commandments which I command thee this day, that the Lord thy God will set thee on high above all nations of the earth: ^{2} And all these blessings shall come on thee, and overtake thee, if thou shalt hearken unto the voice of the Lord thy God. ^{3} Blessed shalt thou be in the city, and blessed shalt thou be in the field. ^{4} Blessed shall be the fruit of thy body, and the fruit of thy ground, and the fruit of thy cattle, the increase of thy kine, and the flocks of thy sheep. ^{5} Blessed shall be thy basket and thy store. ^{6} Blessed shalt thou be when thou comest in, and blessed shalt thou be when thou goest out. ^{7} The Lord shall cause thine enemies that rise up against thee to be smitten before thy face: they shall come out against thee one way, and flee before thee seven ways. ^{8} The Lord shall command the blessing upon thee in thy storehouses, and in all that thou settest thine hand unto; and he shall

bless thee in the land which the Lord thy God giveth thee. ⁹ The Lord shall establish thee an holy people unto himself, as he hath sworn unto thee, if thou shalt keep the commandments of the Lord thy God, and walk in his ways. ¹⁰ And all people of the earth shall see that thou art called by the name of the Lord; and they shall be afraid of thee. ¹¹ And the Lord shall make thee plenteous in goods, in the fruit of thy body, and in the fruit of thy cattle, and in the fruit of thy ground, in the land which the Lord sware unto thy fathers to give thee. ¹² The Lord shall open unto thee his good treasure, the heaven to give the rain unto thy land in his season, and to bless all the work of thine hand: and thou shalt lend unto many nations, and thou shalt not borrow. ¹³ And the Lord shall make thee the head, and not the tail; and thou shalt be above only, and thou shalt not be beneath; if that thou hearken unto the commandments of the Lord thy God, which I command thee this day, to observe and to do them:

† **Psalm 105:15 (KJV)** Saying, Touch not mine anointed, and do my prophets no harm.

† **Psalm 115:15 (KJV)** Ye are blessed of the Lord which made heaven and earth.

† **Proverbs 10:22 (KJV)** The blessing of the Lord, it maketh rich, and he addeth no sorrow with it.

† **Proverbs 10:22 (AMPC)** The blessing of the Lord—it makes [truly] rich, and He adds no sorrow with it [neither does toiling increase it].

† **Isaiah 54:11-17 (MSG)** "Afflicted city, storm-battered, unpitied: I'm about to rebuild you with stones of turquoise, Lay your foundations with sapphires, construct your towers with rubies, Your gates with jewels, and all your walls with precious stones. All your children will have GOD for their teacher—what a mentor for your children! You'll be built solid, grounded in righteousness, far from any trouble—nothing to fear! far from terror—it won't even come close! If anyone attacks you, don't for a moment suppose that I sent them, And if any should attack, nothing will come of it. I create the blacksmith who fires up his forge and makes a weapon designed to kill. I also create the destroyer—but no weapon that can hurt you has ever been forged. Any accuser who takes you to court will be dismissed as a liar. This is what GOD's servants can expect. I'll see to it that everything works out for the best." GOD's Decree.

† **Zechariah 8:1–3 (NASB)** [The Coming Peace and Prosperity of Zion] Then the word of the LORD of hosts came, saying, "Thus says the LORD of hosts, 'I am exceedingly jealous for Zion, yes, with great wrath I am jealous for her.' Thus says the LORD, 'I will return to Zion and will dwell in the midst of Jerusalem. Then Jerusalem will be called the City of Truth, and the mountain of the LORD of hosts *will be called* the Holy Mountain.'

† **Matthew 13:16–17 (AMPC)** But blessed (happy,

fortunate, and to be envied) are your eyes because they do see, and your ears because they do hear. Truly I tell you, many prophets and righteous men [men who were upright and in right standing with God] yearned to see what you see, and did not see it, and to hear what you hear, and did not hear it.

† **John 20:29 (KJV)** Jesus saith unto him, Thomas, because thou hast seen me, thou hast believed: blessed are they that have not seen, and yet have believed.

† **Romans 4:8 (AMPC)** Blessed and happy and to be envied is the person of whose sin the Lord will take no account nor reckon it against him.

† **Romans 4:16 (KJV)** Therefore it is of faith, that it might be by grace; to the end the promise might be sure to all the seed; not to that only which is of the law, but to that also which is of the faith of Abraham; who is the father of us all.

† **Galatians 3:8-9 (ESV)** And the Scripture, foreseeing that God would justify the Gentiles by faith, preached the gospel beforehand to Abraham, saying, "In you shall all the nations be blessed." So then, those who are of faith are blessed along with Abraham, the man of faith.

† **Ephesians 1:3 (KJV)** Blessed be the God and Father of our Lord Jesus Christ, who hath blessed us with all spiritual blessings in heavenly places in Christ:

† **Ephesians 3:5-7 (NASB)** which in other generations

was not made known to the sons of men, as it has now been revealed to His holy apostles and prophets in the Spirit; *to be specific*, that the Gentiles are fellow heirs and fellow members of the body, and fellow partakers of the promise in Christ Jesus through the gospel, of which I was made a minister, according to the gift of God's grace which was given to me according to the working of His power.

† **Hebrews 4:6-11 (KJV)** ⁶ Seeing therefore it remaineth that some must enter therein, and they to whom it was first preached entered not in because of unbelief: ⁷ Again, he limiteth a certain day, saying in David, To day, after so long a time; as it is said, To day if ye will hear his voice, harden not your hearts. ⁸ For if Jesus had given them rest, then would he not afterward have spoken of another day. ⁹ There remaineth therefore a rest to the people of God. ¹⁰ For he that is entered into his rest, he also hath ceased from his own works, as God did from his. ¹¹ Let us labour therefore to enter into that rest, lest any man fall after the same example of unbelief.

† **James 1:12 (AMPC)** Blessed (happy, to be envied) is the man who is patient under trial and stands up under temptation, for when he has stood the test and been approved, he will receive [the victor's] crown of life which God has promised to those who love Him.

Care

If there is anyone who believes that no one cares about them, please read up on (Isaiah 53:5, see under "Jesus Christ"). God cares for you and us all. Jesus willingly gave His body to be crucified. Jesus believed and trusted that God the Father would raise Him up. As a farmer plants seed in the ground, so did Jesus die as a seed for us, so that we can live in Him. He took the sins away for the whole mankind. But each individual has to accept Jesus as their Lord and Savior, in order to partake in this life giving, life changing act. If you want to be set free from a life of sin and death, Jesus is offering eternal life.

† **Deuteronomy 11:11-14 (AMPC)** But the land which you enter to possess is a land of hills and valleys which drinks water of the rain of the heavens, A land for which the Lord your God cares; the eyes of the Lord your God are always upon it from the beginning of the year to the end of the year. And if you will diligently heed My commandments which I command you this day—to love the Lord your God and to serve Him with all your [mind and] heart and with your entire being—I will give the rain for your land in its season, the early rain and the latter rain, that you may gather in your grain, your new wine, and your oil.

- † **Luke 10:29-37 (NKJV)** ²⁹ But he, wanting to justify himself, said to Jesus, "And who is my neighbor?" ³⁰ Then Jesus answered and said: "A certain *man* went down from Jerusalem to Jericho, and fell among thieves, who stripped him of his clothing, wounded *him,* and departed, leaving *him* half dead. ³¹ Now by chance a certain priest came down that road. And when he saw him, he passed by on the other side. ³² Likewise a Levite, when he arrived at the place, came and looked, and passed by on the other side. ³³ But a certain Samaritan, as he journeyed, came where he was. And when he saw him, he had compassion. ³⁴ So he went to *him* and bandaged his wounds, pouring on oil and wine; and he set him on his own animal, brought him to an inn, and took care of him. ³⁵ On the next day, when he departed, he took out two denarii, gave *them* to the innkeeper, and said to him, 'Take care of him; and whatever more you spend, when I come again, I will repay you.' ³⁶ So which of these three do you think was neighbor to him who fell among the thieves?" ³⁷ And he said, "He who showed mercy on him." Then Jesus said to him, "Go and do likewise."

- † **Psalm 8:4 (AMPC)** What is man that You are mindful of him, and the son of [earthborn] man that You care for him?

- † **Proverbs 29:7 (NLT)** The godly care about the rights of the poor; the wicked don't care at all.

† **Romans 5:7–9 (AMPC)** ⁷Now it is an extraordinary thing for one to give his life even for an upright man, though perhaps for a noble *and* lovable *and* generous benefactor someone might even dare to die. ⁸But God shows *and* clearly proves His [own] love for us by the fact that while we were still sinners, Christ (the Messiah, the Anointed One) died for us. ⁹Therefore, since we are now justified (acquitted, made righteous, and brought into right relationship with God) by Christ's blood, how much more [certain is it that] we shall be saved by Him from the indignation *and* wrath of God.

† **2 Corinthians 5:14–15 (AMPC)** For the love of Christ controls *and* urges *and* impels us, because we are of the opinion *and* conviction that [if] One died for all, then all died; And He died for all, so that all those who live might live no longer to *and* for themselves, but to *and* for Him Who died and was raised again for their sake.

† **1 Peter 5:7 (KJV)** Casting all your care upon Him; for He careth for you.

GIVING IS GOD

Cause

Did you know that something without a cause will not come/happen, there has to be a cause? (Proverbs 26:2 says so, see here)

I know you are saying to yourself, "How can that be, when there is so much bad and cruel things happening in the world?" These things are so because the curse is in the world. The curse is the opposite of the blessing. You are probably wondering, like I just did, about the scripture; (Numbers 22:12 see here) that says no one can curse what God has blessed—which is still the truth! I believe, because the devil/curse is controlling the world, the innocent ones has to be covered by prayer of protection. I believe also, in most cases, this is where the freewill comes in, and I believe that the curse affected the mind/soul only (the body has no choice, but to be led to do whatever the mind wants).

Of course, after Adam & Eve fell, this is when sin (the curse) came in the earth. The man (Adam) could no longer depend on the spirit of God, because of fear. His spirit/ inner man as the result/*cause*, his spirit died (disconnected from God). God is only good He had to send Adam and Eve away from the Garden of Eden.

God had already decided, before the foundation of the world, to send His son; Jesus, into the world to redeem us. Before Jesus came in the world, people were only blessed, because they had a sensitive heart to hear and were willing to obey the Lord. God is still inside of us. After all, He created us. So at that time, the Lord came to the willing ones in different ways—a vision, a dream, angels, or through a priest or prophet.

The curse manifested through people, who allowed Satan to work through them, whether they knew it or not. They had been taken over by Satan, who had blinded their minds by fear which prevented them from hearing God.

This is what we are learning today. Once we accept Jesus as our Lord and Savior, we are to renew our mind with the Word of God. This gives the knowledge and strength to know what to do when the devil is trying to attack us through our mind; our thoughts. We are to first calm down, relax by casting our cares upon the Lord, be still so we can hear what God is saying. What God is saying is in the Bible.

The curse is also in things, in the ground, in the environment; this is why the weather is so destructive. Now, when we are strong in the Lord, we will hear the Holy Spirit tell us what to do, such as to command those things to cease, Jesus' name. The Holy Spirit is also here on the earth to comfort us and His angels to protect us.

We have to know that we are not alone; there is also an unseen world (see Hebrews 11:3 under

"Faith"). If an individual does not accept Jesus as the Lord and Savior, the one(s) that doesn't, has chosen Satan as their lord by default. Not to be frightened, especially if you are in Christ; pray Psalms 91 (see under "Safety").

Have you ever noticed how some people or things are doing extremely good? They are either blessed by God and continually keep His word before them, or they are helping Satan build up his kingdom. Again, Satan controls the mind of those who haven't accepted Jesus as the Lord and Savior (2 Corinthians 4:4, see here) and Christians, who are not allowing God to help them, by not building themselves up in His Word. We are supposed to be able to see who God's children are and who is not, by their fruit. Not just by works, but what they are producing to advance the Kingdom of God.

Again, when sin came in the world in the Garden of Eden through the disobedience of Adam, sin (the curse) contaminated everything. The devil, Satan, the fallen angel Lucifer, used a serpent's body to trick Eve. Yes, she was curious—why? I don't know. When they had everything, there should have not been a lack of anything, anywhere, but there was a loose end. God knew that this was the only way to defeat Satan, because we are all spirits that never die. God had to use His redemptive plan; using His son, Jesus, to redeem us. Jesus died for us, so that we can live in

Him, in our born-again spirit. (Galatians 2:20 says so, see here.)

Jesus is the solution for any cause that is not of God, Amen !!!

† **Genesis 3:22–24 (AMPC)** ²² And the Lord God said, Behold, the man has become like one of Us [the Father, Son, and Holy Spirit], to know [how to distinguish between] good and evil *and* blessing and calamity; and now, lest he put forth his hand and take also from the tree of life and eat, and live forever— ²³ Therefore the Lord God sent him forth from the Garden of Eden to till the ground from which he was taken. ²⁴ So [God] drove out the man; and He placed at the east of the Garden of Eden the cherubim and a flaming sword which turned every way, to keep *and* guard the way to the tree of life.

† **Numbers 22:12 (NKJV)** And God said to Balaam, "You shall not go with them; you shall not curse the people, for they are blessed."

† **1 Samuel 17:29 (KJV)** And David said, What have I now done? Is there not a cause?

† **Psalm 35:27 (KJV)** Let them shout for joy, and be glad, that favour my righteous cause: yea, let them say continually, Let the Lord be magnified, which hath pleasure in the prosperity of His servant.

† **Proverbs 26:2 (KJV)** As the bird by wandering, as the swallow by flying, so the curse causeless shall not

come.

† **2 Corinthians 4:4 (NKJV)** whose minds the god of this age has blinded, who do not believe, lest the light of the gospel of the glory of Christ, who is the image of God, should shine on them.

† **Galatians 2:20-21 (KJV)** I am crucified with Christ: nevertheless I live; yet not I, but Christ liveth in me: and the life which I now live in the flesh I live by the faith of the Son of God, who loved me, and gave himself for me. I do not frustrate the grace of God: ...

Character

Before I was born-again (as an adult), I can say my character was okay, but I was lacking in some areas. I was always obedient to my parents and my elders, as taught at home. I got along with my siblings, unlike some of them, who would fight among themselves. I guess I was considered the needy one of the family, so they would take up for me. Growing up, I was tall, very skinny, wore glasses and stuttered, or I would say the end of my sentence before the first, but I got it right when I repeated it. My family and close friends seemed to always want to help me do something. Not so with some friends/classmates, who thought I was weak and naïve. Even though I may have been, now I have learned in those times, I became strong, because God had stepped in. This is funny, when I look back, how one of my classmates in the seventh or eighth grade kicked the leg of my chair out from under me. Of course, I fell, but didn't hurt myself. The funny thing was when we had to go to the principal's office. I had an angry look on my face. My classmate, who I thought was my friend, was crying, making it look like I was the guilty one. I don't even remember why she did it, but I easily forgave.

Now, thinking about it, I believe I was bullied in

school. I remember how in high school, another female classmate, snatched my glasses off, because I believe I wouldn't cheat on our test in class.

Since I am learning who I am in Christ, my character can be found, defined, and corrected in the Holy Bible. I will continually thrive to have the character God says I am. I confess I am one of His sons that He is well pleased with.

† **Proverbs 3:3-5 (NASB)** Do not let kindness and truth leave you; Bind them around your neck, Write them on the tablet of your heart. So you will find favor and good repute In the sight of God and man. Trust in the LORD with all your heart And do not lean on your own understanding.

† **Proverbs 22:1 (KJV)** A good name is rather to be chosen than great riches, and loving favour rather than silver and gold.

† **Proverbs 31:10 (KJV)** Who can find a virtuous woman? for her price is far above rubies.

† **Ezekiel 18:7–9 (NASB)** if a man does not oppress anyone, but restores to the debtor his pledge, does not commit robbery, *but* gives his bread to the hungry and covers the naked with clothing, if he does not lend *money* on interest or take increase, *if* he keeps his hand from iniquity *and* executes true justice between man and man, *if* he walks in My statutes and My ordinances so as to deal faithfully—he is righteous

and will surely live," declares the Lord GOD.

† **Matthew 12:33 (KJV)** Either make the tree good, and his fruit good; or else make the tree corrupt, and his fruit corrupt: for the tree is known by his fruit.

† **1 Corinthians 15:33 (AMPC)** Do not be so deceived and misled! Evil companionships (communion, associations) corrupt and deprave good manners and morals and character.

† **Philippians 1:11 (NASB)** having been filled with the fruit of righteousness which *comes* through Jesus Christ, to the glory and praise of God.

† **Hebrews 1:3 (AMPC)** He is the sole expression of the glory of God [the Light-being, the out-raying or radiance of the divine], and He is the perfect imprint and very image of [God's] nature, upholding and maintaining and guiding and propelling the universe by His mighty word of power. When He had by offering Himself accomplished our cleansing of sins and riddance of guilt, He sat down at the right hand of the divine Majesty on high,

† **1 Peter 4:11-13 (AMPC)** Whoever speaks, [let him do it as one who utters] oracles of God; whoever renders service, [let him do it] as with the strength which God furnishes abundantly, so that in all things God may be glorified through Jesus Christ (the Messiah). To Him be the glory and dominion forever and ever (through endless ages). Amen (so be it).

Beloved, do not be amazed *and* bewildered at the fiery ordeal which is taking place to test your quality, as though something strange (unusual and alien to you and your position) were befalling you. But insofar as you are sharing Christ's sufferings, rejoice, so that when His glory [full of radiance and splendor] is revealed, you may also rejoice with triumph [exultantly].

Choices

Choices are so important. It is truly an honor to God that we can make choices. He gave us free will to choose Him or not to choose Him. I chose Jesus as my Lord and Savior, because He chose me. He sent the Holy Spirit to woo me and I couldn't resist Him. If God loved me enough to come for me, to save me from sin and death, how can I not receive Him?

He is the One who created me and you, we didn't create ourselves. If you think that we came from the boom, or a monkey, shake yourself free now, for you are going the wrong way. Yes, we may be old enough to make our own choices, but I have to give two more things. There is a cause and effect in every decision/choice that we make. We can do things God's way, which leads to Zoe/Life or Satan's life, which leads to destruction/death. There are only these two ways; there is no middle ground.

I believe we all owe it to ourselves, but especially to God to learn what is really going on; the truth. In order to learn, we have to go to a Bible-based teaching church. Also read the Bible for yourself and God will speak to you. Only believe and choose now, Jesus loves you so !!!

† **Deuteronomy 30:19 (KJV)** I call heaven and earth to record this day against you, that I have set before you life and death, blessing and cursing: therefore choose life, that both thou and thy seed may live:

† **Deuteronomy 30:19-20 (NASB)** I call heaven and earth to witness against you today, that I have set before you life and death, the blessing and the curse. So choose life in order that you may live, you and your descendants, by loving the LORD your God, by obeying His voice, and by holding fast to Him; for this is your life and the length of your days, that you may live in the land which the LORD swore to your fathers, to Abraham, Isaac, and Jacob, to give them."

† **Proverbs 14:12 (KJV)** There is a way which seemeth right unto a man, but the end thereof are the ways of death.

† **Matthew 7:13 (NASB)** [The Narrow and Wide Gates] "Enter through the narrow gate; for the gate is wide and the way is broad that leads to destruction, and there are many who enter through it.

† **Philippians 1:21-25 (AMPC)** For me to live is Christ [His life in me], and to die is gain [the gain of the glory of eternity]. If, however, it is to be life in the flesh *and* I am to live on here, that means fruitful service for me; so I can say nothing as to my personal preference [I cannot choose], But I am hard pressed between the two. My yearning desire is to depart (to be free of this world, to set forth) and be with Christ,

for that is far, far better; But to remain in my body is more needful *and* essential for your sake. Since I am convinced of this, I know that I shall remain and stay by you all, to promote your progress and joy in believing,

† **Revelation 3:15-17 (AMPC)** I know your [record of] works and what you are doing; you are neither cold nor hot. Would that you were cold or hot! So, because you are lukewarm and neither cold nor hot, I will spew you out of My mouth! For you say, I am rich; I have prospered and grown wealthy, and I am in need of nothing; and you do not realize and understand that you are wretched, pitiable, poor, blind, and naked.

† **Revelation 3:15–17 (NIV)** I know your deeds, that you are neither cold nor hot. I wish you were either one or the other! So, because you are lukewarm—neither hot nor cold—I am about to spit you out of my mouth. You say, 'I am rich; I have acquired wealth and do not need a thing.' But you do not realize that you are wretched, pitiful, poor, blind and naked.

Commission

I believe each child of God is commissioned to share the good news, the Gospel. For anyone who knows me, they can tell you, I enjoy posting on social media and blogging. I believe one of my strengths lies in communicating in written form. My desire is to share the joy of Jesus; it is like no other, and the peace is indescribable.

Are you one who is willing to take up this great commission to spread the Gospel to all the world (Mark 16:15)? If you don't go and do it personally, support someone who is representing the feet of Jesus (Romans 10:15 see here.)

Let us share our faith in God and the love of God with those who haven't accepted Jesus as Lord and Savior.

† **Isaiah 61:1–4 (AMPC)** The Spirit of the Lord God is upon me, because the Lord has anointed and qualified me to preach the Gospel of good tidings to the meek, the poor, and afflicted; He has sent me to bind up and heal the brokenhearted, to proclaim liberty to the [physical and spiritual] captives and the opening of the prison and of the eyes to those who are bound, To proclaim the acceptable year of the Lord [the year of His favor] and the day of vengeance of our God, to

comfort all who mourn, To grant [consolation and joy] to those who mourn in Zion—to give them an ornament (a garland or diadem) of beauty instead of ashes, the oil of joy instead of mourning, the garment [expressive] of praise instead of a heavy, burdened, and failing spirit—that they may be called oaks of righteousness [lofty, strong, and magnificent, distinguished for uprightness, justice, and right standing with God], the planting of the Lord, that He may be glorified. And they shall rebuild the ancient ruins; they shall raise up the former desolations and renew the ruined cities, the devastations of many generations.

† **Jeremiah 1:4–5 (KJV)** Then the word of the Lord came unto me, saying, Before I formed thee in the belly I knew thee; and before thou camest forth out of the womb I sanctified thee, and I ordained thee a prophet unto the nations.

† **Matthew 24:4–14 (NASB)** ⁴ And Jesus answered and said to them, "See to it that no one misleads you. ⁵ For many will come in My name, saying, 'I am the Christ,' and will mislead many. ⁶ You will be hearing of wars and rumors of wars. See that you are not frightened, for *those things* must take place, but *that* is not yet the end. ⁷ For nation will rise against nation, and kingdom against kingdom, and in various places there will be famines and earthquakes. ⁸ But all these things are *merely* the beginning of birth pangs. ⁹ "Then they will

deliver you to tribulation, and will kill you, and you will be hated by all nations because of My name. [10] At that time many will fall away and will betray one another and hate one another. [11] Many false prophets will arise and will mislead many. [12] Because lawlessness is increased, most people's love will grow cold. [13] But the one who endures to the end, he will be saved. [14] This gospel of the kingdom shall be preached in the whole world as a testimony to all the nations, and then the end will come.

† **Mark 16:15 (KJV)** And He said unto them, Go ye into all the world, and preach the gospel to every creature.

† **Luke 2:49 (KJV)** And He said unto them, How is it that ye sought me? wist ye not that I must be about my Father's business?

† **John 8:30–32 (KJV)** As He spake these words, many believed on Him. Then said Jesus to those Jews which believed on Him, If ye continue in My word, then are ye My disciples indeed; And ye shall know the truth, and the truth shall make you free.

† **Romans 10:15 (KJV)** And how shall they preach, except they be sent? as it is written, How beautiful are the feet of them that preach the gospel of peace, and bring glad tidings of good things!

† **Romans 15:20–21 (NASB)** And thus I aspired to preach the gospel, not where Christ was *already* named, so that I would not build on another man's

foundation; but as it is written, "THEY WHO HAD NO NEWS OF HIM SHALL SEE, AND THEY WHO HAVE NOT HEARD SHALL UNDERSTAND."

Commitment

Commitment to God for me means that I am all in. I have made up my mind, and I am not turning back. The apostle Paul summed up my commitment in Galatians 1:10 (see here for the NLT version).

† **2 Chronicles 16:9 (KJV)** For the eyes of the Lord run to and fro throughout the whole earth, to shew himself strong in the behalf of them whose heart is perfect toward him. Herein thou hast done foolishly: therefore from henceforth thou shalt have wars.

† **Psalm 37:3–5 (KJV)** Trust in the Lord, and do good; so shalt thou dwell in the land, and verily thou shalt be fed. Delight thyself also in the Lord: and He shall give thee the desires of thine heart. Commit thy way unto the Lord; trust also in Him; and He shall bring it to pass.

† **Psalm 105:7–9 (NASB)** He is the LORD our God; His judgments are in all the earth. He has remembered His covenant forever, The word which He commanded to a thousand generations, *The covenant* which He made with Abraham, And His oath to Isaac.

† **Luke 16:10-12 (NKJV)** He who *is* faithful in *what is* least is faithful also in much; and he who is unjust in *what is* least is unjust also in much. [11] Therefore if you

have not been faithful in the unrighteous mammon, who will commit to your trust the true *riches?* ¹² And if you have not been faithful in what is another man's, who will give you what is your own?

† **Luke 23:45-47 (NKJV)** Then the sun was darkened, and the veil of the temple was torn in two. And when Jesus had cried out with a loud voice, He said, "Father, 'into Your hands I commit My spirit.'" Having said this, He breathed His last. So when the centurion saw what had happened, he glorified God, saying, "Certainly this was a righteous Man!"

† **John 5:21-23 (NKJV)** For as the Father raises the dead and gives life to *them,* even so the Son gives life to whom He will. For the Father judges no one, but has committed all judgment to the Son, that all should honor the Son just as they honor the Father. He who does not honor the Son does not honor the Father who sent Him.

† **Galatians 1:10 (NLT)** Obviously, I'm not trying to win the approval of people, but of God. If pleasing people were my goal, I would not be Christ's servant.

Communion

Taking communion is to acknowledge what Jesus had done for me on the cross. I personally enjoy taking communion every day, whether it is bread and water (which it usually is), but whatever it is, it represents Jesus' body and His precious blood. I take communion every day, because Jesus said, as often as I do this, do it in the remembrance of Him. I like to take it early in the morning, because the day can get distracting, but the Holy Spirit would bring to my remembrance, at the front door, if I had not taken communion today. So I thank Him for reminding me and go take communion. I made myself a short prayer confession with 1 Corinthians 11:24-25 (see here), (Galatians 2:20-21 under Cause and 2 Corinthians 5:21 under Righteousness).

† **John 6:53–55 (AMPC)** And Jesus said to them, I assure you, most solemnly I tell you, you cannot have any life in you unless you eat the flesh of the Son of Man and drink His blood [unless you appropriate His life and the saving merit of His blood]. He who feeds on My flesh and drinks My blood has (possesses now) eternal life, and I will raise him up [from the dead] on the last day. For My flesh is true and genuine food, and My blood is true and genuine drink.

† **1 Corinthians 10:15-17 (NKJV)** I speak as to wise men; judge for yourselves what I say. The cup of blessing which we bless, is it not the communion of the blood of Christ? The bread which we break, is it not the communion of the body of Christ? For we, *though* many, are one bread *and* one body; for we all partake of that one bread.

† **1 Corinthians 10:16-17 (NASB)** Is not the cup of blessing which we bless a sharing in the blood of Christ? Is not the bread which we break a sharing in the body of Christ? Since there is one bread, we who are many are one body; for we all partake of the one bread.

† **1 Corinthians 11:24–25 (KJV)** And when He had given thanks, He brake it, and said, Take, eat: this is My body, which is broken for you: this do in remembrance of Me. After the same manner also He took the cup, when He had supped, saying, this cup is the new testament in My blood: this do ye, as oft as ye drink it, in remembrance of Me.

† **2 Corinthians 13:14 (KJV)** The grace of the Lord Jesus Christ, and the love of God, and the communion of the Holy Ghost, be with you all. Amen.

Compassion

In a class I had taken, we were asked to think of an adjective with the same first letter as our first name. So I chose compassionate; Compassionate Claudette was on my desk name card. The dictionary says it means showing feelings of sympathy for the suffering of others, often with a desire to help. My desire to do more than to only have the desire, this is why I am happy to know that God gives me the desires of my heart, so it shall come to pass.

† **Psalm 145:8 (KJV)** The Lord is gracious, and full of compassion; slow to anger, and of great mercy.

† **Matthew 25:44–46 (NASB)** Then they themselves also will answer, 'Lord, when did we see You hungry, or thirsty, or a stranger, or naked, or sick, or in prison, and did not take care of You?' Then He will answer them, 'Truly I say to you, to the extent that you did not do it to one of the least of these, you did not do it to Me.' These will go away into eternal punishment, but the righteous into eternal life."

† **Mark 6:34 (KJV)** And Jesus, when he came out, saw much people, and was moved with compassion toward them, because they were as sheep not having a shepherd: and he began to teach them many things.

† **Luke 10:33–34 (AMPC)** But a certain Samaritan, as he traveled along, came down to where he was; and when he saw him, he was moved with pity and sympathy [for him], And went to him and dressed his wounds, pouring on [them] oil and wine. Then he set him on his own beast and brought him to an inn and took care of him.

† **1 John 3:17 (KJV)** But whoso hath this world's good, and seeth his brother have need, and shutteth up his bowels of compassion from him, how dwelleth the love of God in him?

† **Jude 1:21–23 (KJV)** Keep yourselves in the love of God, looking for the mercy of our Lord Jesus Christ unto eternal life. And of some have compassion, making a difference: And others save with fear, pulling them out of the fire; hating even the garment spotted by the flesh.

Continual

God has a rhythm. *The definition for rhythm: in a regular pattern and in characteristic pattern.*

Regular pattern: *a regularly recurring pattern of activity, e.g. the cycle of the seasons, night and day, or repeated functions of the body.*

Characteristic pattern: *the characteristic pattern of an activity.* **Characteristic:** *a feature or quality that makes somebody or something recognizable.*

I have discovered God uses a pattern, an order, and is consistent. We all should know that what God does, is nowhere near "regular", it is supernatural. There is no other like Him. He created the seasons, so we can know what part of the year we are presently in or which season is next. Seasons has a pattern, arranged in a specific order and is consistently the same every year. Spring, summer, fall, winter, and it repeats in that order. Likewise, keep believing in God, keep hearing the Word of God; for faith comes by hearing and hearing, a continual renewing of the mind. Let us keep loving one another, because faith works by love.

When we are born-again, God bestow upon us His precious promises, principals, processes, and Himself. These will never change; they are forever. All of His gifts (see Romans 11:29 under Gifts) — sowing and reaping, giving and receiving—and Jesus will never change. Know when we sow our seed in good ground, we will reap a good harvest from that seed. (See Matthew 13:23 under Increase)

We as sons of God are required to learn how to get into His flow of things (Matthew 6:33, AMPC, see under God's Way) then we will never fall (2 Peter 1:10, AMPC, see here).

† **Genesis 1:11–12 (AMPC)** ¹¹ And God said, Let the earth put forth [tender] vegetation: plants yielding seed and fruit trees yielding fruit whose seed is in itself, each according to its kind, upon the earth. And it was so. ¹² The earth brought forth vegetation: plants yielding seed according to their own kinds and trees bearing fruit in which was their seed, each according to its kind. And God saw that it was good (suitable, admirable) *and* He approved it.

† **Genesis 1:14–16 (AMPC)** ¹³ And there was evening and there was morning, a third day. ¹⁴ And God said, Let there be lights in the expanse of the heavens to separate the day from the night, and let them be signs *and* tokens [of God's provident care], and [to mark] seasons, days, and years, ¹⁵ And let them be lights in the expanse of the sky to give light upon the earth. And it was so. ¹⁶ And God made the two great lights—the greater light (the sun) to rule the day and the lesser light (the moon) to rule the night. He also made the

stars.

† **Genesis 8:22 (KJV)** While the earth remaineth, seedtime and harvest, and cold and heat, and summer and winter, and day and night shall not cease.

† **Joshua 1:8 (MSG)** And don't for a minute let this Book of The Revelation be out of mind. Ponder and meditate on it day and night, making sure you practice everything written in it. Then you'll get where you're going; then you'll succeed.

† **Psalm 27:13-14 (AMPC)** [What, what would have become of me] had I not believed that I would see the Lord's goodness in the land of the living! Wait *and* hope for *an* expect the Lord; be brave *and* of good courage and let your heart be stout *and* enduring. Yes, wait for *and* hope for *and* expect the Lord.

† **Psalm 70:4 (KJV)** Let all those that seek thee rejoice and be glad in thee: and let such as love thy salvation say continually, Let God be magnified.

† **Psalm 107:1 (KJV)** O give thanks unto the LORD, for he is good: for his mercy endureth for ever.

† **Malachi 3:6 (KJV)** For I am the LORD…

† **Malachi 3:6 (MSG)** "I am GOD—yes, I AM. I haven't changed.

† **Mark 5:28 (AMPC)** For she kept saying, If I only touch His garments, I shall be restored to health.

† **Mark 10:28–30 (KJV)** Then Peter began to say unto

him, Lo, we have left all, and have followed thee. And Jesus answered and said, Verily I say unto you, There is no man that hath left house, or brethren, or sisters, or father, or mother, or wife, or children, or lands, for my sake, and the gospel's, But he shall receive an hundredfold now in this time, houses, and brethren, and sisters, and mothers, and children, and lands, with persecutions; and in the world to come eternal life.

† **Luke 11:8-9 (AMPC)** I tell you, although he will not get up and supply him anything because he is his friend, yet because of his shameless persistence *and* insistence he will get up and give him as much as he needs. So I say to you, Ask *and* keep on asking and it shall be given you; seek *and* keep on seeking and you shall find; knock *and* keep on knocking and the door shall be opened to you.

† **Luke 18:1-3 (MSG)** [The Story of the Persistent Widow] Jesus told them a story showing that it was necessary for them to pray consistently and never quit. He said, "There was once a judge in some city who never gave God a thought and cared nothing for people. A widow in that city kept after him: 'My rights are being violated. Protect me!'

† **Romans 1:9 (KJV)** For God is my witness, whom I serve with my spirit in the gospel of his Son, that without ceasing I make mention of you always in my prayers;

† **Galatians 6:7 (KJV)** Be not deceived; God is not

mocked: for whatsoever a man soweth, that shall he also reap.

† **Galatians 6:8 (KJV)** For he that soweth to his flesh shall of the flesh reap corruption; but he that soweth to the Spirit shall of the Spirit reap life everlasting.

† **Ephesians 5:10 (AMPC)** And try to learn [in your experience] what is pleasing to the Lord [let your lives be constant proofs of what is most acceptable to Him].

† **Philippians 4:15-17 (KJV)** Now ye Philippians know also, that in the beginning of the gospel, when I departed from Macedonia, no church communicated with me as concerning giving and receiving, but ye only. For even in Thessalonica ye sent once and again unto my necessity. Not because I desire a gift: but I desire fruit that may abound to your account.

† **1 Thessalonians 1:3-4 (KJV)** Remembering without ceasing your work of faith, and labour of love, and patience of hope in our Lord Jesus Christ, in the sight of God and our Father; Knowing, brethren beloved, your election of God.

† **Hebrews 13:8 (AMPC)** Jesus Christ (the Messiah) is [always] the same, yesterday, today, [yes] and forever (to the ages).

† **Hebrews 13:15 (NKJV)** Therefore by Him let us continually offer the sacrifice of praise to God, that is, the fruit of *our* lips, giving thanks to His name.

† **2 Peter 1:10 (AMPC)** Because of this, brethren, be all

the more solicitous *and* eager to make sure (to ratify, to strengthen, to make steadfast) your calling and election; for if you do this, you will never stumble *or* fall.

† **James 5:16 (KJV)** Confess your faults one to another, and pray one for another, that ye may be healed. The effectual fervent prayer of a righteous man availeth much.

† **James 5:16 (AMPC)** The earnest (heartfelt, continued) prayer of a righteous man makes tremendous power available [dynamic in its working].

Covenant / Promise / Vow

What an honor to be in covenant with God. To accept Jesus should be a no-brainer for us, because God is doing everything. The Father does the work. Jesus shed His blood for us, gave us power and strength, and now He intercedes for us and the Holy Spirit helps us to do what God has called us to do, when we let Him. All we have to do is first to receive Jesus Christ as our Lord and Savior, learn God's will for our lives, which is the renewing of our minds with the word of God (Holy Bible). This will allow Him to lead us and guide us, as we go to Him in prayer and walk and talk with the Holy Spirit during the day. Thanking Him for watching over us, especially as we sleep. We are Blessed !!!

A vow is a covenant promise that is meant for an agreement to be settled. A done-deal. A vow made to God is certainly a "no turning back" deal, nor an "I changed my mind" moment.

† **Genesis 2:15-17 (KJV)** And the Lord God took the man, and put him into the garden of Eden to dress it and to keep it. And the Lord God commanded the man, saying, Of every tree of the garden thou mayest freely eat: But of the tree of the knowledge of good

and evil, thou shalt not eat of it: for in the day that thou eatest thereof thou shalt surely die.

† **Genesis 9:12-14 (NASB)** God said, "This is the sign of the covenant which I am making between Me and you and every living creature that is with you, for all successive generations; I set My bow in the cloud, and it shall be for a sign of a covenant between Me and the earth. It shall come about, when I bring a cloud over the earth, that the bow will be seen in the cloud,

† **Genesis 17:4-5 (KJV)** As for me, behold, my covenant is with thee, and thou shalt be a father of many nations. Neither shall thy name any more be called Abram, but thy name shall be Abraham; for a father of many nations have I made thee.

† **Joshua 21:45 (GW)** Every single good promise that the Lord had given the nation of Israel came true.

† **1 Samuel 1:11 (KJV)** And she vowed a vow, and said, O Lord of hosts, if Thou wilt indeed look on the affliction of Thine handmaid, and remember me, and not forget Thine handmaid, but wilt give unto Thine handmaid a man child, then I will give him unto the Lord all the days of his life, and there shall no razor come upon his head.

† **1 Kings 8:56 (AMPC)** Blessed be the Lord, Who has given rest to His people Israel, according to all that He promised. Not one word has failed of all His good promise which He promised through Moses His

servant.

† **Ecclesiastes 5:5 (KJV)** Better is it that thou shouldest not vow, than that thou shouldest vow and not pay.

† **Psalm 89:34 (GW)** My covenant will I not break, nor alter the thing that is gone out of My lips.

† **Psalm 116:17-19 (AMPC)** I will offer to You the sacrifice of thanksgiving and will call on the name of the Lord. I will pay my vows to the Lord, yes, in the presence of all His people, In the courts of the Lord's house—in the midst of you, O Jerusalem. Praise the Lord! (Hallelujah!)

† **Isaiah 55:11 (KJV)** So shall my word be that goeth forth out of my mouth: it shall not return unto me void, but it shall accomplish that which I please, and it shall prosper in the thing whereto I sent it.

† **Zechariah 9:11-12 (KJV)** As for thee also, by the blood of Thy covenant I have sent forth thy prisoners out of the pit wherein is no water. Turn you to the strong hold, ye prisoners of hope: even to day do I declare that I will render double unto thee;

† **Romans 4:16 (AMPC)** Therefore, [inheriting] the promise is the outcome of faith *and* depends [entirely] on faith, in order that it might be given as an act of grace (unmerited favor), to make it stable *and* valid *and* guaranteed to all his descendants—not only to the devotees *and* adherents of the Law, but also to those who share the faith of Abraham, who is [thus] the

father of us all.

† **Romans 5:18-20 (KJV)** Therefore as by the offence of one judgment came upon all men to condemnation; even so by the righteousness of One the free gift came upon all men unto justification of life. For as by one man's disobedience many were made sinners, so by the obedience of One shall many be made righteous. Moreover the law entered, that the offence might abound. But where sin abounded, grace did much more abound:

† **2 Corinthians 1:20 (KJV)** For all the promises of God in Him are yea, and in Him Amen, unto the glory of God by us.

† **Galatians 3:14 (KJV)** That the blessing of Abraham might come on the Gentiles through Jesus Christ; that we might receive the promise of the Spirit through faith.

† **Galatians 3:15-17 (KJV)** Brethren, I speak after the manner of men; Though it be but a man's covenant, yet if it be confirmed, no man disannulleth, or addeth thereto. Now to Abraham and his seed were the promises made. He saith not, And to seeds, as of many; but as of One, And to thy seed, which is Christ. And this I say, that the covenant, that was confirmed before of God in Christ, the law, which was four hundred and thirty years after, cannot disannul, that it should make the promise of none effect.

† **1 Thessalonians 5:23-24 (KJV)** And the very God of peace sanctify you wholly; and I pray God your whole spirit and soul and body be preserved blameless unto the coming of our Lord Jesus Christ. Faithful is He that calleth you, who also will do it.

† **Hebrews 8:6-9 (KJV)** But now hath He obtained a more excellent ministry, by how much also He is the mediator of a better covenant, which was established upon better promises. For if that first covenant had been faultless, then should no place have been sought for the second. For finding fault with them, He saith, Behold, the days come, saith the Lord, when I will make a new covenant with the house of Israel and with the house of Judah: Not according to the covenant that I made with their fathers in the day when I took them by the hand to lead them out of the land of Egypt; because they continued not in my covenant, and I regarded them not, saith the Lord.

† **Hebrews 8:9 (AMPC)** It will not be like the covenant that I made with their forefathers on the day when I grasped them by the hand to help and relieve them and to lead them out from the land of Egypt, for they did not abide in My agreement with them, and so I withdrew My favor and disregarded them, says the Lord.

† **James 1:12 (AMPC)** Blessed (happy, to be envied) is the man who is patient under trial and stands up under temptation, for when he has stood the test and been

approved, he will receive [the victor's] crown of life which God has promised to those who love Him.

† **2 Peter 2:21 (AMPC)** For never to have obtained a [full, personal] knowledge of the way of righteousness would have been better for them than, having obtained [such knowledge], to turn back from the holy commandment which was [verbally] delivered to them.

† **Jude 1:24-25 (KJV)** Now unto Him that is able to keep you from falling, and to present you faultless before the presence of His glory with exceeding joy, To the only wise God our Saviour, be glory and majesty, dominion and power, both now and ever. Amen.

† **Revelation 21:5-7 (KJV)** And He that sat upon the throne said, Behold, I make all things new. And He said unto me, Write: for these words are true and faithful. And He said unto me, It is done. I am Alpha and Omega, the beginning and the end. I will give unto him that is athirst of the fountain of the water of life freely. He that overcometh shall inherit all things; and I will be his God, and he shall be My son.

Creating Value

Imagine a world where everyone feels valuable. There would be not lack of any good thing. They would have a sense of value, not arrogance, but a confidence of their dignity intact as it should. We are creative people, because God made us like Him. We have the ability to add value to someone's life. With God, this is possible, so let's create a value-filled world !!!

Value *definition can be money and/or a usefulness of something to somebody.*

† **Proverbs 10:20 (AMPC)** The tongues of those who are upright *and* in right standing with God are as choice silver; the minds of those who are wicked *and* out of harmony with God are of little value.

† **Proverbs 31:10 (AMPC)** A capable, intelligent, *and* virtuous woman—who is he who can find her? She is far more precious than jewels *and* her value is far above rubies *or* pearls.

† **Isaiah 32:14-16 (AMPC)** For the palace shall be forsaken, the populous city shall be deserted; the hill and the watchtower shall become dens [for wild animals] endlessly, a joy for wild donkeys, a pasture for flocks, Until the Spirit is poured upon us from on high, and the wilderness becomes a fruitful field, and

the fruitful field is valued as a forest. Then justice will dwell in the wilderness, and righteousness (moral and spiritual rectitude in every area and relation) will abide in the fruitful field.

† **John 17:23 (AMPC)** I in them and You in Me, in order that they may become one and perfectly united, that the world may know and [definitely] recognize that You sent Me and that You have loved them [even] as You have loved Me.

† **Romans 12:9–11 (NASB)** *Let* love *be* without hypocrisy. Abhor what is evil; cling to what is good. *Be* devoted to one another in brotherly love; ¹give preference to one another in honor; not lagging behind in diligence, fervent in spirit, serving the Lord;

† **Ephesians 4:12 (KJV)** For the perfecting of the saints, for the work of the ministry, for the edifying of the body of Christ:

† **Ephesians 6:2 (AMPC)** Honor (esteem and value as precious) your father and your mother—this is the first commandment with a promise—

† **Ephesians 6:8 (KJV)** Knowing that whatsoever good thing any man doeth, the same shall he receive of the Lord, whether he be bond or free.

† **Ephesians 6:7-8 (NKJV)** … with goodwill doing service, as to the Lord, and not to men, knowing that whatever good anyone does, he will receive the same from the Lord, whether *he is* a slave or free.

† **Colossians 3:16-17 (AMPC)** ¹⁶ Let the word [spoken by] Christ (the Messiah) have its home [in your hearts and minds] *and* dwell in you in [all its] richness, as you teach and admonish *and* train one another in all insight *and* intelligence *and* wisdom [in spiritual things, and as you sing] psalms and hymns and spiritual songs, making melody to God with [His] grace in your hearts. ¹⁷ And whatever you do [no matter what it is] in word or deed, do everything in the name of the Lord Jesus *and* in [dependence upon] His Person, giving praise to God the Father through Him.

† **1 Timothy 4:8 (AMPC)** For physical training is of some value (useful for a little), but godliness (spiritual training) is useful *and* of value in everything *and* in every way, for it holds promise for the present life and also for the life which is to come

Our Daily Living

My daily living is acknowledging God daily by thanking Him for my life and the lives of my family and love ones. My daily reading of His word, and listening to His word being taught by His men and women of God, gives me the confidence that I can do all things through Christ. There is nothing else I would rather do, even when I am among people, I know that I can still have a conversation with the Holy Spirit. This is the good life!

† **Joshua 1:8 (KJV)** This book of the law shall not depart out of thy mouth; but thou shalt meditate therein day and night, that thou mayest observe to do according to all that is written therein: for then thou shalt make thy way prosperous, and then thou shalt have good success.

† **Psalm 67:1–3 (KJV)** God be merciful unto us, and bless us; and cause His face to shine upon us; Selah. That Thy way may be known upon earth, Thy saving health among all nations. Let the people praise Thee, O God; let all the people praise Thee.

† **Psalm 127:2 (KJV)** It is vain for you to rise up early, to sit up late, to eat the bread of sorrows: for so He giveth His beloved sleep.

- † **Matthew 6:11 (KJV)** Give us this day our daily bread.

- † **Matthew 6:33 (KJV)** But seek ye first the kingdom of God, and his righteousness; and all these things shall be added unto you.

- † **Romans 12:1-2 (KJV)** I beseech you therefore, brethren, by the mercies of God, that ye present your bodies a living sacrifice, holy, acceptable unto God, which is your reasonable service. And be not conformed to this world: but be ye transformed by the renewing of your mind, that ye may prove what is that good, and acceptable, and perfect, will of God

Deliverance

God has delivered me from a lot of things. One of those I will share with you is that I was addicted to ice cream. Did you know that it doesn't take much to eat a whole pint of ice cream a night? All you have to do is get a spoon and it just melts in your mouth. No work really, right? Oh, I even got to the point and had a piece of cake with it.

It was so good, I have to admit it; but it wasn't good for my body. Plus, I am spirit, and I tell my mind and body what to do, not the other way.

After God had delivered me, how many of you know that the devil tried to convince me that, since I had stopped for months or years now, it is okay to start back? Thank God for His men and women of God. I heard one of these men of God referring to ice cream. I was thinking, I didn't tell him about that, God must have told him.

Now, I am ice cream free !!!

† **Psalm 34:3–5 (KJV)** O magnify the Lord with me, and let us exalt His name together. I sought the Lord, and He heard me, and delivered me from all my fears. They looked unto Him, and were lightened: and their faces were not ashamed.

† **Psalm 34:19 (KJV)** Many are the afflictions of the righteous: but the Lord delivereth him out of them all.

† **Psalm 40:1–3 (KJV)** I waited patiently for the Lord; and he inclined unto me, and heard my cry. He brought me up also out of an horrible pit, out of the miry clay, and set my feet upon a rock, and established my goings. And he hath put a new song in my mouth, even praise unto our God: many shall see it, and fear, and shall trust in the Lord.

† **Zechariah 9:11–12 (AMPC)** As for you also, because of and for the sake of the [covenant of the Lord with His people, which was sealed with sprinkled] covenant blood, I have released and sent forth your imprisoned people out of the waterless pit. Return to the stronghold [of security and prosperity], you prisoners of hope; even today do I declare that I will restore double your former prosperity to you.

† **Romans 8:31–33 (KJV)** What shall we then say to these things? If God be for us, who can be against us? He that spared not His own Son, but delivered Him up for us all, how shall He not with Him also freely give us all things? Who shall lay any thing to the charge of God's elect? It is God that justifieth.

Diligence

Diligence to me means to continually build my faith in God. To watch what I see, hear, do, and say, so that it would line up with the Word of God. To be quick to repent, when I sin (see Romans 3:23 under Righteousness) and ask God for forgiveness, which He will forgive me, when I confess them to Him.

This may sound like not having any fun, but it is the most rewarding fun imaginable; it's wonderful. I know by staying with God and not compromising, I have a free conscience and that is a peace of mind, like Jesus Christ. I will be able to help others to stand strong in the Lord too, in Jesus' name.

† **Proverbs 4:23 (KJV)** Keep thy heart with all diligence; for out of it are the issues of life.

† **Proverbs 10:4 (AMPC)** He becomes poor who works with a slack and idle hand, but the hand of the diligent makes rich.

† **Proverbs 22:28–29 (KJV)** Remove not the ancient landmark, which thy fathers have set. Seest thou a man diligent in his business? he shall stand before kings; he shall not stand before mean men.

† **2 Corinthians 8:6-8 (NKJV)** But as you abound in

everything—in faith, in speech, in knowledge, in all diligence, and in your love for us—*see* that you abound in this grace also [Christ Our Pattern] I speak not by commandment, but I am testing the sincerity of your love by the diligence of others.

† **Hebrews 6:10–12 (KJV)** For God is not unrighteous to forget your work and labour of love, which ye have shewed toward his name, in that ye have ministered to the saints, and do minister. And we desire that every one of you do shew the same diligence to the full assurance of hope unto the end: That ye be not slothful, but followers of them who through faith and patience inherit the promises.

† **2 Peter 1:2-7 (KJV)** ^{2} Grace and peace be multiplied unto you through the knowledge of God, and of Jesus our Lord, ^{3} According as his divine power hath given unto us all things that pertain unto life and godliness, through the knowledge of him that hath called us to glory and virtue: ^{4} Whereby are given unto us exceeding great and precious promises: that by these ye might be partakers of the divine nature, having escaped the corruption that is in the world through lust. ^{5} And beside this, giving all diligence, add to your faith virtue; and to virtue knowledge; ^{6} And to knowledge temperance; and to temperance patience; and to patience godliness; ^{7} And to godliness brotherly kindness; and to brotherly kindness charity.

† **2 Peter 1:10-11 (NKJV)** Therefore, brethren, be even

more diligent to make your call and election sure, for if you do these things you will never stumble; for so an entrance will be supplied to you abundantly into the everlasting kingdom of our Lord and Savior Jesus Christ.

Direction

I don't know about you, but I've always wanted to know the right direction to go. I have already used up a lot of years, but now since I know the right direction. I am on the right road and I am not getting off. I am blessed, I am happy, I am at peace, and I am full of joy, no matter what is going on around me.

† **Psalm 1:1–2 (KJV)** Blessed is the man that walketh not in the counsel of the ungodly, nor standeth in the way of sinners, nor sitteth in the seat of the scornful. But his delight is in the law of the Lord; and in his law doth he meditate day and night.

† **Psalm 1:3 (KJV)** And he shall be like a tree planted by the rivers of water, that bringeth forth his fruit in his season; his leaf also shall not wither; and whatsoever he doeth shall prosper.

† **Psalm 32:8 (KJV)** I will instruct thee and teach thee in the way which thou shalt go: I will guide thee with mine eye.

† **Psalm 32:8 (AMPC)** I [the Lord] will instruct you and teach you in the way you should go; I will counsel you with My eye upon you.

† **Proverbs 3:5–7 (KJV)** Trust in the Lord with all thine heart; and lean not unto thine own understanding. In

all thy ways acknowledge Him, and He shall direct thy paths.

† **Proverbs 3:11 (KJV)** My son, despise not the chastening of the Lord; neither be weary of his correction:

† **Proverbs 16:9 (KJV)** A man's heart deviseth his way: but the Lord directeth his steps.

† **Proverbs 29:18 (KJV)** Where there is no vision, the people perish: but he that keepeth the law, happy is he.

† **Proverbs 29:18 (AMPC)** Where there is no vision [no redemptive revelation of God], the people perish; but he who keeps the law [of God, which includes that of man]—blessed (happy, fortunate, and enviable) is he.

† **Isaiah 30:21 (KJV)** And thine ears shall hear a word behind thee, saying, This is the way, walk ye in it, when ye turn to the right hand, and when ye turn to the left.

† **Isaiah 48:17 (KJV)** Thus saith the Lord, thy Redeemer, the Holy One of Israel; I am the Lord thy God which teacheth thee to profit, which leadeth thee by the way that thou shouldest go.

† **Mark 4:35 (KJV)** And the same day, when the even was come, He saith unto them, Let us pass over unto the other side.

Discern / Discernment

Discernment is so very important to God. He wants us to hear Him when He is talking to us. Of course, God already know the things we will say and do before we even think about them, but He wants us to know when He speaks. He knows the things that we react to, but the bad thing is that Satan figures this out when he tries things that gets the response he wants that will open the door for him to kill, steal or destroy us.

Discernment is to know the difference between God and the devil and the difference between good and evil. God wants us to learn to obey His Voice only, which is His Will in His Word; the Holy Bible (see Romans 12:1-2 here).

To learn to discern the voice of God, we must first accept His Son; Jesus as our Lord and Savior (see Romans 10:9-10 under Life). Jesus is the Golden Open Door. Also God gives us the opportunity to receive His Spirit (see Acts 2:38 under Gifts). When we allow the Holy Spirit to lead us, He is teaching us the things of God, which allows the Blessings of God to flow freely in our lives (see Deuteronomy 28:1-2 here). On the other side, when we don't learn God's voice, this blocks our Blessings (see Deuteronomy 28:15 here).

The curse is not from God, it is certainly from the devil, who by deception tries to make us think it is from God.

We must ON PURPOSE seek to learn to discern God's voice, if not we automatically by default choose the ways of the devil. We, as individuals must learn to discern God's voice, because our life may or a worthwhile life will depend on it.

† **Deuteronomy 28:1-2 (NKJV)** Now it shall come to pass, if you diligently obey the voice of the LORD your God, to observe carefully all His commandments which I command you today, that the LORD your God will set you high above all nations of the earth. And all these blessings shall come upon you and overtake you, because you obey the voice of the LORD your God:

† **Deuteronomy 28:15 (NKJV)** "But it shall come to pass, if you do not obey the voice of the LORD your God, to observe carefully all His commandments and His statutes which I command you today, that all these curses will come upon you and overtake you:

† **Proverbs 28:1-2 (AMPC)** The wicked flee when no man pursues them, but the [uncompromisingly] righteous are bold as a lion. When a land transgresses, it has many rulers, but when the ruler is a man of discernment, understanding, *and* knowledge, its stability will long continue.

† **Malachi 3:17-18 (AMPC)** And they shall be Mine,

says the Lord of hosts, in that day when I publicly recognize *and* openly declare them to be My jewels (My special possession, My peculiar treasure). And I will spare them, as a man spares his own son who serves him. Then shall you return and discern between the righteous and the wicked, between him who serves God and him who does not serve Him.

† **John 6:6 (KJV)** And this he said to prove him: for he himself knew what he would do.

† **Romans 12:1-2 (NKJV)** [Living Sacrifices to God] I beseech you therefore, brethren, by the mercies of God, that you present your bodies a living sacrifice, holy, acceptable to God, *which is* your reasonable service. And do not be conformed to this world, but be transformed by the renewing of your mind, that you may prove what *is* that good and acceptable and perfect will of God.

† **1 Corinthians 2:14 (KJV)** But the natural man receiveth not the things of the Spirit of God: for they are foolishness unto him: neither can he know them, because they are spiritually discerned.

† **1 Corinthians 12:9–11 (KJV)** But the manifestation of the Spirit is given to every man to profit withal. For to one is given by the Spirit the word of wisdom; to another the word of knowledge by the same Spirit; To another faith by the same Spirit; to another the gifts of healing by the same Spirit; To another the working of miracles; to another prophecy; to another discerning of

spirits; to another divers kinds of tongues; to another the interpretation of tongues: But all these worketh that One and the selfsame Spirit, dividing to every man severally as He will.

† **2 Corinthians 4:2–4 (AMPC)** We have renounced disgraceful ways (secret thoughts, feelings, desires and underhandedness, the methods and arts that men hide through shame); we refuse to deal craftily (to practice trickery and cunning) or to adulterate or handle dishonestly the Word of God, but we state the truth openly (clearly and candidly). And so we commend ourselves in the sight and presence of God to every man's conscience. But even if our Gospel (the glad tidings) also be hidden (obscured and covered up with a veil that hinders the knowledge of God), it is hidden [only] to those who are perishing and obscured [only] to those who are spiritually dying and veiled [only] to those who are lost. For the god of this world has blinded the unbelievers' minds [that they should not discern the truth], preventing them from seeing the illuminating light of the Gospel of the glory of Christ (the Messiah), Who is the Image and Likeness of God.

† **Ephesians 1:17 (KJV)** That the God of our Lord Jesus Christ, the Father of glory, may give unto you the spirit of wisdom and revelation in the knowledge of him:

† **Philippians 1:9-10 (AMPC)** And this I pray: that your love may abound yet more and more *and* extend

to its fullest development in knowledge and all keen insight [that your love may display itself in greater depth of acquaintance and more comprehensive discernment], So that you may surely learn to sense what is vital, *and* approve *and* prize what is excellent *and* of real value [recognizing the highest and the best, and distinguishing the moral differences], and that you may be untainted *and* pure and unerring *and* blameless [so that with hearts sincere and certain and unsullied, you may approach] the day of Christ [not stumbling *nor* causing others to stumble].

† **Hebrews 4:12 (KJV)** For the word of God is quick, and powerful, and sharper than any twoedged sword, piercing even to the dividing asunder of soul and spirit, and of the joints and marrow, and is a discerner of the thoughts and intents of the heart.

† **Hebrews 5:12-14 (KJV)** For when for the time ye ought to be teachers, ye have need that one teach you again which be the first principles of the oracles of God; and are become such as have need of milk, and not of strong meat. For every one that useth milk is unskilful in the word of righteousness: for he is a babe. But strong meat belongeth to them that are of full age, even those who by reason of use have their senses exercised to discern both good and evil.

† **1 John 2:20 (KJV)** But ye have an unction from the Holy One, and ye know all things.

† **1 John 2:26-28 (AMPC)** I write this to you with

reference to those who would deceive you [seduce and lead you astray]. But as for you, the anointing (the sacred appointment, the unction) which you received from Him abides [permanently] in you; [so] then you have no need that anyone should instruct you. But just as His anointing teaches you concerning everything and is true and is no falsehood, so you must abide in (live in, never depart from) Him [being rooted in Him, knit to Him], just as [His anointing] has taught you [to do]. And now, little children, abide (live, remain permanently) in Him, so that when He is made visible, we may have *and* enjoy perfect confidence (boldness, assurance) and not be ashamed *and* shrink from Him at His coming.

Do / Doer / Doing

I thought I knew what to do, but I discovered I was doing things that I shouldn't have been doing that wasn't the will of God. Now, I continually thrive to be a doer of God's word and not a hearer only.

† **Deuteronomy 6:1–3 (KJV)** Now these are the commandments, the statutes, and the judgments, which the Lord your God commanded to teach you, that ye might do them in the land whither ye go to possess it: That thou mightest fear the Lord thy God, to keep all His statutes and his commandments, which I command thee, thou, and thy son, and thy son's son, all the days of thy life; and that thy days may be prolonged. Hear therefore, O Israel, and observe to do it; that it may be well with thee, and that ye may increase mightily, as the Lord God of thy fathers hath promised thee, in the land that floweth with milk and honey.

† **Psalm 31:23-24 (KJV)** O love the LORD, all ye his saints: for the LORD preserveth the faithful, and plentifully rewardeth the proud doer. Be of good courage, and he shall strengthen your heart, all ye that hope in the LORD.

† **Daniel 11:32 (AMPC)** And such as violate the

covenant he shall pervert *and* seduce with flatteries, but the people who know their God shall prove themselves strong and shall stand firm and do exploits [for God].

† **Mark 16:19–20 (KJV)** So then after the Lord had spoken unto them, he was received up into heaven, and sat on the right hand of God. And they went forth, and preached every where, the Lord working with them, and confirming the word with signs following. Amen.

† **John 2:5 (CEV)** Mary then said to the servants, "Do whatever Jesus tells you to do."

† **John 2:4-5 (GW)** His mother told the servers, "Do whatever he tells you."

† **John 2:5 (NKJV)** His mother said to the servants, "Whatever He says to you, do *it*."

† **2 Thessalonians 3:3-5 (AMPC)** Yet the Lord is faithful, and He will strengthen [you] and set you on a firm foundation and guard you from the evil [one]. And we have confidence in the Lord concerning you, that you are doing and will continue to do the things which we suggest and with which we charge you. May the Lord direct your hearts into [realizing and showing] the love of God and into the steadfastness and patience of Christ and in waiting for His return.

† **James 1:22 (KJV)** But be ye doers of the word, andnot hearers only, deceiving your own selves.

Dominion

Sons of God, our Father God has been ready for us to take dominion over the earth which He has given to us through His son, Jesus Christ.

He first gave us dominion through Adam in the Garden of Eden, but it was given to Satan. We now have this great opportunity to take it back by faith, by walking out, what Jesus died for on the cross, went to hell and God raised Him up so that we can have dominion, through Him.

Don't you want to come back home to God? Why do you want to continue to struggle to death? Are we not the manifested sons of God? Claim it by faith and let's be about our Father's business!

† **Genesis 1:26 (KJV)** And God said, Let us make man in our image, after our likeness: and let them have dominion over the fish of the sea, and over the fowl of the air, and over the cattle, and over all the earth, and over every creeping thing that creepeth upon the earth.

† **Genesis 13:14–15 (NASB)** The LORD said to Abram, after Lot had separated from him, "Now lift up your eyes and look from the place where you are, northward and southward and eastward and westward;

for all the land which you see, I will give it to you and to your descendants forever.

† **Deuteronomy 28:8–10 (KJV)** The Lord shall command the blessing upon thee in thy storehouses, and in all that thou settest thine hand unto; and He shall bless thee in the land which the Lord thy God giveth thee. The Lord shall establish thee an holy people unto Himself, as He hath sworn unto thee, if thou shalt keep the commandments of the Lord thy God, and walk in His ways. And all people of the earth shall see that thou art called by the name of the Lord; and they shall be afraid of thee.

† **Joshua 1:3 (KJV)** Every place that the sole of your foot shall tread upon, that have I given unto you, as I said unto Moses.

† **Joshua 6:2 (AMPC)** And the Lord said to Joshua, See, I have given Jericho, its king and mighty men of valor, into your hands.

† **Psalm 8:6 (AMPC)** You made him to have dominion over the works of Your hands; You have put all things under his feet:

† **Psalm 8:6 (CEV)** You let us rule everything your hands have made. And you put all of it under our power—

† **Psalm 115:16 (KJV)** The heaven, even the heavens, are the Lord's: but the earth hath he given to the children of men.

† **John 2:14–16 (KJV)** And found in the temple those that sold oxen and sheep and doves, and the changers of money sitting: And when He had made a scourge of small cords, He drove them all out of the temple, and the sheep, and the oxen; and poured out the changers' money, and overthrew the tables; And said unto them that sold doves, Take these things hence; make not my Father's house an house of merchandise.

† **Romans 5:17 (KJV)** For if by one man's offence death reigned by one; much more they which receive abundance of grace and of the gift of righteousness shall reign in life by One, Jesus Christ.)

† **1 Corinthians 3:21–23 (NASB)** So then let no one boast in men. For all things belong to you, whether Paul or Apollos or Cephas or the world or life or death or things present or things to come; all things belong to you, and you belong to Christ; and Christ belongs to God.

† **1 Corinthians 15:25–28 (NASB)** For He must reign until He has put all His enemies under His feet. The last enemy that will be abolished is death. For HE HAS PUT ALL THINGS IN SUBJECTION UNDER HIS FEET. But when He says, "All things are put in subjection," it is evident that He is excepted who put all things in subjection to Him. When all things are subjected to Him, then the Son Himself also will be subjected to the One who subjected all things to Him, so that God may be all in all.

- † **Hebrews 11:1 (AMPC)** Now faith is the assurance (the confirmation, the title deed) of the things [we] hope for, being the proof of things [we] do not see and the conviction of their reality [faith perceiving as real fact what is not revealed to the senses].
- † **Revelation 1:6 (KJV)** And hath made us kings and priests unto God and his Father; to him be glory and dominion for ever and ever. Amen.

Dying / Eternity

What more to say ... see the following scriptures. Our born-again spirit lives for all eternity, because of our Lord and Savior Jesus Christ. If you are not born again, it is not too late. Say these scriptures *out loud*, Romans 10:9-10 (see under Life), because Jesus loves you! (See John 3:16, under Love).

† **Romans 8:10-11 (NASB)** If Christ is in you, though the body is dead because of sin, yet the spirit is alive because of righteousness. But if the Spirit of Him who raised Jesus from the dead dwells in you, He who raised Christ Jesus from the dead will also give life to your mortal bodies through His Spirit who dwells in you.

† **1 Corinthians 13:12 (AMPC)** For now we are looking in a mirror that gives only a dim (blurred) reflection [of reality as in a riddle or enigma], but then [when perfection comes] we shall see in reality *and* face to face! Now I know in part (imperfectly), but then I shall know *and* understand fully *and* clearly, even in the same manner as I have been fully *and* clearly known *and* understood [by God].

† **1 Corinthians 15:20–26 (AMPC)** But the fact is that Christ (the Messiah) has been raised from the dead,

and He became the firstfruits of those who have fallen asleep [in death]. For since [it was] through a man that death [came into the world, it is] also through a Man that the resurrection of the dead [has come]. For just as [because of their union of nature] in Adam all people die, so also [by virtue of their union of nature] shall all in Christ be made alive. But each in his own rank and turn: Christ (the Messiah) [is] the firstfruits, then those who are Christ's [own will be resurrected] at His coming. After that comes the end (the completion), when He delivers over the kingdom to God the Father after rendering inoperative and abolishing every [other] rule and every authority and power. For [Christ] must be King and reign until He has put all [His] enemies under His feet. The last enemy to be subdued and abolished is death.

† **1 Corinthians 15:30–33 (MSG)** And why do you think I keep risking my neck in this dangerous work? I look death in the face practically every day I live. Do you think I'd do this if I wasn't convinced of your resurrection and mine as guaranteed by the resurrected Messiah Jesus? Do you think I was just trying to act heroic when I fought the wild beasts at Ephesus, hoping it wouldn't be the end of me? Not on your life! It's resurrection, resurrection, always resurrection, that undergirds what I do and say, the way I live. If there's no resurrection, "We eat, we drink, the next day we die," and that's all there is to it. But don't fool yourselves. Don't let yourselves be poisoned by this

anti-resurrection loose talk. "Bad company ruins good manners."

† **1 Corinthians 15:44–46 (AMPC)** It is sown a natural (physical) body; it is raised a supernatural (a spiritual) body. [As surely as] there is a physical body, there is also a spiritual body. Thus it is written, The first man Adam became a living being (an individual personality); the last Adam (Christ) became a life-giving Spirit [restoring the dead to life]. But it is not the spiritual life which came first, but the physical and then the spiritual.

† **2 Corinthians 5:8 (KJV)** We are confident, I say, and willing rather to be absent from the body, and to be present with the Lord.

Eradicating Poverty

I refuse to accept that a person would not give food, clothing, and shelter to someone in need, especially if that person were in their right mind. When we have the mind of Christ, even the little that we have, we would share it. But no small thinking here, because the earth is the Lord's and the fullness thereof and He has given it to us !!! (see 1 Corinthians 2:16 and Psalm 115:16 under Image ...) IT IS TIME TO GET BACK TO EDEN !!!

† **Numbers 11:17 (KJV)** And I will come down and talk with thee there: and I will take of the spirit which is upon thee, and will put it upon them; and they shall bear the burden of the people with thee, that thou bear it not thyself alone.

† **Numbers 11:17 (AMPC)** And I will come down and talk with you there; and I will take of the Spirit which is upon you and will put It upon them; and they shall bear the burden of the people with you, so that you may not have to bear it yourself alone.

† **Proverbs 11:23–24 (MSG)** The world of the generous gets larger and larger; the world of the stingy gets smaller and smaller. The one who blesses others is abundantly blessed; those who help others are helped.

† **Proverbs 11:23–24 (NIV)** One person gives freely,

yet gains even more; another withholds unduly, but comes to poverty. A generous person will prosper; whoever refreshes others will be refreshed.

† **Proverbs 31:8–9 (MSG)** Don't walk on the poor just because they're poor, and don't use your position to crush the weak, Because GOD will come to their defense; the life you took, he'll take from you and give back to them.

† **Proverbs 31:8–9 (KJV)** Open thy mouth, judge righteously, and plead the cause of the poor and needy.

† **Proverbs 31:8–9 (MSG)** "Speak up for the people who have no voice, for the rights of all the down-and-outers. Speak out for justice! Stand up for the poor and destitute!"

† **Psalm 72:12–14 (NASB)** For he will deliver the needy when he cries for help, The afflicted also, and him who has no helper. He will have compassion on the poor and needy, And the lives of the needy he will save. He will rescue their life from oppression and violence, And their blood will be precious in his sight;

† **Isaiah 58:6–8 (KJV)** ^{6} Is not this the fast that I have chosen? to loose the bands of wickedness, to undo the heavy burdens, and to let the oppressed go free, and that ye break every yoke? ^{7} Is it not to deal thy bread to the hungry, and that thou bring the poor that are cast out to thy house? when thou seest the naked, that thou cover him; and that thou hide not thyself from thine

own flesh? ⁸ Then shall thy light break forth as the morning, and thine health shall spring forth speedily: and thy righteousness shall go before thee; the glory of the LORD shall be thy reward.

† **Isaiah 58:12 (KJV)** And they that shall be of thee shall build the old waste places: thou shalt raise up the foundations of many generations; and thou shalt be called, The repairer of the breach, The restorer of paths to dwell in.

† **Ezekiel 36:33-36 (KJV)** ³³ Thus saith the Lord GOD; In the day that I shall have cleansed you from all your iniquities I will also cause you to dwell in the cities, and the wastes shall be builded. ³⁴ And the desolate land shall be tilled, whereas it lay desolate in the sight of all that passed by. ³⁵ And they shall say, This land that was desolate is become like the garden of Eden; and the waste and desolate and ruined cities are become fenced, and are inhabited. ³⁶ Then the heathen that are left round about you shall know that I the LORD build the ruined places, and plant that that was desolate: I the LORD have spoken it, and I will do it.

† **Ezekiel 36:33-36 (AMPC)** ³³ Thus says the Lord God: In the day that I cleanse you from all your iniquities I will [also] cause [Israel's] cities to be inhabited, and the waste places shall be rebuilt. ³⁴ And the desolate land shall be tilled, that which had lain desolate in the sight of all who passed by. ³⁵ And they shall say, This land that was desolate has become like the garden of

Eden, and the waste and desolate and ruined cities are fortified and inhabited. ³⁶ Then the nations that are left round about you shall know that I the Lord have rebuilt the ruined places and replanted that which was desolate. I the Lord have spoken it, and I will do it.

† **Ezekiel 36:33-36 (NASB)** ³³ 'Thus says the Lord GOD, "On the day that I cleanse you from all your iniquities, I will cause the cities to be inhabited, and the waste places will be rebuilt. ³⁴ The desolate land will be cultivated instead of being a desolation in the sight of everyone who passes by. ³⁵ They will say, 'This desolate land has become like the garden of Eden; and the waste, desolate and ruined cities are fortified *and* inhabited.' ³⁶ Then the nations that are left round about you will know that I, the LORD, have rebuilt the ruined places *and* planted that which was desolate; I, the LORD, have spoken and will do it."

Faith

God is so faithful! I am convinced and confess and believe that I am one of the ones Jesus died to save. Jesus indeed saved me, now I have no desire to live in my past. Forward for me, until I see my Lord face to face. Only believe we can, that's faith! (Having Faithfulness is a Fruit of the Spirit attribute)

† **Habakkuk 2:4 (MSG)** "Look at that man, bloated by self-importance — full of himself but soul - empty. But the person in right standing before God through loyal and steady believing is fully alive, really alive.

† **Habakkuk 2:4 (AMPC)** Look at the proud; his soul is not straight or right within him, but the [rigidly] just and the [uncompromisingly] righteous man shall live by his faith and in his faithfulness.

† **Habakkuk 3:17-18 (NKJV)** [A Hymn of Faith] Though the fig tree may not blossom, Nor fruit be on the vines; Though the labor of the olive may fail, And the fields yield no food; Though the flock may be cut off from the fold, And there be no herd in the stalls —Yet I will rejoice in the LORD, I will joy in the God of my salvation.

† **Matthew 9:27-29 (KJV)** And when Jesus departed thence, two blind men followed him, crying, and

saying, Thou son of David, have mercy on us. And when he was come into the house, the blind men came to him: and Jesus saith unto them, Believe ye that I am able to do this? They said unto him, Yea, Lord. Then touched he their eyes, saying, According to your faith be it unto you.

† **Matthew 17:20 (AMPC)** He said to them, Because of the littleness of your faith [that is, your lack of firmly relying trust]. For truly I say to you, if you have faith [that is living] like a grain of mustard seed, you can say to this mountain, Move from here to yonder place, and it will move; and nothing will be impossible to you.

† **Matthew 21:21 (AMPC)** And Jesus answered them, Truly I say to you, if you have faith (a firm relying trust) and do not doubt, you will not only do what has been done to the fig tree, but even if you say to this mountain, Be taken up and cast into the sea, it will be done.

† **Matthew 25:21 (KJV)** His lord said unto him, Well done, thou good and faithful servant: thou hast been faithful over a few things, I will make thee ruler over many things: enter thou into the joy of thy lord.

† **Mark 5:25-34 (AMPC)** ^{25} And there was a woman who had had a flow of blood for twelve years, ^{26} And who had endured much suffering under [the hands of] many physicians and had spent all that she had, and was no better but instead grew worse. ^{27} She had heard

the reports concerning Jesus, and she came up behind Him in the throng and touched His garment, ²⁸ For she kept saying, If I only touch His garments, I shall be restored to health.²⁹ And immediately her flow of blood was dried up at the source, and [suddenly] she felt in her body that she was healed of her [distressing] ailment. ³⁰ And Jesus, recognizing in Himself that the power proceeding from Him had gone forth, turned around immediately in the crowd and said, Who touched My clothes? ³¹ And the disciples kept saying to Him, You see the crowd pressing hard around You from all sides, and You ask, Who touched Me? ³² Still He kept looking around to see her who had done it. ³³ But the woman, knowing what had been done for her, though alarmed *and* frightened and trembling, fell down before Him and told Him the whole truth. ³⁴ And He said to her, Daughter, your faith (your trust and confidence in Me, springing from faith in God) has restored you to health. Go in (into) peace and be continually healed *and* freed from your [distressing bodily] disease.

† **Mark 5:34 (KJV)** And he said unto her, Daughter, thy faith hath made thee whole; go in peace, and be whole of thy plague.

† **Mark 10:52 (KJV)** And Jesus said unto him, Go thy way; thy faith hath made thee whole. And immediately he received his sight, and followed Jesus in the way.

† **Mark 11:22-24 (KJV)** And Jesus answering saith

unto them, Have faith in God. For verily I say unto you, That whosoever shall say unto this mountain, Be thou removed, and be thou cast into the sea; and shall not doubt in his heart, but shall believe that those things which he saith shall come to pass; he shall have whatsoever he saith. Therefore I say unto you, What things soever ye desire, when ye pray, believe that ye receive them, and ye shall have them.

† **Mark 11:22-24 (AMPC)** And Jesus, replying, said to them, Have faith in God [constantly]. Truly I tell you, whoever says to this mountain, Be lifted up and thrown into the sea! and does not doubt at all in his heart but believes that what he says will take place, it will be done for him. For this reason I am telling you, whatever you ask for in prayer, believe (trust and be confident) that it is granted to you, and you will [get it].

† **Romans 4:17–18 (KJV)** (As it is written, I have made thee a father of many nations,) before him whom he believed, even God, who quickeneth the dead, and calleth those things which be not as though they were. Who against hope believed in hope, that he might become the father of many nations, according to that which was spoken, So shall thy seed be.

† **Romans 4:19–21 (AMPC)** He did not weaken in faith when he considered the [utter] impotence of his own body, which was as good as dead because he was about a hundred years old, or [when he considered] the

barrenness of Sarah's [deadened] womb. No unbelief or distrust made him waver (doubtingly question) concerning the promise of God, but he grew strong and was empowered by faith as he gave praise and glory to God, Fully satisfied and assured that God was able and mighty to keep His word and to do what He had promised.

† **Romans 10:17 (KJV)** So then faith cometh by hearing, and hearing by the word of God.

† **Romans 12:3 (KJV)** For I say, through the grace given unto me, to every man that is among you, not to think of himself more highly than he ought to think; but to think soberly, according as God hath dealt to every man the measure of faith.

† **Romans 16:16–18 (AMPC)** [16] Greet one another with a holy (consecrated) kiss. All the churches of Christ (the Messiah) wish to be remembered to you. [17] I appeal to you, brethren, to be on your guard concerning those who create dissensions and difficulties *and* cause divisions, in opposition to the doctrine (the teaching) which you have been taught. [I warn you to turn aside from them, to] avoid them. [18] For such persons do not serve our Lord Christ but their own appetites *and* base desires, and by ingratiating and flattering speech, they beguile the hearts of the unsuspecting *and* simpleminded [people].

† **1 Corinthians 13:12-13 (MSG)** We don't yet see things clearly. We're squinting in a fog, peering

through a mist. But it won't be long before the weather clears and the sun shines bright! We'll see it all then, see it all as clearly as God sees us, knowing him directly just as he knows us! But for right now, until that completeness, we have three things to do to lead us toward that consummation: Trust steadily in God, hope unswervingly, love extravagantly. And the best of the three is love.

† **2 Corinthians 5:7 (KJV)** (For we walk by faith, not by sight:)

† **Ephesians 4:5 (KJV)** One Lord, one faith, one baptism,

† **1 Thessalonians 1:2–6 (NASB)** ² We give thanks to God always for all of you, making mention *of you* in our prayers; ³ constantly bearing in mind your work of faith and labor of love and steadfastness of hope in our Lord Jesus Christ in the presence of our God and Father,⁴ knowing, brethren beloved by God, *His* choice of you; ⁵ for our gospel did not come to you in word only, but also in power and in the Holy Spirit and with full conviction; just as you know what kind of men we proved to be among you for your sake.⁶ You also became imitators of us and of the Lord, having received the word in much tribulation with the joy of the Holy Spirit,

† **1 Timothy 6:12 (NLT)** Fight the good fight of faith; take hold of the eternal life to which you were called, and you made the good confession in the presence of

many witnesses.

† **2 Timothy 2:13 (AMPC)** If we are faithless [do not believe and are untrue to Him], He remains true (faithful to His Word and His righteous character), for He cannot deny Himself.

† **2 Timothy 4:6–8 (KJV)** For I am now ready to be offered, and the time of my departure is at hand. I have fought a good fight, I have finished my course, I have kept the faith: Henceforth there is laid up for me a crown of righteousness, which the Lord, the righteous judge, shall give me at that day: and not to me only, but unto all them also that love His appearing.

† **Hebrews 11:1 (AMPC)** Now faith is the assurance (the confirmation, the title deed) of the things [we] hope for, being the proof of things [we] do not see and the conviction of their reality [faith perceiving as real fact what is not revealed to the senses].

† **Hebrews 11:6 (KJV)** But without faith it is impossible to please Him: for he that cometh to God must believe that He is, and that He is a rewarder of them that diligently seek Him.

† **Hebrews 11:6 (MSG)** It's impossible to please God apart from faith. And why? Because anyone who wants to approach God must believe both that He exists and that He cares enough to respond to those who seek Him.

† **Hebrews 11:11 (AMPC)** Because of faith also Sarah

herself received physical power to conceive a child, even when she was long past the age for it, because she considered [God] Who had given her the promise to be reliable and trustworthy and true to His word.

† **Hebrews 12:2 (KJV)** Looking unto Jesus the author and finisher of our faith; Who for the joy that was set before Him endured the cross, despising the shame, and is set down at the right hand of the throne of God.

† **2 Peter 1:1 (KJV)** Simon Peter, a servant and an apostle of Jesus Christ, to them that have obtained like precious faith with us through the righteousness of God and our Saviour Jesus Christ:

† **2 Peter 1:3–7 (KJV)** ^{3} According as his divine power hath given unto us all things that pertain unto life and godliness, through the knowledge of him that hath called us to glory and virtue: ^{4} Whereby are given unto us exceeding great and precious promises: that by these ye might be partakers of the divine nature, having escaped the corruption that is in the world through lust. ^{5} And beside this, giving all diligence, add to your faith virtue; and to virtue knowledge; ^{6} And to knowledge temperance; and to temperance patience; and to patience godliness; ^{7} And to godliness brotherly kindness; and to brotherly kindness charity.

† **Hebrews 10:23, 25 (AMPC)** So let us seize and hold fast and retain without wavering the hope we cherish and confess and our acknowledgment of it, for He Who promised is reliable (sure) and faithful to His

word. Not forsaking or neglecting to assemble together [as believers], as is the habit of some people, but admonishing (warning, urging, and encouraging) one another, and all the more faithfully as you see the day approaching.

† **Revelation 3:7–8 (KJV)** And to the angel of the church in Philadelphia write; These things saith He that is holy, He that is true, He that hath the key of David, He that openeth, and no man shutteth; and shutteth, and no man openeth; I know thy works: behold, I have set before thee an open door, and no man can shut it: for thou hast a little strength, and hast kept My word, and hast not denied My name.

Family

Family is so important. Even if there is no physical family, know that when we are born-again, we have a spiritual family. We are not alone and orphaned; we are brothers and sisters in Christ, we are family.

I've learned that my earthly father's brother passed today, he lived in Detroit. He died exactly six months to the date that Daddy died. I called his wife, I made her laugh, as we remembered the times we had as me and my siblings were growing up. Daddy would take us on road trips to see them. Daddy and his brother were very close now since they had accepted Jesus as their Lord and Savior, they are together again.

† **Genesis 2:24 (AMPC)** Therefore a man shall leave his father and his mother and shall become united and cleave to his wife, and they shall become one flesh.

† **Genesis 45:9-11 (NKJV)** "Hurry and go up to my father, and say to him, 'Thus says your son Joseph: "God has made me lord of all Egypt; come down to me, do not tarry. You shall dwell in the land of Goshen, and you shall be near to me, you and your children, your children's children, your flocks and your herds, and all that you have. There I will provide for you, lest you and your household, and all that you

have, come to poverty; for *there are* still five years of famine.'"

† **Genesis 47:6 (MSG)** Pharaoh looked at Joseph. "So, your father and brothers have arrived—a reunion! Egypt welcomes them. Settle your father and brothers on the choicest land—yes, give them Goshen.

† **Proverbs 3:12 (KJV)** For whom the Lord loveth He correcteth; even as a father the son in whom he delighteth.

† **Proverbs 13:24 (NASB)** He who withholds his rod hates his son, But he who loves him disciplines him diligently.

† **Proverbs 22:6 (KJV)** Train up a child in the way he should go: and when he is old, he will not depart from it.

† **Proverbs 23:12-14 (NASB)** Apply your heart to discipline And your ears to words of knowledge. [13] Do not hold back discipline from the child, Although you strike him with the rod, he will not die. [14] You shall strike him with the rod And rescue his soul from Sheol.

† **Proverbs 22:15 (AMPC)** Foolishness is bound up in the heart of a child, but the rod of discipline will drive it far from him.

† **Proverbs 29:17 (KJV)** Correct thy son, and he shall give thee rest; yea, he shall give delight unto thy soul.

† **Matthew 10:37 (NKJV)** He who loves father or

mother more than Me is not worthy of Me. And he who loves son or daughter more than Me is not worthy of Me.

† **Matthew 12:47–50 (NASB)** Someone said to Him, "Behold, Your mother and Your brothers are standing outside seeking to speak to You." But Jesus answered the one who was telling Him and said, "Who is My mother and who are My brothers?" And stretching out His hand toward His disciples, He said, "Behold My mother and My brothers! For whoever does the will of My Father who is in heaven, he is My brother and sister and mother."

† **Matthew 15:3–4 (AMPC)** He replied to them, And why also do you transgress and violate the commandment of God for the sake of the rules handed down to you by your forefathers (the elders)? For God commanded, Honor your father and your mother, and, He who curses or reviles or speaks evil of or abuses or treats improperly his father or mother, let him surely come to his end by death.

† **Romans 12:4–5 (NASB)** For just as we have many members in one body and all the members do not have the same function, so we, who are many, are one body in Christ, and individually members one of another.

† **1 Corinthians 7:3–5 (AMPC)** The husband should give to his wife her conjugal rights (goodwill, kindness, and what is due her as his wife), and likewise the wife to her husband. For the wife does not

have [exclusive] authority and control over her own body, but the husband [has his rights]; likewise also the husband does not have [exclusive] authority and control over his body, but the wife [has her rights]. Do not refuse and deprive and defraud each other [of your due marital rights], except perhaps by mutual consent for a time, so that you may devote yourselves unhindered to prayer. But afterwards resume marital relations, lest Satan tempt you [to sin] through your lack of restraint of sexual desire.

† **Ephesians 4:26 (KJV)** Be ye angry, and sin not: let not the sun go down upon your wrath:

† **Ephesians 5:21–26 (AMPC)** Be subject to one another out of reverence for Christ (the Messiah, the Anointed One). Wives, be subject (be submissive and adapt yourselves) to your own husbands as [a service] to the Lord. For the husband is head of the wife as Christ is the Head of the church, Himself the Savior of [His] body. As the church is subject to Christ, so let wives also be subject in everything to their husbands. Husbands, love your wives, as Christ loved the church and gave Himself up for her, So that He might sanctify her, having cleansed her by the washing of water with the Word,

† **Ephesians 5:29–33 (NASB)** for no one ever hated his own flesh, but nourishes and cherishes it, just as Christ also *does* the church, because we are members of His body. FOR THIS REASON A MAN SHALL LEAVE HIS

FATHER AND MOTHER AND SHALL BE JOINED TO HIS WIFE, AND THE TWO SHALL BECOME ONE FLESH. This mystery is great; but I am speaking with reference to Christ and the church Nevertheless, each individual among you also is to love his own wife even as himself, and the wife must *see to it* that she respects her husband.

† **Ephesians 6:4 (NASB)** Fathers, do not provoke your children to anger, but bring them up in the discipline and instruction of the Lord.

† **Colossians 3:20 (KJV)** Children, obey your parents in all things: for this is well pleasing unto the Lord.

† **Colossians 3:21 (KJV)** Fathers, provoke not your children to anger, lest they be discouraged.

† **2 Timothy 1:5 (KJV)** When I call to remembrance the unfeigned faith that is in thee, which dwelt first in thy grandmother Lois, and thy mother Eunice; and I am persuaded that in thee also.

† **Hebrews 13:4 (AMPC)** Let marriage be held in honor (esteemed worthy, precious, of great price, and especially dear) in all things. And thus let the marriage bed be undefiled (kept undishonored); for God will judge and punish the unchaste [all guilty of sexual vice] and adulterous.

† **1 Peter 3:1 (KJV)** Likewise, ye wives, be in subjection to your own husbands; that, if any obey not the word, they also may without the word be won by

the conversation of the wives;

† **1 Peter 3:7 (KJV)** Likewise, ye husbands, dwell with them according to knowledge, giving honour unto the wife, as unto the weaker vessel, and as being heirs together of the grace of life; that your prayers be not hindered.

Favor

I believe having favor is so wonderful. Favor is when someone has received something good, maybe unexpectedly; like an open door. Favor is getting the yes, one was always hoping and praying for (See Jabez in 1 Chronicles 4:10 under Receiving).

Favor is a gift from God. Jesus is God's greatest gift to us, for He is the Light Who dominates the darkness in the world.

Thank You, Lord for Your favor in the sight of God and man !!!

† **Genesis 39:21 (NASB)** But the LORD was with Joseph and extended kindness to him, and gave him favor in the sight of the chief jailer.

† **Exodus 3:21 (KJV)** And I will give this people favour in the sight of the Egyptians: and it shall come to pass, that, when ye go, ye shall not go empty.

† **Exodus 12:35-36 (AMPC)** The Israelites did according to the word of Moses; and they [urgently] asked of the Egyptians jewels of silver and of gold, and clothing. The Lord gave the people favor in the sight of the Egyptians, so that they gave them what they asked. And they stripped the Egyptians [of those

things].

† **1 Samuel 16:22 (KJV)** And Saul sent to Jesse, saying, Let David, I pray thee, stand before me; for he hath found favour in my sight.

† **Esther 2:17 (AMPC)** And the king loved Esther more than all the women, and she obtained grace and favor in his sight more than all the maidens, so that he set the royal crown on her head and made her queen instead of Vashti.

† **Esther 5:8 (KJV)** If I have found favour in the sight of the king, and if it please the king to grant my petition, and to perform my request, let the king and Haman come to the banquet that I shall prepare for them, and I will do to morrow as the king hath said.

† **Esther 8:5 (KJV)** And said, If it please the king, and if I have favour in his sight, and the thing seem right before the king, and I be pleasing in his eyes, let it be written to reverse the letters devised by Haman the son of Hammedatha the Agagite, which he wrote to destroy the Jews which are in all the king's provinces:

† **Psalm 5:12 (KJV)** For Thou, Lord, wilt bless the righteous; with favour wilt Thou compass him as with a shield.

† **Psalm 44:3 (KJV)** For they got not the land in possession by their own sword, neither did their own arm save them: but Thy right hand, and Thine arm, and the light of Thy countenance, because Thou hadst

a favour unto them.

† **Psalm 75:6-7 (KJV)** For promotion cometh neither from the east, nor from the west, nor from the south. But God is the judge: he putteth down one, and setteth up another.

† **Proverbs 3:4 (KJV)** So shalt thou find favour and good understanding in the sight of God and man.

† **Proverbs 8:35 (AMPC)** For whoever finds me [Wisdom] finds life and draws forth and obtains favor from the Lord.

† **Proverbs 18:22 (CEV)** A man's greatest treasure is his wife—she is a gift from the LORD.

† **Isaiah 61:1-2 (KJV)** The Spirit of the Lord God is upon me; because the Lord hath anointed me to preach good tidings unto the meek; he hath sent me to bind up the brokenhearted, to proclaim liberty to the captives, and the opening of the prison to them that are bound; To proclaim the acceptable year of the LORD, and the day of vengeance of our God; to comfort all that mourn;

† **Luke 1:28 (KJV)** And the angel came in unto her, and said, Hail, thou that art highly favoured, the Lord is with thee: blessed art thou among women.

† **Luke 4:19 (AMPC)** To proclaim the accepted *and* acceptable year of the Lord [the day when salvation and the free favors of God profusely abound].

† **Galatians 3:9 (KJV)** So then they which be of faith

are blessed with faithful Abraham.

† **Galatians 3:13-14 (KJV)** Christ hath redeemed us from the curse of the law, being made a curse for us: for it is written, Cursed is every one that hangeth on a tree: That the blessing of Abraham might come on the Gentiles through Jesus Christ; that we might receive the promise of the Spirit through faith.

† **Galatians 3:29 (KJV)** And if ye be Christ's, then are ye Abraham's seed, and heirs according to the promise.

Fear of the Lord

The "fear" of the Lord is not the scary kind of fear. It means to have "respect" or "reverential fear" for God.

Respectful: *feeling or expressing deep respect or awe. Deserving respect: worthy of deep respect or awe.*

Growing up, I have never had a sense of being scared of God. I've always had this respect for His Presence, even though I didn't know Who He was or knew anything about Him, nor had I seen Him. I know now that I obtained the reverential fear (respect) for God from my mother, because she was always talking about Him or to Him. No one seemed to question His Presence, I know I didn't nor had I the thought to ask. He was always a part of the family, so since then I have acknowledged that He is always with me. I can now relate with Romans 1:19-21, see here. Thank You Lord God !!!

† **Psalm 19:9 (AMPC)** The [reverent] fear of the Lord is clean, enduring forever; the ordinances of the Lord are true and righteous altogether.

† **Proverbs 1:7 (KJV)** The fear of the LORD is the beginning of knowledge: but fools despise wisdom and instruction.

† **Proverbs 3:7-9 (KJV)** Be not wise in thine own eyes: fear the LORD, and depart from evil. It shall be health to thy navel, and marrow to thy bones. Honour the LORD with thy substance, and with the firstfruits of all thine increase:

† **Proverbs 31:30 (NKJV)** Charm *is* deceitful and beauty *is* passing, But a woman *who* fears the LORD, she shall be praised.

† **Psalm 34:11 (AMPC)** Come, you children, listen to me; I will teach you to fear the LORD [with awe-inspired reverence and worship Him with obedience].

† **Isaiah 11:1-3 (KJV)** And there shall come forth a rod out of the stem of Jesse, and a Branch shall grow out of his roots: And the spirit of the LORD shall rest upon him, the spirit of wisdom and understanding, the spirit of counsel and might, the spirit of knowledge and of the fear of the LORD; And shall make him of quick understanding in the fear of the LORD: and he shall not judge after the sight of his eyes, neither reprove after the hearing of his ears:

† **Isaiah 33:5-6 (AMPC)** ⁵ The Lord is exalted, for He dwells on high; He will fill Zion with justice and righteousness (moral and spiritual rectitude in every area and relation). ⁶ And there shall be stability in your times, an abundance of salvation, wisdom, and knowledge; the reverent fear *and* worship of the Lord is your treasure *and* His.

† **Acts 9:31 (KJV)** Then had the churches rest throughout all Judaea and Galilee and Samaria, and were edified; and walking in the fear of the Lord, and in the comfort of the Holy Ghost, were multiplied.

† **Romans 1:19-21 (AMPC)** [19] For that which is known about God is evident to them *and* made plain in their inner consciousness, because God [Himself] has shown it to them. [20] For ever since the creation of the world His invisible nature *and* attributes, that is, His eternal power and divinity, have been made intelligible *and* clearly discernible in *and* through the things that have been made (His handiworks). So [men] are without excuse [altogether without any defense or justification], [21] Because when they knew *and* recognized Him as God, they did not honor *and* glorify Him as God or give Him thanks. But instead they became futile *and* godless in their thinking [with vain imaginings, foolish reasoning, and stupid speculations] and their senseless minds were darkened.

Fearless

Fear is not good. Fear is a bad thing. God wants us to think on good things (see Philippians 4:8 here). When we think, dwell, meditate, do good things, there is no room for the bad. Yes, bad always seems to want to come and try to stay, but we are children of God. We have been given the ability to first, submit ourselves to God, cast down imaginations, cast our cares upon the Lord, and other confessions of faith in the reality of who we are in Christ. We are bold as a lion, so fear not, for God is with us! (See 2 Kings 6:15–17 under "Protection").

† **Isaiah 41:10 (KJV)** Fear thou not; for I am with thee: be not dismayed; for I am thy God: I will strengthen thee; yea, I will help thee; yea, I will uphold thee with the right hand of my righteousness.

† **Jeremiah 1:7–8 (KJV)** But the Lord said unto me, Say not, I am a child: for thou shalt go to all that I shall send thee, and whatsoever I command thee thou shalt speak. Be not afraid of their faces: for I am with thee to deliver thee, saith the Lord.

† **Proverbs 28:1-2 (AMPC)** The wicked flee when no man pursues them, but the [uncompromisingly] righteous are bold as a lion. When a land transgresses,

it has many rulers, but when the ruler is a man of discernment, understanding, *and* knowledge, its stability will long continue.

† **Proverbs 30:30 (KJV)** A lion which is strongest among beasts, and turneth not away for any;

† **Proverbs 30:30 (NIV)** a lion, mighty among beasts, who retreats before nothing;

† **Proverbs 30:30 (AMPC)** The lion, which is mightiest among beasts and turns not back before any;

† **Matthew 6:25 (KJV)** Therefore I say unto you, Take no thought for your life, what ye shall eat, or what ye shall drink; nor yet for your body, what ye shall put on. Is not the life more than meat, and the body than raiment?

† **Romans 8:15 (KJV)** For ye have not received the spirit of bondage again to fear; but ye have received the Spirit of adoption, whereby we cry, Abba, Father.

† **Philippians 4:8 (KJV)** Finally, brethren, whatsoever things are true, whatsoever things are honest, whatsoever things are just, whatsoever things are pure, whatsoever things are lovely, whatsoever things are of good report; if there be any virtue, and if there be any praise, think on these things.

† **Philippians 4:6–8 (AMPC)** Do not fret or have any anxiety about anything, but in every circumstance and in everything, by prayer and petition (definite requests), with thanksgiving, continue to make your

wants known to God. And God's peace [shall be yours, that tranquil state of a soul assured of its salvation through Christ, and so fearing nothing from God and being content with its earthly lot of whatever sort that is, that peace] which transcends all understanding shall garrison and mount guard over your hearts and minds in Christ Jesus. For the rest, brethren, whatever is true, whatever is worthy of reverence and is honorable and seemly, whatever is just, whatever is pure, whatever is lovely and lovable, whatever is kind and winsome and gracious, if there is any virtue and excellence, if there is anything worthy of praise, think on and weigh and take account of these things [fix your minds on them].

† **2 Timothy 1:7 (KJV)** For God hath not given us the spirit of fear; but of power, and of love, and of a sound mind.

† **Hebrews 13:6 (KJV)** So that we may boldly say, The Lord is my helper, and I will not fear what man shall do unto me.

† **James 4:7 (NASB)** Submit therefore to God. Resist the devil and he will flee from you.

† **1 John 4:18 (AMPC)** There is no fear in love [dread does not exist], but full-grown (complete, perfect) love turns fear out of doors *and* expels every trace of terror! For fear brings with it the thought of punishment, and [so] he who is afraid has not reached the full maturity of love [is not yet grown into love's complete

perfection].

† **Revelation 5:5 (AMPC)** Then one of the elders [of the heavenly Sanhedrin] said to me, Stop weeping! See, the Lion of the tribe of Judah, the Root (Source) of David, has won (has overcome and conquered)! He can open the scroll and break its seven seals!

Focus

Focus is a very important word. Whatever we desire to be, have, or give we have to focus on one thing at a time. When we do this we can successfully get that one thing accomplished, and then go to the next task, instead of doing a little on each of the many things in our lives. When we try to concentrate on many things, nothing is finished successfully. Some things are strictly distractions from the devil, even if it comes through a person close to us. Know who is responsible for this interference. Love the person, but hate the devil's strategy and don't come off the wall. Our God-given destiny takes focus; Jesus will help us, so seek God and be led by the Holy Spirit.

† **Nehemiah 6:1-9 (NKJV)** [Conspiracy Against Nehemiah] ¹ Now it happened when Sanballat, Tobiah, Geshem the Arab, and the rest of our enemies heard that I had rebuilt the wall, and *that* there were no breaks left in it (though at that time I had not hung the doors in the gates), ² that Sanballat and Geshem sent to me, saying, "Come, let us meet together among the villages in the plain of Ono." But they thought to do me harm. ³ So I sent messengers to them, saying, "I *am* doing a great work, so that I cannot come down. Why should the work cease while I leave it and go down to

you?" ⁴ But they sent me this message four times, and I answered them in the same manner. ⁵ Then Sanballat sent his servant to me as before, the fifth time, with an open letter in his hand. ⁶ In it *was* written: It is reported among the nations, and Geshem says, *that* you and the Jews plan to rebel; therefore, according to these rumors, you are rebuilding the wall, that you may be their king. ⁷ And you have also appointed prophets to proclaim concerning you at Jerusalem, saying, "*There is* a king in Judah!" Now these matters will be reported to the king. So come, therefore, and let us consult together. ⁸ Then I sent to him, saying, "No such things as you say are being done, but you invent them in your own heart." ⁹ For they all *were trying to* make us afraid, saying, "Their hands will be weakened in the work, and it will not be done." Now therefore, *O God,* strengthen my hands.

† **Ecclesiastes 7:8 (MSG)** Endings are better than beginnings. Sticking to it is better than standing out.

† **Isaiah 26:3 (KJV)** Thou wilt keep him in perfect peace, whose mind is stayed on thee: because he trusteth in thee.

† **Isaiah 26:2-4 (AMPC)** Open the gates, that the [uncompromisingly] righteous nation which keeps her faith *and* her troth [with God] may enter in. You will guard him *and* keep him in perfect *and* constant peace whose mind [both its inclination and its character] is stayed on You, because he commits himself to You,

leans on You, *and* hopes confidently in You. So trust in the Lord (commit yourself to Him, lean on Him, hope confidently in Him) forever; for the Lord God is an everlasting Rock [the Rock of Ages].

† **Luke 10:38-42 (KJV)** [38] Now it came to pass, as they went, that he entered into a certain village: and a certain woman named Martha received him into her house. [39] And she had a sister called Mary, which also sat at Jesus' feet, and heard his word. [40] But Martha was cumbered about much serving, and came to him, and said, Lord, dost thou not care that my sister hath left me to serve alone? bid her therefore that she help me. [41] And Jesus answered and said unto her, Martha, Martha, thou art careful and troubled about many things: [42] But one thing is needful: and Mary hath chosen that good part, which shall not be taken away from her.

† **John 16:33 (NIV)** "I have told you these things, so that in me you may have peace. In this world you will have trouble. But take heart! I have overcome the world."

† **John 16:31-33 (MSG)** Jesus answered them, "Do you finally believe? In fact, you're about to make a run for it—saving your own skins and abandoning me. But I'm not abandoned. The Father is with me. I've told you all this so that trusting me, you will be unshakable and assured, deeply at peace. In this godless world you will continue to experience difficulties. But take heart!

I've conquered the world."

† **Philippians 4:13 (KJV)** I can do all things through Christ which strengtheneth me.

† **Hebrews 12:2 (KJV)** Looking unto Jesus the author and finisher of our faith; who for the joy that was set before him endured the cross, despising the shame, and is set down at the right hand of the throne of God.

† **Hebrews 12:2 (AMPC)** Looking away [from all that will distract] to Jesus, Who is the Leader *and* the Source of our faith [giving the first incentive for our belief] and is also its Finisher [bringing it to maturity and perfection]. He, for the joy [of obtaining the prize] that was set before Him, endured the cross, despising *and* ignoring the shame, and is now seated at the right hand of the throne of God.

† **Hebrews 12:2-3 (MSG)** Do you see what this means—all these pioneers who blazed the way, all these veterans cheering us on? It means we'd better get on with it. Strip down, start running—and never quit! No extra spiritual fat, no parasitic sins. Keep your eyes on *Jesus*, who both began and finished this race we're in. Study how he did it. Because he never lost sight of where he was headed—that exhilarating finish in and with God—he could put up with anything along the way: Cross, shame, whatever. And now he's *there*, in the place of honor, right alongside God. When you find yourselves flagging in your faith, go over that story again, item by item, that long litany of

hostility he plowed through. *That* will shoot adrenaline into your souls!

Forgiving

Since being born-again, I have learned how important forgiving someone is. God had been working with me on forgiveness, even before I confess Him as my Lord and Savior. I began to see that I couldn't stay mad with anyone too long. If it was possible, I may not associate with them anymore, but I had learned to release the bitterness. I can see it now, how I was covered with this hard shell and I realized how God was sending His word, like a dart via His laborers, TV and/or nature, and He finally penetrated that hard shell. I thank God !!! I am a happy person now. No one can bring me down, unless I allow it through unforgiveness. I choose to forgive, because I refuse to go backward. I am a new creation in Christ (See 2 Corinthians 5:17 under Letting Go).

† **Isaiah 43:25-26 (AMPC)** I, even I, am He Who blots out and cancels your transgressions, for My own sake, and I will not remember your sins. Put Me in remembrance [remind Me of your merits]; let us plead and argue together. Set forth your case, that you may be justified (proved right).

† **Matthew 6:14-15 (KJV)** For if ye forgive men their trespasses, your heavenly Father will also forgive you:

But if ye forgive not men their trespasses, neither will your Father forgive your trespasses.

† **Matthew 18:21–22 (NIV)** Then Peter came to Jesus and asked, "Lord, how many times shall I forgive my brother or sister who sins against me? Up to seven times?" Jesus answered, "I tell you, not seven times, but seventy-seven times.

† **Mark 11:24–26 (KJV)** Therefore I say unto you, What things soever ye desire, when ye pray, believe that ye receive them, and ye shall have them. And when ye stand praying, forgive, if ye have ought against any: that your Father also which is in heaven may forgive you your trespasses. But if ye do not forgive, neither will your Father which is in heaven forgive your trespasses.

† **Ephesians 4:25–27 (AMPC)** Therefore, rejecting all falsity and being done now with it, let everyone express the truth with his neighbor, for we are all parts of one body and members one of another. When angry, do not sin; do not ever let your wrath (your exasperation, your fury or indignation) last until the sun goes down. Leave no [such] room or foothold for the devil [give no opportunity to him].

† **1 John 2:12 (AMPC)** I am writing to you, little children, because for His name's sake your sins are forgiven [pardoned through His name and on account of confessing His name].

Freedom

Freedom in Christ to me is the greatest gift One can ever give to anyone. It is such a relief to be free; to have no restraint, no boundaries, and no borders. I am free to do more and have freedom to dream bigger. I may not know the full extent of these scriptures (see 2 Corinthians 5:17, under Letting Go and Philippians 4:13, under Victorious) but, I believe I can do all things through Christ which strengthens me. **All I can say is, "Thank You Jesus for my Freedom !!!"**

† **John 8:36 (NKJV)** Therefore if the Son makes you free, you shall be free indeed.

† **Romans 6:23 (KJV)** For the wages of sin is death; but the gift of God is eternal life through Jesus Christ our Lord.

† **Romans 8:1 (KJV)** There is therefore now no condemnation to them which are in Christ Jesus, who walk not after the flesh, but after the Spirit.

† **2 Corinthians 3:17 (AMPC)** Now the Lord is the Spirit, and where the Spirit of the Lord is, there is liberty (emancipation from bondage, freedom).

† **Galatians 5:1 (NKJV)** [Christian Liberty] Stand fast therefore in the liberty by which Christ has made us

free, and do not be entangled again with a yoke of bondage.

† **Galatians 5:13-15 (MSG)** It is absolutely clear that God has called you to a free life. Just make sure that you don't use this freedom as an excuse to do whatever you want to do and destroy your freedom. Rather, use your freedom to serve one another in love; that's how freedom grows. For everything we know about God's Word is summed up in a single sentence: Love others as you love yourself. That's an act of true freedom.

† **1 John 1:7 (AMPC)** But if we [really] are living and walking in the Light, as He [Himself] is in the Light, we have [true, unbroken] fellowship with one another, and the blood of Jesus Christ His Son cleanses (removes) us from all sin and guilt [keeps us cleansed from sin in all its forms and manifestations].

Fruit of the Spirit

The Fruit of the Spirit is Love, Joy, Peace, Patience, Kindness, Goodness, Faithfulness, Gentleness, Self-control. The fruit of the Spirit attributes are the requirements for us to be effective for and in the kingdom of God. When we allow the Holy Spirit to help us by leading us in every way, everyday, we will be able to accomplish the things of God in the Earth as it is in Heaven.

(See all of these attributes listed separately in alphabetical order, along with scriptures).

† **Proverbs 20:5-6 (AMPC)** Counsel in the heart of man is like water in a deep well, but a man of understanding draws it out. Many a man proclaims his own loving-kindness *and* goodness, but a faithful man who can find?

† **Galatians 5:22–23 (AMPC)** But the fruit of the [Holy] Spirit [the work which His presence within accomplishes] is love, joy (gladness), peace, patience (an even temper, forbearance), kindness, goodness (benevolence), faithfulness, Gentleness (meekness, humility), self-control (self-restraint, continence). Against such things there is no law [that can bring a charge].

- † **Galatians 5:22-23 (KJV)** But the fruit of the Spirit is love, joy, peace, longsuffering, gentleness, goodness, faith, Meekness, temperance: against such there is no law.

- † **Galatians 5:22–23 (MSG)** But what happens when we live God's way? He brings gifts into our lives, much the same way that fruit appears in an orchard—things like affection for others, exuberance about life, serenity. We develop a willingness to stick with things, a sense of compassion in the heart, and a conviction that a basic holiness permeates things and people. We find ourselves involved in loyal commitments, not needing to force our way in life, able to marshal and direct our energies wisely. Legalism is helpless in bringing this about; it only gets in the way.

- † **Ephesians 4:1-3 (KJV)** [1] I therefore, the prisoner of the Lord, beseech you that ye walk worthy of the vocation wherewith ye are called, [2] With all lowliness and meekness, with longsuffering, forbearing one another in love; [3] Endeavouring to keep the unity of the Spirit in the bond of peace.

- † **Colossians 3:12-13 (NASB)** So, as those who have been chosen of God, holy and beloved, put on a heart of compassion, kindness, humility, gentleness and patience; bearing with one another, and forgiving each other, whoever has a complaint against anyone; just as the Lord forgave you, so also should you.

Fulfilling a Need

By fulfilling a need for someone, this act is showing the love of God. We are to be willing vessels for God to use, so that we can help people in need, that's what advancing the Kingdom of God is all about. We may think or even say, why? We haven't experience anyone giving or showing love to us. But that can't be true; there have been times when we ourselves have indeed experienced love. We may not have recognized them, and Love is always working in our lives. If we are able to do anything, like read this book, someone has shown the love of God to us at some point of our lives. Always remember God's law; seedtime and harvest; we have to give to receive. What we sow is the type of thing we will reap. Let us sow a seed to fulfill a need in someone's life, so that we can reap a harvest that will fill the need in our own lives !!!

† **Proverbs 13:23 (CEB)** A poor person's land might produce much food, but it is unjustly swept away.

† **Proverbs 31:8–9 (AMPC)** Open your mouth for the dumb [those unable to speak for themselves], for the rights of all who are left desolate and defenseless; Open your mouth, judge righteously, and administer justice for the poor and needy.

† **Matthew 6:4 (KJV)** That thine alms may be in secret: and thy Father which seeth in secret Himself shall reward thee openly.

† **Matthew 6:4 (MSG)** When you help someone out, don't think about how it looks. Just do it—quietly and unobtrusively. That is the way your God, who conceived you in love, working behind the scenes, helps you out.

† **2 Corinthians 9:7 (KJV)** Every man according as he purposeth in his heart, so let him give; not grudgingly, or of necessity: for God loveth a cheerful giver.

† **2 Corinthians 9:9 (NKJV)** As it is written: "He has dispersed abroad, He has given to the poor; His righteousness endures forever."

† **2 Corinthians 9:12–13 (AMPC)** For the service that the ministering of this fund renders does not only fully supply what is lacking to the saints (God's people), but it also overflows in many [cries of] thanksgiving to God. Because at [your] standing of the test of this ministry, they will glorify God for your loyalty and obedience to the Gospel of Christ which you confess, as well as for your generous- hearted liberality to them and to all [the other needy ones].

Gentleness

If you ever held a baby before, this is a good example for gentleness. We would hold the baby with the upmost care and gentleness. Being careful to move slowly and/or don't make any awkward movements, because babies can sense insecurity. When in gentle arms, they will actually fall to sleep and even give a smile. (A Fruit of the Spirit attribute)

† **Psalm 18:34-36 (KJV)** He teacheth my hands to war, so that a bow of steel is broken by mine arms. Thou hast also given me the shield of thy salvation: and thy right hand hath holden me up, and thy gentleness hath made me great. Thou hast enlarged my steps under me, that my feet did not slip.

† **Proverbs 15:1 (KJV)** A soft answer turneth away wrath: but grievous words stir up anger.

† **Philippians 4:5 (AMPC)** Let all men know *and* perceive *and* recognize your unselfishness (your considerateness, your forbearing spirit). The Lord is near [He is coming soon].

† **Colossians 3:12 (AMPC)** Clothe yourselves therefore, as God's own chosen ones (His own picked representatives), [who are] purified *and* holy and well-beloved [by God Himself, by putting on behavior

marked by] tenderhearted pity *and* mercy, kind feeling, a lowly opinion of yourselves, gentle ways, [and] patience [which is tireless and long-suffering, and has the power to endure whatever comes, with good temper].

† **James 3:16-18 (KJV)** But the wisdom that is from above is first pure, then peaceable, gentle, and easy to be intreated, full of mercy and good fruits, without partiality, and without hypocrisy.

Gifts

The gifts of God are freely given to us (see 1 Corinthians 2:12 here). God has Blessed us with these wonderful gifts, but if we don't know and learn about them, we will continue to live a defeated life. We had been lied to by the devil (Satan, the enemy), that we are nobody; we are below normal, when the truth is we are supernatural beings.

We are all spirits, but to be able to partake of these gifts, we have to be born-again. The only way to return to God is we must accept Jesus as our Lord and Savior. Then it is an automatic Blessing, but we still have to learn and receive—We are the righteousness of God in Christ! We are somebody! We are a child of God! In order to learn and build our faith to operate in our new life in Christ is through renewing our minds with the Word of God. These gifts are spiritual, some that can become tangible, such as in Deuteronomy 8:18, which the Lord gives us the power to get wealth (see under Remember).

† **Ecclesiastes 3:13 (KJV)** And also that every man should eat and drink, and enjoy the good of all his labour, it is the gift of God.

† **Ecclesiastes 5:19 (KJV)** Every man also to whom

God hath given riches and wealth, and hath given him power to eat thereof, and to take his portion, and to rejoice in his labour; this is the gift of God.

† **Matthew 7:11 (KJV)** If ye then, being evil, know how to give good gifts unto your children, how much more shall your Father which is in heaven give good things to them that ask Him?

† **Matthew 10:8 (KJV)** Heal the sick, cleanse the lepers, raise the dead, cast out devils: freely ye have received, freely give.

† **Acts 2:2-4 (KJV)** And suddenly there came a sound from heaven as of a rushing mighty wind, and it filled all the house where they were sitting. And there appeared unto them cloven tongues like as of fire, and it sat upon each of them. And they were all filled with the Holy Ghost, and began to speak with other tongues, as the Spirit gave them utterance.

† **Acts 2:38 (KJV)** Then Peter said unto them, Repent, and be baptized every one of you in the name of Jesus Christ for the remission of sins, and ye shall receive the gift of the Holy Ghost.

† **Romans 5:17 (KJV)** For if by one man's offence death reigned by one; much more they which receive abundance of grace and of the gift of righteousness shall reign in life by one, Jesus Christ.)

† **Romans 11:28-30 (AMPC)** From the point of view of the Gospel (good news), they [the Jews, at present]

are enemies [of God], which is for your advantage and benefit. But from the point of view of God's choice (of election, of divine selection), they are still the beloved (dear to Him) for the sake of their forefathers. For God's gifts and His call are irrevocable. [He never withdraws them when once they are given, and He does not change His mind about those to whom He gives His grace or to whom He sends His call.] Just as you were once disobedient and rebellious toward God but now have obtained [His] mercy, through their disobedience,

† **Romans 11:29 (CEV)** God doesn't take back the gifts he has given or forget about the people he has chosen.

† **Romans 12:5–9 (KJV)** So we, being many, are one body in Christ, and every one members one of another. Having then gifts differing according to the grace that is given to us, whether prophecy, let us prophesy according to the proportion of faith; Or ministry, let us wait on our ministering: or he that teacheth, on teaching; Or he that exhorteth, on exhortation: he that giveth, let him do it with simplicity; he that ruleth, with diligence; he that sheweth mercy, with cheerfulness. Let love be without dissimulation. Abhor that which is evil; cleave to that which is good.

† **1 Corinthians 2:12 (KJV)** Now we have received, not the spirit of the world, but the spirit which is of God; that we might know the things that are freely given to us of God.

† **1 Corinthians 12:1–3 (AMPC)** Now about the spiritual gifts (the special endowments of supernatural energy), brethren, I do not want you to be misinformed. You know that when you were heathen, you were led off after idols that could not speak [habitually] as impulse directed and whenever the occasion might arise. Therefore I want you to understand that no one speaking under the power and influence of the [Holy] Spirit of God can [ever] say, Jesus be cursed! And no one can [really] say, Jesus is [my] Lord, except by and under the power and influence of the Holy Spirit.

† **1 Corinthians 12:9–11 (KJV)** To another faith by the same Spirit; to another the gifts of healing by the same Spirit; To another the working of miracles; to another prophecy; to another discerning of spirits; to another divers kinds of tongues; to another the interpretation of tongues: But all these worketh that One and the selfsame Spirit, dividing to every man severally as He will.

† **Ephesians 4:11–13 (KJV)** And he gave some, apostles; and some, prophets; and some, evangelists; and some, pastors and teachers; For the perfecting of the saints, for the work of the ministry, for the edifying of the body of Christ: Till we all come in the unity of the faith, and of the knowledge of the Son of God, unto a perfect man, unto the measure of the stature of the fulness of Christ

Giving What Is Due

We give You, Lord, what is due to You. We glorify and honor You and give You all of our praise. May God be the glory forever! God is so worthy to be praised. He is such a giving God; He has given us the opportunity to be worthy of walking with Him (also see Colossians 1:9-10 under Pleasing). *When we give God what is due to Him, He gives what is due to the giver !!!*

† **Leviticus 27:30-31 (NKJV)** And all the tithe of the land, *whether* of the seed of the land *or* of the fruit of the tree, *is* the LORD's. It *is* holy to the LORD. If a man wants at all to redeem *any* of his tithes, he shall add one-fifth to it.

† **Psalm 7:17 (AMPC)** I will give to the Lord the thanks due to His rightness and justice, and I will sing praise to the name of the Lord Most High.

† **Proverbs 3:9-10 (NKJV)** Honor the LORD with your possessions, And with the firstfruits of all your increase; So your barns will be filled with plenty, And your vats will overflow with new wine.

† **Ecclesiastes 12:13 (KJV)** Let us hear the conclusion of the whole matter: Fear God, and keep his commandments: for this is the whole duty of man.

† **Matthew 22:21 (AMPC)** They said, Caesar's. Then He said to them, Pay therefore to Caesar the things that are due to Caesar, and pay to God the things that are due to God.

† **Romans 13:8 (NKJV)** Owe no one anything except to love one another, for he who loves another has fulfilled the law.

† **Romans 14:11 (KJV)** For it is written, As I live, saith the Lord, every knee shall bow to me, and every tongue shall confess to God.

† **2 Thessalonians 1:10–12 (NKJV)** when He comes, in that Day, to be glorified in His saints and to be admired among all those who believe, because our testimony among you was believed. Therefore we also pray always for you that our God would count you worthy of this calling, and fulfill all the good pleasure of His goodness and the work of faith with power, that the name of our Lord Jesus Christ may be glorified in you, and you in Him, according to the grace of our God and the Lord Jesus Christ.

† **1 Timothy 4:8–10 (NKJV)** For bodily exercise profits a little, but godliness is profitable for all things, having promise of the life that now is and of that which is to come. This is a faithful saying and worthy of all acceptance. For to this end we both labor and suffer reproach, because we trust in the living God, who is the Savior of all men, especially of those who believe.

† **<u>1 John 5:21 (AMPC)</u>** Little children, keep yourselves from idols (false gods)—[from anything and everything that would occupy the place in your heart due to God, from any sort of substitute for Him that would take first place in your life]. *Amen (so let it be).*

God, the Father

Father God is our Creator and He is Spirit (see John 4:24 here). I am pleased to call God my Father; often I call Him Papa. He is my Source of life and I am so honored that He chose me. I acknowledge He is real. He is more real than anyone who doubts His existence. Thank You, Father, for Your Love for us, in Jesus' name.

Father God has many names for His many attributes. God is Three Persons in One; TRINITY; God the Father, God the Son-Jesus and God the Holy Spirit.

Also see in the **Contents** for Their own chapter (but not really, because we know They are still sharing, but separately working in Their/His purpose).

Listed are just some of God's names with scripture(s).

GOD'S NAME	MEANING	SCRIPTURE
Abba	Father	Galatians 4:6
Alpha and Omega	Beginning and End	Relevation 1:8
Ancient of Days	I AM	Daniel 7:9
El Chayil	Lord of Armies King of Glory	1 Samuel 17:45
El Chuwl	God Formed us	Psalm 139:13-18
El Deah	God of Knowledge	1 Samuel 2:3
El Elyon	God Most High	Genesis 14:18-20
El Olam	Everlasting God	Psalm 90:1-2
El Roi	God Who Sees	Genesis 16:13
El Shaddai	God Almighty	Genesis 17:1-2
Elohim	Our Creator	Genesis 1:1-3
Jehovah / Yahweh	Self-Existing One	Exodus 6:1-4
Jehovah Nissi	Lord my Banner	Exodus 17:15
Jehovah Rajah	Lord my Shepherd	Psalm 23
Jehovah Rapha	Lord our Healer	Exodus 15:26
Jehovah Shalom	Prince of Peace	Judges 6:23-24
Jehovah Shammah	Lord is There	Ezekiel 48:35
Jehovah Tsidkenu	Lord our Righteousness	Jeremiah 23:6
Jehovah Jireh	Lord will Provide	Genesis 22:14

www.GivingIsGodbook.com

† **Genesis 1:1-3 (KJV)** In the beginning God created the heaven and the earth. And the earth was without form, and void; and darkness was upon the face of the deep. And the Spirit of God moved upon the face of the waters. And God said, Let there be light: and there was light.

† **Genesis 1:26 (AMPC)** God said, Let Us [Father, Son, and Holy Spirit] make mankind in Our image, after Our likeness, and let them have complete authority over the fish of the sea, the birds of the air, the [tame] beasts, and over all of the earth, and over everything that creeps upon the earth.

† **Genesis 3:22 (KJV)** And the LORD God said, Behold, the man is become as one of us, to know good and evil: and now, lest he put forth his hand, and take also of the tree of life, and eat, and live for ever:

† **Genesis 14:18-20, 22 (KJV)** [18] And Melchizedek king of Salem brought forth bread and wine: and he was the priest of the **most high** God. [19] And he blessed him, and said, Blessed be Abram of the most high God, possessor of heaven and earth: [20] And blessed be the most high God, which hath delivered thine enemies into thy hand. And he gave him tithes of all. [22] And Abram said to the king of Sodom, I have lift up mine hand unto the LORD, the most high God, the possessor of heaven and earth,

† **Genesis 16:13 (NKJV)** Then she called the name of the LORD who spoke to her, You-Are-the-**God-Who-**

Sees; for she said, "Have I also here seen Him who sees me?"

† **Genesis 17:1-2 (NASB)** Now when Abram was ninety-nine years old, the LORD appeared to Abram and said to him, "I am **God Almighty**; Walk before Me, and be blameless. "I will establish My covenant between Me and you, And I will multiply you exceedingly."

† **Genesis 21:33 (KJV)** And Abraham planted a grove in Beersheba, and called there on the name of the LORD, the **everlasting God**.

† **Genesis 22:14 (KJV)** And Abraham called the name of that place **Jehovahjireh**: as it is said to this day, In the mount of the LORD it shall be seen.

† **Genesis 28:15 (NASB)** Behold, I am with you and will keep you wherever you go, and will bring you back to this land; for I will not leave you until I have done what I have promised you."

† **Exodus 3:13-14 (KJV)** And Moses said unto God, Behold, when I come unto the children of Israel, and shall say unto them, The God of your fathers hath sent me unto you; and they shall say to me, What is his name? what shall I say unto them? And God said unto Moses, **I AM THAT I AM**: and he said, Thus shalt thou say unto the children of Israel, I AM hath sent me unto you.

† **Exodus 6:1-4 (KJV)** Then the LORD said unto Moses,

Now shalt thou see what I will do to Pharaoh: for with a strong hand shall he let them go, and with a strong hand shall he drive them out of his land. And God spake unto Moses, and said unto him, I am the LORD: And I appeared unto Abraham, unto Isaac, and unto Jacob, by the name of God Almighty, but by my name **JEHOVAH** was I not known to them. And I have also established my covenant with them, to give them the land of Canaan, the land of their pilgrimage, wherein they were strangers.

† **Exodus 15:26 (KJV)** And said, If thou wilt diligently hearken to the voice of the LORD thy God, and wilt do that which is right in his sight, and wilt give ear to his commandments, and keep all his statutes, I will put none of these diseases upon thee, which I have brought upon the Egyptians: for I am the **LORD that healeth thee**.

† **Exodus 17:14-15 (KJV)** And the LORD said unto Moses, Write this for a memorial in a book, and rehearse it in the ears of Joshua: for I will utterly put out the remembrance of Amalek from under heaven. And Moses built an altar, and called the name of it **Jehovahnissi**:

† **Deuteronomy 32:18 (NASB)** "You neglected the Rock who begot you, And forgot the God who gave you birth.

† **Deuteronomy 32:18 (KJV)** Of the Rock that begat thee thou art unmindful, and hast forgotten God that

formed thee.

† **Judges 6:23-24 (KJV)** And the LORD said unto him, Peace be unto thee; fear not: thou shalt not die. Then Gideon built an altar there unto the LORD, and called it **Jehovahshalom:** unto this day it is yet in Ophrah of the Abiezrites.

† **1 Samuel 2:3 (KJV)** Talk no more so exceeding proudly; let not arrogancy come out of your mouth: for the **LORD is a God of knowledge**, and by him actions are weighed.

† **1 Samuel 17:45 (KJV)** Then said David to the Philistine, Thou comest to me with a sword, and with a spear, and with a shield: but I come to thee in the **name of the LORD of hosts, the God of the armies of Israel**, whom thou hast defied.

† **2 Chronicles 7:14 (KJV)** If my people, which are called by my name, shall humble themselves, and pray, and seek my face, and turn from their wicked ways; then will I hear from heaven, and will forgive their sin, and will heal their land.

† **Psalm 23:1 (KJV)** The LORD is my shepherd; I shall not want.

† **Psalm 46:10 (KJV)** Be still, and know that I am God: I will be exalted among the heathen, I will be exalted in the earth.

† **Psalm 90:1-2 (KJV)** Lord, thou hast been our dwelling place in all generations. Before the

mountains were brought forth, or ever thou hadst formed the earth and the world, even from everlasting to **everlasting, thou art God**.

† **Psalm 92:1 (KJV)** It is a good thing to give thanks unto the LORD, and to sing praises unto thy name, O Most High:

† **Psalm 139:13-18 (AMPC)** ¹³ For You did **form** my inward parts; You did knit me together in my mother's womb. ¹⁴ I will confess *and* praise You *for You are fearful and wonderful and* for the awful wonder of my birth! Wonderful are Your works, and that my inner self knows right well. ¹⁵ My frame was not hidden from You when I was being formed in secret [and] intricately *and* curiously wrought [as if embroidered with various colors] in the depths of the earth [a region of darkness and mystery]. ¹⁶ Your eyes saw my unformed substance, and in Your book all the days [of my life] were written before ever they took shape, when as yet there was none of them. ¹⁷ How precious *and* weighty also are Your thoughts to me, O God! How vast is the sum of them! ¹⁸ If I could count them, they would be more in number than the sand. When I awoke, [could I count to the end] I would still be with You.

† **Isaiah 40:28 (KJV)** Hast thou not known? hast thou not heard, that the everlasting God, the LORD, the Creator of the ends of the earth, fainteth not, neither is weary? there is no searching of his understanding.

† **Isaiah 46:9-10 (KJV)** Remember the former things of old: for I am God, and there is none else; I am God, and there is none like me, Declaring the end from the beginning, and from ancient times the things that are not yet done, saying, My counsel shall stand, and I will do all my pleasure:

† **Isaiah 55:9 (KJV)** For as the heavens are higher than the earth, so are my ways higher than your ways, and my thoughts than your thoughts.

† **Jeremiah 23:6 (KJV)** In his days Judah shall be saved, and Israel shall dwell safely: and this is his name whereby he shall be called, THE LORD OUR RIGHTEOUSNESS.

† **Ezekiel 48:35 (KJV)** It was round about eighteen thousand measures: and the name of the city from that day shall be, **The LORD is there.**

† **Daniel 7:9 (KJV)** I beheld till the thrones were cast down, and the **Ancient of days** did sit, whose garment was white as snow, and the hair of his head like the pure wool: his throne was like the fiery flame, and his wheels as burning fire.

† **Daniel 7:13-14 (KJV)** I saw in the night visions, and, behold, one like the Son of man came with the clouds of heaven, and came to the Ancient of days, and they brought him near before him. And there was given him dominion, and glory, and a kingdom, that all people, nations, and languages, should serve him: his

dominion is an everlasting dominion, which shall not pass away, and his kingdom that which shall not be destroyed.

† **Matthew 6:9 (KJV)** After this manner therefore pray ye: Our **Father** which art in heaven, Hallowed be thy name.

† **Matthew 6:33 (NASB)** But seek first His kingdom and His righteousness, and all these things will be added to you.

† **Matthew 8:7 (KJV)** And Jesus saith unto him, I will come and heal him.

† **Matthew 10:1 (KJV)** And when he had called unto him his twelve disciples, he gave them power against unclean spirits, to cast them out, and to heal all manner of sickness and all manner of disease.

† **Matthew 25:32 (KJV)** And before him shall be gathered all nations: and he shall separate them one from another, as a shepherd divideth his sheep from the goats:

† **Mark 10:27 (KJV)** And Jesus looking upon them saith, With men it is impossible, but not with God: for with God all things are possible.

† **Mark 14:36 (KJV)** And he said, Abba, Father, all things are possible unto thee; take away this cup from me: nevertheless not what I will, but what thou wilt.

† **Luke 4:18 (KJV)** The Spirit of the Lord is upon me, because he hath anointed me to preach the gospel to

the poor; he hath sent me to heal the brokenhearted, to preach deliverance to the captives, and recovering of sight to the blind, to set at liberty them that are bruised,

† **John 1:1-2 (AMPC)** In the beginning [before all time] was the Word (Christ), and the Word was with God, and the Word was God Himself. He was present originally with God.

† **John 1:12-14 (AMPC)** ^{12} But to as many as did receive *and* welcome Him, He gave the authority (power, privilege, right) to become the children of God, that is, to those who believe in (adhere to, trust in, and rely on) His name— ^{13} Who owe their birth neither to bloods nor to the will of the flesh [that of physical impulse] nor to the will of man [that of a natural father], but to God. [They are born of God!] ^{14} And the Word (Christ) became flesh (human, incarnate) and tabernacled (fixed His tent of flesh, lived awhile) among us; and we [actually] saw His glory (His honor, His majesty), such glory as an only begotten son receives from his father, full of grace (favor, loving-kindness) and truth.

† **John 4:24 (KJV)** God is a Spirit: and they that worship him must worship him in spirit and in truth.

† **John 4:23–24 (AMPC)** A time will come, however, indeed it is already here, when the true (genuine) worshipers will worship the Father in spirit and in truth (reality); for the Father is seeking just such

people as these as His worshipers. God is a Spirit (a spiritual Being) and those who worship Him must worship *Him* in spirit and in truth (reality).

† **John 5:30 (AMPC)** I am able to do nothing from Myself [independently, of My own accord—but only as I am taught by God and as I get His orders]. Even as I hear, I judge [I decide as I am bidden to decide. As the voice comes to Me, so I give a decision], and My judgment is right (just, righteous), because I do not seek *or* consult My own will [I have no desire to do what is pleasing to Myself, My own aim, My own purpose] but only the will *and* pleasure of the Father Who sent Me.

† **John 10:11 (KJV)** I am the good shepherd: the good shepherd giveth his life for the sheep.

† **John 14:10 (KJV)** Believest thou not that I am in the Father, and the Father in me? the words that I speak unto you I speak not of myself: but the Father that dwelleth in me, he doeth the works.

† **John 14:8-10 (NKJV)** [8] Philip said to Him, "Lord, show us the Father, and it is sufficient for us." [9] Jesus said to him, "Have I been with you so long, and yet you have not known Me, Philip? He who has seen Me has seen the Father; so how can you say, 'Show us the Father'? [10] Do you not believe that I am in the Father, and the Father in Me? The words that I speak to you I do not speak on My own *authority;* but the Father who dwells in Me does the works.

† **John 14:16-17 (NASB)** ^{16} I will ask the Father, and He will give you another Helper, that He may be with you forever; ^{17} *that is* the Spirit of truth, whom the world cannot receive, because it does not see Him or know Him, *but* you know Him because He abides with you and will be in you.

† **John 15:16–17 (NKJV)** You did not choose Me, but I chose you and appointed you that you should go and bear fruit, and that your fruit should remain, that whatever you ask the Father in My name He may give you. These things I command you, that you love one another.

† **John 17:11 (KJV)** And now I am no more in the world, but these are in the world, and I come to thee. Holy Father, keep through thine own name those whom thou hast given me, that they may be one, as we are.

† **Acts 17:24-28 (KJV)** ^{24} God that made the world and all things therein, seeing that he is Lord of heaven and earth, dwelleth not in temples made with hands; ^{25} Neither is worshipped with men's hands, as though he needed any thing, seeing he giveth to all life, and breath, and all things; ^{26} And hath made of one blood all nations of men for to dwell on all the face of the earth, and hath determined the times before appointed, and the bounds of their habitation; ^{27} That they should seek the Lord, if haply they might feel after him, and find him, though he be not far from every one of us:

²⁸ For in him we live, and move, and have our being; as certain also of your own poets have said, For we are also his offspring.

† **Acts 7:48-49 (KJV)** ⁴⁸ Howbeit the most High dwelleth not in temples made with hands; as saith the prophet, ⁴⁹ Heaven is my throne, and earth is my footstool: what house will ye build me? saith the Lord: or what is the place of my rest?

† **Romans 1:20 (AMPC)** For ever since the creation of the world His invisible nature *and* attributes, that is, His eternal power and divinity, have been made intelligible *and* clearly discernible in *and* through the things that have been made (His handiworks). So [men] are without excuse [altogether without any defense or justification],

† **Romans 5:18 (KJV)** Therefore as by the offence of one judgment came upon all men to condemnation; even so by the righteousness of one the free gift came upon all men unto justification of life.

† **Romans 8:10 (KJV)** And if Christ be in you, the body is dead because of sin; but the Spirit is life because of righteousness.

† **Romans 8:9-11 (AMPC)** ⁹ But you are not living the life of the flesh, you are living the life of the Spirit, if the [Holy] Spirit of God [really] dwells within you [directs and controls you]. But if anyone does not possess the [Holy] Spirit of Christ, he is none of His

[he does not belong to Christ, is not truly a child of God]. ¹⁰ But if Christ lives in you, [then although] your [natural] body is dead by reason of sin *and* guilt, the spirit is alive because of [the] righteousness [that He imputes to you]. ¹¹ And if the Spirit of Him Who raised up Jesus from the dead dwells in you, [then] He Who raised up Christ *Jesus* from the dead will also restore to life your mortal (short-lived, perishable) bodies through His Spirit Who dwells in you.

† **Romans 8:13-14 (AMPC)** ¹³ For if you live according to [the dictates of] the flesh, you will surely die. But if through the power of the [Holy] Spirit you are [habitually] putting to death (making extinct, deadening) the [evil] deeds prompted by the body, you shall [really and genuinely] live forever. ¹⁴ For all who are led by the Spirit of God are sons of God.

† **Romans 8:15 (KJV)** For ye have not received the spirit of bondage again to fear; but ye have received the Spirit of adoption, whereby we cry, **Abba, Father.**

† **Romans 8:16-17 (AMPC)** ¹⁶ The Spirit Himself [thus] testifies together with our own spirit, [assuring us] that we are children of God. ¹⁷ And if we are [His] children, then we are [His] heirs also: heirs of God and fellow heirs with Christ [sharing His inheritance with Him]; only we must share His suffering if we are to share His glory.

† **Romans 8:19 (KJV)** ¹⁹ For the earnest expectation of the creature waiteth for the manifestation of the sons

of God.

† **Romans 11:33 (KJV)** ³³ O the depth of the riches both of the wisdom and knowledge of God! how unsearchable are his judgments, and his ways past finding out!

† **1 Corinthians 1:18-31 (KJV)** ¹⁸ For the preaching of the cross is to them that perish foolishness; but unto us which are saved it is the power of God. ¹⁹ For it is written, I will destroy the wisdom of the wise, and will bring to nothing the understanding of the prudent. ²⁰ Where is the wise? where is the scribe? where is the disputer of this world? hath not God made foolish the wisdom of this world? ²¹ For after that in the wisdom of God the world by wisdom knew not God, it pleased God by the foolishness of preaching to save them that believe. ²² For the Jews require a sign, and the Greeks seek after wisdom: ²³ But we preach Christ crucified, unto the Jews a stumblingblock, and unto the Greeks foolishness; ²⁴ But unto them which are called, both Jews and Greeks, Christ the power of God, and the wisdom of God. ²⁵ Because the foolishness of God is wiser than men; and the weakness of God is stronger than men. ²⁶ For ye see your calling, brethren, how that not many wise men after the flesh, not many mighty, not many noble, are called: ²⁷ But God hath chosen the foolish things of the world to confound the wise; and God hath chosen the weak things of the world to confound the things which are mighty; ²⁸ And base

things of the world, and things which are despised, hath God chosen, yea, and things which are not, to bring to nought things that are: ²⁹ That no flesh should glory in his presence. ³⁰ But of him are ye in Christ Jesus, who of God is made unto us wisdom, and righteousness, and sanctification, and redemption: ³¹ That, according as it is written, He that glorieth, let him glory in the Lord.

† **1 Corinthians 8:5–7 (AMPC)** For although there may be so-called gods, whether in heaven or on earth, as indeed there are many of them, both of gods and of lords and masters, Yet for us there is [only] one God, the Father, Who is the Source of all things and for Whom we [have life], and one Lord, Jesus Christ, through and by Whom are all things and through and by Whom we [ourselves exist]. Nevertheless, not all [believers] possess this knowledge. But some, through being all their lives until now accustomed to [thinking of] idols [as real and living], still consider the food [offered to an idol] as that sacrificed to an [actual] god; and their weak consciences become defiled and injured if they eat [it].

† **2 Corinthians 6:18 (KJV)** And will be a Father unto you, and ye shall be my sons and daughters, saith the Lord Almighty.

† **Galatians 4:6 (KJV)** And because ye are sons, God hath sent forth the Spirit of his Son into your hearts, crying, **Abba, Father**.

- † **Ephesians 1:5 (AMPC)** For He foreordained us (destined us, planned in love for us) to be adopted (revealed) as His own children through Jesus Christ, in accordance with the purpose of His will [because it pleased Him and was His kind intent]—

- † **Ephesians 4:6 (KJV)** One God and Father of all, who is above all, and through all, and in you all.

- † **Colossians 1:16-17 (KJV)** For by him were all things created, that are in heaven, and that are in earth, visible and invisible, whether they be thrones, or dominions, or principalities, or powers: all things were created by him, and for him: And he is before all things, and by him all things consist.

- † **2 Thessalonians 3:16 (KJV)** Now the Lord of peace himself give you peace always by all means. The Lord be with you all.

- † **Hebrews 1:8 (KJV)** But unto the Son he saith, Thy throne, O God, is for ever and ever: a sceptre of righteousness is the sceptre of thy kingdom.

- † **Hebrews 11:3 (KJV)** Through faith we understand that the worlds were framed by the word of God, so that things which are seen were not made of things which do appear.

- † **Hebrews 13:20-21 (AMPC)** [20] Now may the God of peace [Who is the Author and the Giver of peace], Who brought again from among the dead our Lord Jesus, that great Shepherd of the sheep, by the blood [that sealed, ratified] the everlasting agreement (covenant, testament), ²¹ Strengthen (complete, perfect) *and* make you what you ought to be *and* equip you with everything good that you may carry out His will; [while He Himself] works in you *and* accomplishes that which is pleasing in His sight, through Jesus Christ (the Messiah); to Whom be the glory forever and ever (to the ages of the ages). Amen (so be it).

† **1 Peter 2:25 (NASB)** For you were continually straying like sheep, but now you have returned to the Shepherd and Guardian of your souls.

† **1 John 1:1-3 (AMPC)** ¹ [We are writing] about the Word of Life [in] Him Who existed from the beginning, Whom we have heard, Whom we have seen with our [own] eyes, Whom we have gazed upon [for ourselves] and have touched with our [own] hands. ² And the Life [an aspect of His being] was revealed (made manifest, demonstrated), and we saw [as eyewitnesses] and are testifying to and declare to you the Life, the eternal Life [in Him] Who already existed with the Father and Who [actually] was made visible (was revealed) to us [His followers]. ³ What we have seen and [ourselves] heard, we are also telling you, so that you too may realize *and* enjoy fellowship as partners *and* partakers with us. And [this] fellowship that we have [which is a distinguishing mark of Christians] is with the Father and with His

Son Jesus Christ (the Messiah).

† **1 John 5:6-8 (KJV)** ⁶This is he that came by water and blood, even Jesus Christ; not by water only, but by water and blood. And it is the Spirit that beareth witness, because the Spirit is truth. ⁷For there are three that bear record in heaven, the Father, the Word, and the Holy Ghost: and these three are one. ⁸And there are three that bear witness in earth, the Spirit, and the water, and the blood: and these three agree in one.

† **Revelation 1:8 (KJV)** I am **Alpha and Omega**, the beginning and the ending, saith the Lord, which is, and which was, and which is to come, the Almighty.

† **Revelation 1:11 (KJV)** Saying, I am Alpha and Omega, the first and the last: and, What thou seest, write in a book, and send it unto the seven churches which are in Asia; unto Ephesus, and unto Smyrna, and unto Pergamos, and unto Thyatira, and unto Sardis, and unto Philadelphia, and unto Laodicea.

† **Revelation 21:6 (KJV)** And he said unto me, It is done. I am Alpha and Omega, the beginning and the end. I will give unto him that is athirst of the fountain of the water of life freely.

† **Revelation 22:13 (KJV) I am Alpha and Omega**, the beginning and the end, the first and the last.

God's Way

God's way is Who He is. God is love, for He is a good God. God is a just God, for He hates injustice. He is Holy. God is not a man, that He should lie. God is merciful and He is righteous. God is so faithful, He does what He says He will do.

God made everything in seed form, so that the seed can reproduce after its own kind. God has already made available every seed we will ever need, before the foundation of the world.

God created us, He breathe part of Himself into us (Life-seed) in the beginning (See Image ... & see Increase ...). All that God is, we are if we are born again. God is good and we have the ability to be good. Anything other than good is evil.

We have to give God a seed to work with; to reproduce it, and/or multiply it, according to our giving and by our faith. When we sow God's word in prayer, He will watch over it to perform it. The kind of seed that we sow will be the kind of harvest we reap and even reap multiplied, so give with a willing heart, cheerfully is preferred. So, what kind of seeds are you sowing? And remember, it is returned back to you and even multiplied. ***Everything that we do is a seed, let's*** *sow seed as unto the Lord !!!*

God Is Love.

† **1 John 4:10 (AMPC)** In this is love: not that we loved God, but that He loved us and sent His Son to be the propitiation (the atoning sacrifice) for our sins.

God Is Good.

† **Psalm 34:8 (NIV)** Taste and see that the Lord is good; blessed is the one who takes refuge in him.

God Is a God of Justice.

† **Hebrews 10:30 (AMPC)** For we know Him Who said, Vengeance is Mine [retribution and the meting out of full justice rest with Me]; I will repay [I will exact the compensation], *says the Lord*. And again, The Lord will judge *and* determine *and* solve *and* settle the cause *and* the cases of His people.

God Is Holy.

† **Leviticus 23:2 (KJV)** And the Lord spake unto Moses, saying, Speak unto the children of Israel, and say unto them, Concerning the feasts of the Lord, which ye shall proclaim to be holy convocations, even these are My feasts.

God Is Not a Man, That He Should Lie.

† **Numbers 23:19 (KJV)** God is not a man, that He should lie; neither the Son of man, that He should repent: hath He said, and shall He not do it? or hath He

spoken, and shall He not make it good?

God Is Merciful.

† **Psalm 109:21 (KJV)** But do thou for me, O God the Lord, for thy name's sake: because thy mercy is good, deliver thou me.

God Is Righteous.

† **Matthew 6:33 (AMPC)** But seek (aim at and strive after) first of all His kingdom and His righteousness (His way of doing and being right), and then all these things taken together will be given you besides.

God Is Faithful.

† **1 Corinthians 1:8–10 (KJV)** Who shall also confirm you unto the end, that ye may be blameless in the day of our Lord Jesus Christ. God is faithful, by whom ye were called unto the fellowship of His Son Jesus Christ our Lord. Now I beseech you, brethren, by the name of our Lord Jesus Christ, that ye all speak the same thing, and that there be no divisions among you; but that ye be perfectly joined together in the same mind and in the same judgment.

God Is The Giver of Seed.

† **Genesis 1:11-12 (AMPC)** And God said, Let the earth put forth [tender] vegetation: plants yielding seed and fruit trees yielding fruit whose seed is in itself, each according to its kind, upon the earth. And it was so. The earth brought forth vegetation: plants yielding seed according to their own kinds and trees bearing

fruit in which was their seed, each according to its kind. And God saw that it was good (suitable, admirable) *and* He approved it.

† **Genesis 8:22 (NKJV)** "While the earth remains, Seedtime and harvest, Cold and heat, Winter and summer, And day and night Shall not cease.

† **Genesis 26:3-5 (KJV)** Sojourn in this land, and I will be with thee, and will bless thee; for unto thee, and unto thy seed, I will give all these countries, and I will perform the oath which I sware unto Abraham thy father; And I will make thy seed to multiply as the stars of heaven, and will give unto thy seed all these countries; and in thy seed shall all the nations of the earth be blessed; Because that Abraham obeyed my voice, and kept my charge, my commandments, my statutes, and my laws.

† **Ecclesiastes 11:6 (KJV)** In the morning sow thy seed, and in the evening withhold not thine hand: for thou knowest not whether shall prosper, either this or that, or whether they both shall be alike good.

† **Isaiah 55:10-11 (AMPC)** For as the rain and snow come down from the heavens, and return not there again, but water the earth and make it bring forth and sprout, that it may give seed to the sower and bread to the eater, So shall My word be that goes forth out of My mouth: it shall not return to Me void [without producing any effect, useless], but it shall accomplish that which I please *and* purpose, and it shall prosper in

the thing for which I sent it.

† **Isaiah 61:8 (KJV)** For I the LORD love judgment, I hate robbery for burnt offering; and I will direct their work in truth, and I will make an everlasting covenant with them.

† **Isaiah 61:7-9 (AMPC)** Instead of your [former] shame you shall have a twofold recompense; instead of dishonor *and* reproach [your people] shall rejoice in their portion. Therefore in their land they shall possess double [what they had forfeited]; everlasting joy shall be theirs. For I the Lord love justice; I hate robbery *and* wrong with violence *or* a burnt offering. And I will faithfully give them their recompense in truth, and I will make an everlasting covenant *or* league with them. And their offspring shall be known among the nations and their descendants among the peoples. All who see them [in their prosperity] will recognize *and* acknowledge that they are the people whom the Lord has blessed.

† **2 Corinthians 9:9-11 (NIV)** As it is written: "They have freely scattered their gifts to the poor; their righteousness endures forever." Now he who supplies seed to the sower and bread for food will also supply and increase your store of seed and will enlarge the harvest of your righteousness. You will be enriched in every way so that you can be generous on every occasion, and through us your generosity will result in thanksgiving to God.

God's Will

My only desire, since I have been saved/born again (actually made free) is to seek to do God's will. I had an okay worldly life, but I had sensed something was missing. Now that I have found out the truth, that I am a spirit, I possess a soul, and I live in a body, I desired to learn more.

So far, I have learned that I am not independent of myself, I have to rely on a head, master, or lord, spiritually. God is a Spirit, Who requires a vessel; my body. The devil is also a spirit who needs a body. I made the choice to accepted Jesus as my Lord and Savior, so that the Holy Spirit can dwell in me. My body is the temple of the Holy Ghost. God's will is for us all to be saved, but the choice has to be made by each person. When a person doesn't directly choose Jesus, that person indirectly chose Satan to be their lord and master, so their life belongs to the devil to do his will.

† **Ecclesiastes 10:20 (KJV)** Curse not the king, no not in thy thought; and curse not the rich in thy bedchamber: for a bird of the air shall carry the voice, and that which hath wings shall tell the matter.

† **Matthew 6:10 (KJV)** Thy kingdom come, Thy will be

done in earth, as it is in heaven.

† **Mark 3:32–35 (AMPC)** And a crowd was sitting around Him, and they said to Him, Your mother and Your brothers *and Your sisters* are outside asking for You. ³³ And He replied, Who are My mother and My brothers? ³⁴ And looking around on those who sat in a circle about Him, He said, See! Here are My mother and My brothers; ³⁵ For whoever does the things God wills is My brother and sister and mother!

† **Mark 16:15 (KJV)** And He said unto them, Go ye into all the world, and preach the gospel to every creature.

† **Luke 22:42 (KJV)** Saying, Father, if Thou be willing, remove this cup from Me: nevertheless not My will, but Thine, be done.

† **Philippians 2:13 (KJV)** For it is God which worketh in you both to will and to do of his good pleasure.

† **1 Timothy 2:3–5 (NKJV)** For this is good and acceptable in the sight of God our Savior, who desires all men to be saved and to come to the knowledge of the truth. For there is one God and one Mediator between God and men, the Man Christ Jesus,

† **2 Peter 3:8 (KJV)** But, beloved, be not ignorant of this one thing, that one day is with the Lord as a thousand years, and a thousand years as one day.

† **Revelation 21:6 (KJV)** And He said unto me, It is done. I am Alpha and Omega, the beginning and the

end. I will give unto him that is athirst of the fountain of the water of life freely.

God's Word

The *Giving Is God* book is used by God to help inspire us to search the Holy Bible to fully explain His Word; which is His Way and His Will. By using several translations, especially the original languages; Hebrew and Greek, we can get a greater understanding. The written word is logos, but it is the Holy Spirit Who gives us the rhema word, which comes directly from God.

We will all find many of our favorite and familiar scriptures in *Giving Is God*, but like a precious man of God has said, "Read it over and over again, like we never seen it before, we will be amazed of how much more revelation we will receive."

† **Psalm 19:8 (AMPC)** The precepts of the Lord are right, rejoicing the heart; the commandment of the Lord is pure *and* bright, enlightening the eyes.

† **Isaiah 55:11 (AMPC)** So shall My word be that goes forth out of My mouth: it shall not return to Me void [without producing any effect, useless], but it shall accomplish that which I please *and* purpose, and it shall prosper in the thing for which I sent it.

† **Jeremiah 23:29 (KJV)** Is not my word like as a fire? saith the Lord; and like a hammer that breaketh the rock in pieces?

† **Matthew 8:8 (KJV)** The centurion answered and said, Lord, I am not worthy that thou shouldest come under my roof: but speak the word only, and my servant shall be healed.

† **Luke 8:11 (KJV)** Now the parable is this: The seed is the word of God.

† **John 1:1–4 (KJV)** In the beginning was the Word, and the Word was with God, and the Word was God. The same was in the beginning with God. All things were made by Him; and without Him was not any thing made that was made. In Him was life; and the life was the light of men.

† **John 17:14–16 (KJV)** I have given them Thy word; and the world hath hated them, because they are not of the world, even as I am not of the world. I pray not that Thou shouldest take them out of the world, but that Thou shouldest keep them from the evil. They are not of the world, even as I am not of the world.

† **1 Thessalonians 1:5-6 (KJV)** For our gospel came not unto you in word only, but also in power, and in the Holy Ghost, and in much assurance; as ye know what manner of men we were among you for your sake. And ye became followers of us, and of the Lord, having received the word in much affliction, with joy of the Holy Ghost.

† **2 Timothy 2:15 (KJV)** Study to shew thyself approved unto God, a workman that needeth not to be

ashamed, rightly dividing the word of Truth.

† **2 Timothy 3:16–17 (NASB)** All Scripture is inspired by God and profitable for teaching, for reproof, for correction, for training in righteousness; so that the man of God may be adequate, equipped for every good work.

† **Hebrews 4:12 (AMPC)** For the Word that God speaks is alive and full of power [making it active, operative, energizing, and effective]; it is sharper than any two-edged sword, penetrating to the dividing line of the breath of life (soul) and [the immortal] spirit, and of joints and marrow [of the deepest parts of our nature], exposing and sifting and analyzing and judging the very thoughts and purposes of the heart.

Good / Goodness

God is so good !!! His desire is for us to imitate Him. By giving to people in need, we are manifesting the sons of God.

There is a lot of good in the world, but since things are not organized enough in unity, it is hard to see our progress. By faith, I decree unity is in the earth in such a way that the whole world will see God, through the advancement of the Kingdom of God, in Jesus' Name, Amen !!!. (A Fruit of the Spirit attribute)

† **Genesis 1:4, 10, 12, 18, 21, 25, 31 (KJV)** [4] And God saw the light, that it was good: and God divided the light from the darkness. [10] And God called the dry land Earth; and the gathering together of the waters called he Seas: and God saw that it was good. [12] And the earth brought forth grass, and herb yielding seed after his kind, and the tree yielding fruit, whose seed was in itself, after his kind: and God saw that it was good. [18] And to rule over the day and over the night, and to divide the light from the darkness: and God saw that it was good. [21] And God created great whales, and every living creature that moveth, which the waters brought forth abundantly, after their kind, and every winged fowl after his kind: and God saw that it was good. [25] And God made the beast of the earth after his kind,

and cattle after their kind, and every thing that creepeth upon the earth after his kind: and God saw that it was good. ³¹ And God saw every thing that he had made, and, behold, it was very good. And the evening and the morning were the sixth day.

† **Genesis 2:9, 12 (KJV)** ⁹ And out of the ground made the LORD God to grow every tree that is pleasant to the sight, and good for food; the tree of life also in the midst of the garden, and the tree of knowledge of good and evil. ¹² And the gold of that land is good: there is bdellium and the onyx stone.

† **Psalm 23:5–6 (KJV)** Thou preparest a table before me in the presence of mine enemies: thou anointest my head with oil; my cup runneth over. Surely goodness and mercy shall follow me all the days of my life: and I will dwell in the house of the Lord for ever.

† **Psalm 27:13 (AMPC)** [What, what would have become of me] had I not believed that I would see the Lord's goodness in the land of the living!

† **Psalm 27:13-14 (MSG)** I'm sure now I'll see God's goodness in the exuberant earth. Stay with GOD! Take heart. Don't quit. I'll say it again: Stay with GOD.

† **Psalm 34:8 (KJV)** O taste and see that the Lord is good: blessed is the man that trusteth in Him.

† **Proverbs 13:22 (KJV)** A good man leaveth an inheritance to his children's children: and the wealth of the sinner is laid up for the just.

- † **Proverbs 15:23 (KJV)** A man hath joy by the answer of his mouth: and a word spoken in due season, how good is it!

- † **Ecclesiastes 2:26 (KJV)** For God giveth to a man that is good in His sight wisdom, and knowledge, and joy: but to the sinner He giveth travail, to gather and to heap up, that he may give to him that is good before God.

- † **Romans 8:28 (AMPC)** We are assured *and* know that [God being a partner in their labor] all things work together *and* are [fitting into a plan] for good to *and* for those who love God and are called according to [His] design *and* purpose.

- † **2 Corinthians 9:9–11 (AMPC)** [9] As it is written, He [the benevolent person] scatters abroad; He gives to the poor; His deeds of justice *and* goodness *and* kindness *and* benevolence will go on *and* endure forever! [10] And [God] Who provides seed for the sower and bread for eating will also provide and multiply your [resources for] sowing and increase the fruits of your righteousness [which manifests itself in active goodness, kindness, and charity]. [11] Thus you will be enriched in all things *and* in every way, so that you can be generous, and [your generosity as it is] administered by us will bring forth thanksgiving to God.

Good Success

I don't know who said this, in order to give credit to the person, but the question was, "Have you ever wondered why some people are rich and some are not?" The answer is "the way a person thinks"! What are we constantly thinking about? What are we letting repeat over and over in our minds? Some of us have been wasting precious time and resources. Are we thinking about more money in a greedy kind of way, rather than thinking about how many people we can help if finances were not an issue.

God has always had the answer for us in His word; the Bible. Let us meditate on scriptures, for this is what we are supposed to do; renew our minds with the Word of God! Jesus died for us to have the abundant life, right? That is, if we have the right mind to do it.

Sons of God, we do have the mind of Christ, let us prove it with manifestation !!!

† **Deuteronomy 30:15-16 (NASB)** [Choose Life] "See, I have set before you today life and prosperity, and death and adversity; in that I command you today to love the LORD your God, to walk in His ways and to keep His commandments and His statutes and His judgments, that you may live and multiply, and that the LORD your God may bless you in the land where

you are entering to possess it.

- † **Deuteronomy 11:18–21 (KJV)** Therefore shall ye lay up these my words in your heart and in your soul, and bind them for a sign upon your hand, that they may be as frontlets between your eyes. And ye shall teach them your children, speaking of them when thou sittest in thine house, and when thou walkest by the way, when thou liest down, and when thou risest up. And thou shalt write them upon the door posts of thine house, and upon thy gates: That your days may be multiplied, and the days of your children, in the land which the Lord sware unto your fathers to give them, as the days of heaven upon the earth.

- † **Joshua 1:8 (KJV)** This book of the law shall not depart out of thy mouth; but thou shalt meditate therein day and night, that thou mayest observe to do according to all that is written therein: for then thou shalt make thy way prosperous, and then thou shalt have good success.

- † **Proverbs 3:5-6 (NKJV)** Trust in the Lord with all your heart, And lean not on your own understanding; In all your ways acknowledge Him, And He shall direct your paths.

- † **Proverbs 3:9-10 (NKJV)** It will be health to your flesh, And strength to your bones. Honor the Lord with your possessions, And with the firstfruits of all your increase; So your barns will be filled with plenty, And your vats will overflow with new wine.

- † **Proverbs 4:6-8 (AMPC)** Forsake not [Wisdom], and she will keep, defend, *and* protect you; love her, and she will guard you. The beginning of Wisdom is: get Wisdom (skillful and godly Wisdom)! [For skillful *and* godly Wisdom is the principal thing.] And with all you have gotten, get understanding (discernment, comprehension, and interpretation). Prize Wisdom highly *and* exalt her, and she will exalt *and* promote you; she will bring you to honor when you embrace her.

- † **Isaiah 48:17 (NKJV)** Thus says the LORD, your Redeemer, The Holy One of Israel: "I *am* the LORD your God, Who teaches you to profit, Who leads you by the way you should go.

- † **John 10:10 (AMPC)** The thief comes only in order to steal and kill and destroy. I came that they may have and enjoy life, and have it in abundance (to the full, till it overflows).

- † **Romans 8:14 (NKJV)** For as many as are led by the Spirit of God, these are sons of God.

- † **Hebrews 1:3 (KJV)** Who being the brightness of his glory, and the express image of his person, and upholding all things by the word of his power, when he had by himself purged our sins, sat down on the right hand of the Majesty on high:

Grace

I would go to spend time with my mother, several times a week. When I ask her how she is doing, she answers, "I am hanging in there, by the grace of God." I don't know about that hanging part, but I do enjoy hearing her put God in there.

I rely and am dependent on the grace of God; I know that I can do nothing without Him. The scripture that has helped me a many of times is 2 Corinthians 12:9 (see here), for His grace is sufficient for me.

Grace is like the impossible suddenly became possible !!!

† **Acts 4:33 (KJV)** And with great power gave the apostles witness of the resurrection of the Lord Jesus: and great grace was upon them all.

† **Acts 20:24 (KJV)** But none of these things move me, neither count I my life dear unto myself, so that I might finish my course with joy, and the ministry, which I have received of the Lord Jesus, to testify the gospel of the grace of God.

† **Acts 20:32 (AMPC)** And now [brethren], I commit you to God [I deposit you in His charge, entrusting you to His protection and care]. And I commend you to the Word of His grace [to the commands and

counsels and promises of His unmerited favor]. It is able to build you up and to give you [your rightful] inheritance among all God's set-apart ones (those consecrated, purified, and transformed of soul).

† **Acts 26:15-18 (NASB)** ¹⁵ And I said, 'Who are You, Lord?' And the Lord said, 'I am Jesus whom you are persecuting. ¹⁶ But get up and stand on your feet; for this purpose I have appeared to you, to appoint you a minister and a witness not only to the things which you have seen, but also to the things in which I will appear to you; ¹⁷ rescuing you from the *Jewish* people and from the Gentiles, to whom I am sending you, ¹⁸ to open their eyes so that they may turn from darkness to light and from the dominion of Satan to God, that they may receive forgiveness of sins and an inheritance among those who have been sanctified by faith in Me.'

† **Romans 3:24 (AMPC)** [All] are justified and made upright and in right standing with God, freely and gratuitously by His grace (His unmerited favor and mercy), through the redemption which is [provided] in Christ Jesus,

† **Romans 6:14 (KJV)** For sin shall not have dominion over you: for ye are not under the law, but under grace.

† **2 Corinthians 8:9 (KJV)** For ye know the grace of our Lord Jesus Christ, that, though He was rich, yet for your sakes He became poor, that ye through His poverty might be rich.

† **2 Corinthians 9:8 (AMPC)** And God is able to make all grace (every favor and earthly blessing) come to you in abundance, so that you may always and under all circumstances and whatever the need be self-sufficient [possessing enough to require no aid or support and furnished in abundance for every good work and charitable donation].

† **2 Corinthians 12:9 (KJV)** And He said unto me, My grace is sufficient for thee: for My strength is made perfect in weakness. Most gladly therefore will I rather glory in my infirmities, that the power of Christ may rest upon me.

† **Galatians 2:21 (KJV)** I do not frustrate the grace of God: for if righteousness come by the law, then Christ is dead in vain.

† **Ephesians 1:6-7 (AMPC)** ⁶[So that we might be] to the praise *and* the commendation of His glorious grace (favor and mercy), which He so freely bestowed on us in the Beloved. ⁷In Him we have redemption (deliverance and salvation) through His blood, the remission (forgiveness) of our offenses (shortcomings and trespasses), in accordance with the riches *and* the generosity of His gracious favor,

† **Ephesians 2:8–9 (KJV)** For by grace are ye saved through faith; and that not of yourselves: it is the gift of God: Not of works, lest any man should boast.

† **2 Thessalonians 1:11-12 (NKJV)** Therefore we also

pray always for you that our God would count you worthy of *this* calling, and fulfill all the good pleasure of *His* goodness and the work of faith with power, that the name of our Lord Jesus Christ may be glorified in you, and you in Him, according to the grace of our God and the Lord Jesus Christ.

† **Hebrews 4:16 (KJV)** Let us therefore come boldly unto the throne of grace, that we may obtain mercy, and find grace to help in time of need.

† **Hebrews 8:8-9 (KJV)** For finding fault with them, he saith, Behold, the days come, saith the Lord, when I will make a new covenant with the house of Israel and with the house of Judah: Not according to the covenant that I made with their fathers in the day when I took them by the hand to lead them out of the land of Egypt; because they continued not in my covenant, and I regarded them not, saith the Lord.

† **Hebrews 8:13 (KJV)** In that he saith, A new covenant, he hath made the first old. Now that which decayeth and waxeth old is ready to vanish away.

† **Hebrews 8:13 (AMPC)** When God speaks of a new [covenant or agreement], He makes the first one obsolete (out of use). And what is obsolete (out of use and annulled because of age) is ripe for disappearance *and* to be dispensed with altogether.

Healing / Health

I enjoy seeing Jesus flow through me, when I place my hand on myself and the symptom or pain goes away. I look forward to learning more on health and healing, for I confess to be in the living when Jesus comes for us.

I have learned that I can't go against a person's will, but I am here for family and loved ones to show them by example; how good it is to be totally sold out for the Lord. I will continue to pray, and by praying in the spirit, I am confident that I'm praying according to God's word.

† **Exodus 15:26 (AMPC)** Saying, If you will diligently hearken to the voice of the Lord your God and will do what is right in His sight, and will listen to and obey His commandments and keep all His statutes, I will put none of the diseases upon you which I brought upon the Egyptians, for I am the Lord Who heals you.

† **Exodus 23:25 (AMPC)** You shall serve the Lord your God; He shall bless your bread and water, and I will take sickness from your midst.

† **Deuteronomy 7:15 (AMPC)** And the Lord will take away from you all sickness, and none of the evil diseases of Egypt which you knew will He put upon you, but will lay them upon all who hate you.

† **Psalm 103:3 (AMPC)** Who forgives [every one of] all your iniquities, Who heals [each one of] all your diseases,

† **Psalm 105:37 (KJV)** He brought them forth also with silver and gold: and there was not one feeble person among their tribes.

† **Psalm 107:20 (NLT)** He sent his word, and healed them, and delivered them from their destructions.

† **Proverbs 4:20–23 (AMPC)** My son, attend to My words; consent and submit to My sayings. Let them not depart from your sight; keep them in the center of your heart. For they are life to those who find them, healing and health to all their flesh. Keep and guard your heart with all vigilance and above all that you guard, for out of it flow the springs of life.

† **Isaiah 53:4–5 (AMPC)** Surely He has borne our griefs (sicknesses, weaknesses, and distresses) and carried our sorrows and pains [of punishment], yet we [ignorantly] considered Him stricken, smitten, and afflicted by God [as if with leprosy]. But He was wounded for our transgressions, He was bruised for our guilt and iniquities; the chastisement [needful to obtain] peace and well-being for us was upon Him, and with the stripes [that wounded] Him we are healed and made whole.

† **Matthew 15:29-31 (KJV)** And Jesus departed from thence, and came nigh unto the sea of Galilee; and

went up into a mountain, and sat down there. And great multitudes came unto him, having with them those that were lame, blind, dumb, maimed, and many others, and cast them down at Jesus' feet; and he healed them: Insomuch that the multitude wondered, when they saw the dumb to speak, the maimed to be whole, the lame to walk, and the blind to see: and they glorified the God of Israel.

† **Mark 16:18 (KJV)** They shall take up serpents; and if they drink any deadly thing, it shall not hurt them; they shall lay hands on the sick, and they shall recover.

† **John 5:2-9 (KJV)** ² Now there is at Jerusalem by the sheep market a pool, which is called in the Hebrew tongue Bethesda, having five porches. ³ In these lay a great multitude of impotent folk, of blind, halt, withered, waiting for the moving of the water. ⁴ For an angel went down at a certain season into the pool, and troubled the water: whosoever then first after the troubling of the water stepped in was made whole of whatsoever disease he had. ⁵ And a certain man was there, which had an infirmity thirty and eight years. ⁶ When Jesus saw him lie, and knew that he had been now a long time in that case, he saith unto him, Wilt thou be made whole? ⁷ The impotent man answered him, Sir, I have no man, when the water is troubled, to put me into the pool: but while I am coming, another steppeth down before me. ⁸ Jesus saith unto him, Rise,

take up thy bed, and walk. ⁹ And immediately the man was made whole, and took up his bed, and walked: and on the same day was the sabbath.

† **James 5:14–15 (AMPC)** Is anyone among you sick? He should call in the church elders (the spiritual guides). And they should pray over him, anointing him with oil in the Lord's name. And the prayer [that is] of faith will save him who is sick, and the Lord will restore him; and if he has committed sins, he will be forgiven.

† **1 Peter 2:24 (KJV)** Who his own self bare our sins in his own body on the tree, that we, being dead to sins, should live unto righteousness: by whose stripes ye were healed.

Holiness / Holy

It is good to be holy; to do the right thing. It is not hard to do, just make the decision to do good. We did so many things wrong; now is the time to choose to do the right things. **Let us be holy for He is Holy !!!**

† **Isaiah 29:23–24 (NIV)** When they see among them their children, the work of my hands, they will keep my name holy; they will acknowledge the holiness of the Holy One of Jacob, and will stand in awe of the God of Israel. Those who are wayward in spirit will gain understanding; those who complain will accept instruction."

† **Isaiah 57:15 (KJV)** For thus saith the high and lofty One that inhabiteth eternity, whose name is Holy; I dwell in the high and holy place, with him also that is of a contrite and humble spirit, to revive the spirit of the humble, and to revive the heart of the contrite ones.

† **Galatians 5:22–23 (AMPC)** ^{22} But the fruit of the [Holy] Spirit [the work which His presence within accomplishes] is love, joy (gladness), peace, patience (an even temper, forbearance), kindness, goodness (benevolence), faithfulness, ^{23} Gentleness (meekness, humility), self-control (self-restraint, continence).

Against such things there is no law [that can bring a charge].

† **Ephesians 4:23–24 (AMPC)** And be constantly renewed in the spirit of your mind [having a fresh mental and spiritual attitude], And put on the new nature (the regenerate self) created in God's image, [Godlike] in true righteousness and holiness.

† **1 Thessalonians 3:12–13 (AMPC)** And may the Lord make you to increase and excel and overflow in love for one another and for all people, just as we also do for you, So that He may strengthen and confirm and establish your hearts faultlessly pure and unblamable in holiness in the sight of our God and Father, at the coming of our Lord Jesus Christ (the Messiah) with all His saints (the holy and glorified people of God)! Amen, (so be it)!

† **1 Thessalonians 4:3 (AMPC)** For this is the will of God, that you should be consecrated (separated and set apart for pure and holy living): that you should abstain *and* shrink from all sexual vice,

† **1 Peter 1:14–16 (AMPC)** ^{14}[Live] as children of obedience [to God]; do not conform yourselves to the evil desires [that governed you] in your former ignorance [when you did not know the requirements of the Gospel]. ^{15} But as the One Who called you is holy, you yourselves also be holy in all your conduct *and* manner of living.^{16} For it is written, You shall be holy, for I am holy.

Holy Spirit

Holy Spirit, Holy Ghost: I call Him my sweet Holy Spirit, because He helps me out so much. I don't want to think about where I would be without Him. I enjoy being in His Presence. Thank You, my sweet Holy Spirit for allowing me to reside with You !!!

† **Genesis 1:1–2 (KJV)** In the beginning God created the heaven and the earth. And the earth was without form, and void; and darkness was upon the face of the deep. And the Spirit of God moved upon the face of the waters.

† **Isaiah 61:1–4 (KJV)** The Spirit of the Lord GOD is upon me; because the Lord hath anointed me to preach good tidings unto the meek; he hath sent me to bind up the brokenhearted, to proclaim liberty to the captives, and the opening of the prison to them that are bound; To proclaim the acceptable year of the Lord, and the day of vengeance of our God; to comfort all that mourn; To appoint unto them that mourn in Zion, to give unto them beauty for ashes, the oil of joy for mourning, the garment of praise for the spirit of heaviness; that they might be called trees of righteousness, the planting of the Lord, that he might be glorified. And they shall build the old wastes, they

shall raise up the former desolations, and they shall repair the waste cities, the desolations of many generations.

† **Matthew 1:20 (KJV)** But while he thought on these things, behold, the angel of the Lord appeared unto him in a dream, saying, Joseph, thou son of David, fear not to take unto thee Mary thy wife: for that which is conceived in her is of the Holy Ghost.

† **Matthew 3:16–17 (KJV)** And Jesus, when He was baptized, went up straightway out of the water: and, lo, the heavens were opened unto Him, and He saw the Spirit of God descending like a dove, and lighting upon Him: And lo a Voice from Heaven, saying, This is My beloved Son, in whom I am well pleased.

† **Luke 4:17–19 (KJV)** And there was delivered unto Him the book of the prophet Esaias. And when He had opened the book, He found the place where it was written, The Spirit of the Lord is upon Me, because He hath anointed Me to preach the gospel to the poor; He hath sent Me to heal the brokenhearted, to preach deliverance to the captives, and recovering of sight to the blind, to set at liberty them that are bruised, To preach the acceptable year of the Lord.

† **John 14:26 (KJV)** But the Comforter, which is the Holy Ghost, whom the Father will send in My name, He shall teach you all things, and bring all things to your remembrance, whatsoever I have said unto you.

† **Acts 2:2–4 (NASB)** And suddenly there came from heaven a noise like a violent rushing wind, and it filled the whole house where they were sitting. And there appeared to them tongues as of fire distributing themselves, and they rested on each one of them. And they were all filled with the Holy Spirit and began to speak with other tongues, as the Spirit was giving them utterance.

† **Acts 2:38 (NASB)** Peter *said* to them, "Repent, and each of you be baptized in the name of Jesus Christ for the forgiveness of your sins; and you will receive the gift of the Holy Spirit.

† **Romans 8:14, 16 (KJV)** For as many as are led by the Spirit of God, they are the sons of God. The Spirit itself beareth witness with our spirit, that we are the children of God:

† **Romans 8:26–27 (KJV)** Likewise the Spirit also helpeth our infirmities: for we know not what we should pray for as we ought: but the Spirit itself maketh intercession for us with groanings which cannot be uttered. And he that searcheth the hearts knoweth what is the mind of the Spirit, because he maketh intercession for the saints according to the will of God.

† **Romans 14:17 (KJV)** For the kingdom of God is not meat and drink; but righteousness, and peace, and joy in the Holy Ghost.

† **Romans 15:13 (NIV)** May the God of hope fill you with all joy and peace as you trust in him, so that you may overflow with hope by the power of the Holy Spirit.

† **1 Corinthians 2:14 (KJV)** But the natural man receiveth not the things of the Spirit of God: for they are foolishness unto him: neither can he know them, because they are spiritually discerned.

† **1 Corinthians 12:1–11 (KJV)** ¹Now concerning spiritual gifts, brethren, I would not have you ignorant. ² Ye know that ye were Gentiles, carried away unto these dumb idols, even as ye were led. ³ Wherefore I give you to understand, that no man speaking by the Spirit of God calleth Jesus accursed: and that no man can say that Jesus is the Lord, but by the Holy Ghost. ⁴ Now there are diversities of gifts, but the same Spirit. ⁵ And there are differences of administrations, but the same Lord. ⁶ And there are diversities of operations, but it is the same God which worketh all in all. ⁷ But the manifestation of the Spirit is given to every man to profit withal. ⁸ For to one is given by the Spirit the word of wisdom; to another the word of knowledge by the same Spirit; ⁹ To another faith by the same Spirit; to another the gifts of healing by the same Spirit; ¹⁰ To another the working of miracles; to another prophecy; to another discerning of spirits; to another divers kinds of tongues; to another the interpretation of tongues: ¹¹ But all these worketh that one and the selfsame

Spirit, dividing to every man severally as he will.

† **2 Corinthians 13:14 (AMPC)** The grace (favor and spiritual blessing) of the Lord Jesus Christ and the love of God and the presence and fellowship (the communion and sharing together, and participation) in the Holy Spirit be with you all. Amen (so be it).

† **Ephesians 4:4 (KJV)** There is one body, and one Spirit, even as ye are called in one hope of your calling;

† **Jude 1:20 (KJV)** But ye, beloved, building up yourselves on your most holy faith, praying in the Holy Ghost,

† **Revelation 1:10 (KJV)** I was in the Spirit on the Lord's day, and heard behind me a great voice, as of a trumpet,

† **Revelation 2:7 (KJV)** He that hath an ear, let him hear what the Spirit saith unto the churches; To him that overcometh will I give to eat of the tree of life, which is in the midst of the paradise of God.

Honor / Respect

When someone honors and shows respect to another person, the one who is on the receiving end feels so loved. For someone to highly value another person is great, I believe everyone should experience this, in both roles.

† **Leviticus 19:32 (MSG)** "Show respect to the aged; honor the presence of an elder; fear your God. I am God.

† **Exodus 20:12 (KJV)** Honour thy father and thy mother: that thy days may be long upon the land which the Lord thy God giveth thee.

† **1 Samuel 2:30 (KJV)** Wherefore the Lord God of Israel saith, I said indeed that thy house, and the house of thy father, should walk before Me for ever: but now the Lord saith, Be it far from Me; for them that honour Me I will honour, and they that despise Me shall be lightly esteemed.

† **Proverbs 3:9 (KJV)** Honour the Lord with thy substance, and with the firstfruits of all thine increase:

† **Proverbs 14:26 (KJV)** In the fear of the Lord is strong confidence: and his children shall have a place of refuge.

† **Proverbs 21:21 (KJV)** He that followeth after righteousness and mercy findeth life, righteousness, and honour.

† **Psalm 86:11 (NIV)** Teach me your way, LORD, that I may rely on your faithfulness; give me an undivided heart, that I may fear your name.

† **Matthew 10:40–41 (KJV)** He that receiveth you receiveth Me, and he that receiveth Me receiveth Him that sent Me. He that receiveth a prophet in the name of a prophet shall receive a prophet's reward; and he that receiveth a righteous man in the name of a righteous man shall receive a righteous man's reward.

† **1 Thessalonians 5:12 (KJV)** And we beseech you, brethren, to know them which labour among you, and are over you in the Lord, and admonish you;

† **1 Thessalonians 5:15 (KJV)** See that none render evil for evil unto any man; but ever follow that which is good, both among yourselves, and to all men.

† **1 Thessalonians 5:20 (KJV)** Despise not prophesyings.

† **1 Peter 5:6 (KJV)** Humble yourselves therefore under the mighty hand of God, that He may exalt you in due time:

Hope

Hope is a word of expectancy. When someone is hopeful and they can be at their weakest, hope in the Lord, shall sustain them. This word brings to mind Job 14:9 (see here what it says).

† **Job 14:9 (NKJV)** Yet at the scent of water it will bud And bring forth branches like a plant.

† **Psalm 31:23-24 (NKJV)** Oh, love the LORD, all you His saints! *For* the LORD preserves the faithful, And fully repays the proud person. Be of good courage, And He shall strengthen your heart, All you who hope in the LORD.

† **Psalm 33:17-19 (AMPC)** A horse is devoid of value for victory; neither does he deliver any by his great power. Behold, the Lord's eye is upon those who fear Him [who revere and worship Him with awe], who wait for Him *and* hope in His mercy *and* lovingkindness, To deliver them from death and keep them alive in famine.

† **Psalm 33:21-22 (NLT)** In him our hearts rejoice, for we trust in his holy name. Let your unfailing love surround us, LORD, for our hope is in you alone.

† **Psalm 38:14-16 (AMPC)** Yes, I have become like a

man who hears not, in whose mouth are no arguments *or* replies. For in You, O Lord, do I hope; You will answer, O Lord my God.

† **Psalm 78:6-7 (KJV)** That the generation to come might know them, even the children which should be born; who should arise and declare them to their children: That they might set their hope in God, and not forget the works of God, but keep his commandments:

† **Proverbs 13:12 (KJV)** Hope deferred maketh the heart sick: but when the desire cometh, it is a tree of life.

† **Jeremiah 17:7 (KJV)** Blessed is the man that trusteth in the Lord, and whose hope the Lord is.

† **Jeremiah 29:11 (NLT)** For I know the thoughts that I think toward you, saith the LORD, thoughts of peace, and not of evil, to give you an expected end.

† **Romans 5:1-2 (KJV)** Therefore being justified by faith, we have peace with God through our Lord Jesus Christ: By whom also we have access by faith into this grace wherein we stand, and rejoice in hope of the glory of God.

† **Romans 5:4-5 (KJV)** And patience, experience; and experience, hope: And hope maketh not ashamed; because the love of God is shed abroad in our hearts by the Holy Ghost which is given unto us.

† **Romans 8:24-25 (NASB)** For in hope we have been

saved, but hope that is seen is not hope; for who hopes for what he *already* sees? But if we hope for what we do not see, with perseverance we wait eagerly for it.

† **Romans 15:13 (NIV)** May the God of hope fill you with all joy and peace as you trust in him, so that you may overflow with hope by the power of the Holy Spirit.

† **Galatians 5:5 (KJV)** For we through the Spirit wait for the hope of righteousness by faith.

† **Ephesians 1:18 (KJV)** The eyes of your understanding being enlightened; that ye may know what is the hope of his calling, and what the riches of the glory of his inheritance in the saints,

† **Ephesians 4:4 (KJV)** There is one body, and one Spirit, even as ye are called in one hope of your calling;

† **1 Corinthians 13:13 (KJV)** And now abideth faith, hope, charity, these three; but the greatest of these is charity.

† **Colossians 1:27 (NKJV)** To them God willed to make known what are the riches of the glory of this mystery among the Gentiles: which is Christ in you, the hope of glory.

† **Hebrews 6:18–20 (NASB)** so that by two unchangeable things in which it is impossible for God to lie, we who have taken refuge would have strong encouragement to take hold of the hope set before us.

This hope we have as an anchor of the soul, a *hope* both sure and steadfast and one which enters within the veil, where Jesus has entered as a forerunner for us, having become a high priest forever according to the order of Melchizedek.

† **1 Peter 1:13 (AMPC)** So brace up your minds; be sober (circumspect, morally alert); set your hope wholly and unchangeably on the grace (divine favor) that is coming to you when Jesus Christ (the Messiah) is revealed.

Image / Identity / Sons of God / Body of Christ / the Church

We, the Church, must know who we are. We must learn our identity in Christ. The Church is not a building. The Church is a people who have accepted Jesus as their Lord and Savior. We, each a born-again child of God is a piece, a member (as in a leg or an eye of a human body) of Christ's body. We calculative make up Jesus Christ's body, leaving Him as our head. Jesus controls us when we let Him. We have the mind of Christ, so what we think about should pertain to what His word says. When we daily renew our minds with the word of God, and we walk in love, we live by faith and not by sight, we are confident that we are doing God's will.

† **Genesis 1:26–28 (KJV)** And God said, Let Us make man in Our image, after Our likeness: and let them have dominion over the fish of the sea, and over the fowl of the air, and over the cattle, and over all the earth, and over every creeping thing that creepeth upon the earth. So God created man in His own image, in the image of God created he him; male and female created he them. And God blessed them, and God said unto them, Be fruitful, and multiply, and replenish the

earth, and subdue it: and have dominion over the fish of the sea, and over the fowl of the air, and over every living thing that moveth upon the earth.

† **Psalm 8:4 (KJV)** What is man, that Thou art mindful of him? and the son of man, that Thou visitest him?

† **Psalm 8:4–6 (KJV)** ⁴ What is man, that thou art mindful of him? and the son of man, that thou visitest him? ⁵ For thou hast made him a little lower than the angels, and hast crowned him with glory and honour. ⁶ Thou madest him to have dominion over the works of thy hands; thou hast put all things under his feet:

† **Psalm 115:16 (KJV)** The heaven, even the heavens, are the Lord's: but the earth hath He given to the children of men.

† **Matthew 5:13 (KJV)** Ye are the salt of the earth: but if the salt have lost his savour, wherewith shall it be salted? it is thenceforth good for nothing, but to be cast out, and to be trodden under foot of men.

† **Matthew 16:18 (KJV)** And I say also unto thee, That thou art Peter, and upon this rock I will build my church; and the gates of hell shall not prevail against it

† **Luke 18:1 (KJV)** And he spake a parable unto them to this end, that men ought always to pray, and not to faint;

† **John 1:12 (KJV)** But as many as received him, to them gave he power to become the sons of God, even to them that believe on his name:

- † **Acts 5:14 (AMPC)** More and more there were being added to the Lord those who believed [those who acknowledged Jesus as their Savior and devoted themselves to Him joined and gathered with them], crowds both of men and of women,

- † **Acts 17:28–30 (AMPC)** For in Him we live and move and have our being; as even some of your [own] poets have said, For we are also His offspring. Since then we are God's offspring, we ought not to suppose that Deity (the Godhead) is like gold or silver or stone, [of the nature of] a representation by human art and imagination, or anything constructed or invented. Such [former] ages of ignorance God, it is true, ignored and allowed to pass unnoticed; but now He charges all people everywhere to repent (to change their minds for the better and heartily to amend their ways, with abhorrence of their past sins),

- † **Romans 8:16–17 (KJV)** The Spirit itself beareth witness with our spirit, that we are the children of God: And if children, then heirs; heirs of God, and joint-heirs with Christ; if so be that we suffer with him, that we may be also glorified together.

- † **Romans 8:19 (KJV)** For the earnest expectation of the creature waiteth for the manifestation of the sons of God.

- † **Romans 8:19 (AMPC)** For [even the whole] creation (all nature) waits expectantly *and* longs earnestly for God's sons to be made known [waits for the revealing, the disclosing of their sonship].

† **Romans 12:4–8 (KJV)** ⁴For as we have many members in one body, and all members have not the same office: ⁵So we, being many, are one body in Christ, and every one members one of another. ⁶Having then gifts differing according to the grace that is given to us, whether prophecy, let us prophesy according to the proportion of faith; ⁷Or ministry, let us wait on our ministering: or he that teacheth, on teaching; ⁸Or he that exhorteth, on exhortation: he that giveth, let him do it with simplicity; he that ruleth, with diligence; he that sheweth mercy, with cheerfulness.

† **1 Corinthians 2:16 (AMPC)** For who has known or understood the mind (the counsels and purposes) of the Lord so as to guide and instruct Him and give Him knowledge? But we have the mind of Christ (the Messiah) and do hold the thoughts (feelings and purposes) of His heart.

† **1 Corinthians 3:21 (KJV)** Therefore let no man glory in men. For all things are your's;

† **1 Corinthians 6:20 (KJV)** For ye are bought with a price: therefore glorify God in your body, and in your spirit, which are God's.

† **1 Corinthians 12:12 (KJV)** For as the body is one, and hath many members, and all the members of that one body, being many, are one body: so also is Christ.

† **1 Corinthians 12:14-18 (KJV)** For the body is not one member, but many. If the foot shall say, Because I am not the hand, I am not of the body; is it therefore not of the body? And if the ear shall say, Because I am not the eye, I am not of the body; is it therefore not of the body? If the whole body were an eye, where were the hearing? If the whole were hearing, where were the smelling? But now hath God set the members every one of them in the body, as it hath pleased Him.

† **1 Corinthians 12:27-28 (KJV)** Now ye are the body of Christ, and members in particular. And God hath set some in the church, first apostles, secondarily prophets, thirdly teachers, after that miracles, then gifts of healings, helps, governments, diversities of tongues.

† **2 Corinthians 3:18 (KJV)** But we all, with open face beholding as in a glass the glory of the Lord, are changed into the same image from glory to glory, even as by the Spirit of the Lord.

† **2 Corinthians 3:18 (AMPC)** And all of us, as with unveiled face, [because we] continued to behold [in the Word of God] as in a mirror the glory of the Lord, are constantly being transfigured into His very own image in ever increasing splendor and from one degree of glory to another; [for this comes] from the Lord [Who is] the Spirit.

† **2 Corinthians 3:18 (NASB)** But we all, with unveiled face, beholding as in a mirror the glory of the Lord,

are being transformed into the same image from glory to glory, just as from the Lord, the Spirit.

† **2 Corinthians 5:15-17 (NKJV)** and He died for all, that those who live should live no longer for themselves, but for Him who died for them and rose again. Therefore, from now on, we regard no one according to the flesh. Even though we have known Christ according to the flesh, yet now we know *Him thus* no longer. Therefore, if anyone *is* in Christ, *he is* a new creation; old things have passed away; behold, all things have become new.

† **2 Corinthians 5:15-17 (AMPC)** And He died for all, so that all those who live might live no longer to *and* for themselves, but to *and* for Him Who died and was raised again for their sake. Consequently, from now on we estimate *and* regard no one from a [purely] human point of view [in terms of natural standards of value]. [No] even though we once did estimate Christ from a human viewpoint *and* as a man, yet now [we have such knowledge of Him that] we know Him no longer [in terms of the flesh]. Therefore if any person is [ingrafted] in Christ (the Messiah) he is a new creation (a new creature altogether); the old [previous moral and spiritual condition] has passed away. Behold, the fresh *and* new has come!

† **2 Corinthians 5:19-21 (AMPC)** It was God [personally present] in Christ, reconciling *and* restoring the world to favor with Himself, not counting

up *and* holding against [men] their trespasses [but cancelling them], and committing to us the message of reconciliation (of the restoration to favor). So we are Christ's ambassadors, God making His appeal as it were through us. We [as Christ's personal representatives] beg you for His sake to lay hold of the divine favor [now offered you] *and* be reconciled to God. For our sake He made Christ [virtually] to be sin Who knew no sin, so that in *and* through Him we might become [endued with, viewed as being in, and examples of] the righteousness of God [what we ought to be, approved and acceptable and in right relationship with Him, by His goodness].

- † **2 Corinthians 5:21 (NKJV)** For He made Him who knew no sin *to be* sin for us, that we might become the righteousness of God in Him.

- † **Galatians 4:1 (KJV)** Now I say, That the heir, as long as he is a child, differeth nothing from a servant, though he be lord of all;

- † **Galatians 4:1 (AMPC)** Now what I mean is that as long as the inheritor (heir) is a child and under age, he does not differ from a slave, although he is the master of all the estate;

- † **Galatians 4:6–7 (AMPC)** And because you [really] are [His] sons, God has sent the [Holy] Spirit of His Son into our hearts, crying, Abba (Father)! Father! Therefore, you are no longer a slave (bond servant) but a son; and if a son, then [it follows that you are] an heir by the aid of God, through Christ.

† **Ephesians 1:18–23 (NKJV)** The eyes of your understanding being enlightened; that you may know what is the hope of His calling, what are the riches of the glory of His inheritance in the saints, and what is the exceeding greatness of His power toward us who believe, according to the working of His mighty power which He worked in Christ when He raised Him from the dead and seated Him at His right hand in the heavenly places, far above all principality and power and might and dominion, and every name that is named, not only in this age but also in that which is to come. And He put all things under His feet, and gave Him to be head over all things to the church, which is His body, the fullness of Him who fills all in all.

† **Ephesians 2:5-6 (KJV)** Even when we were dead in sins, hath quickened us together with Christ, (by grace ye are saved;) And hath raised us up together, and made us sit together in heavenly places in Christ Jesus:

† **Ephesians 2:10 (AMPC)** For we are God's [own] handiwork (His workmanship), recreated in Christ Jesus, [born anew] that we may do those good works which God predestined (planned beforehand) for us [taking paths which He prepared ahead of time], that we should walk in them [living the good life which He prearranged and made ready for us to live].

† **Ephesians 2:12–14 (KJV)** That at that time ye were without Christ, being aliens from the commonwealth

of Israel, and strangers from the covenants of promise, having no hope, and without God in the world: But now in Christ Jesus ye who sometimes were far off are made nigh by the blood of Christ. For he is our peace, who hath made both one, and hath broken down the middle wall of partition between us;

† **Ephesians 3:9-12 (NASB)** and to bring to light what is the administration of the mystery which for ages has been hidden in God who created all things; so that the manifold wisdom of God might now be made known through the church to the rulers and the authorities in the heavenly *places. This was* in accordance with the eternal purpose which He carried out in Christ Jesus our Lord, in whom we have boldness and confident access through faith in Him.

† **Ephesians 4:4–6 (AMPC)** [There is] one body and one Spirit—just as there is also one hope [that belongs] to the calling you received—[There is] one Lord, one faith, one baptism, One God and Father of [us] all, Who is above all [Sovereign over all], pervading all and [living] in [us] all.

† **Ephesians 5:1 (NASB)** Therefore be imitators of God, as beloved children;

† **Ephesians 5:1–3 (KJV)** Be ye therefore followers of God, as dear children; And walk in love, as Christ also hath loved us, and hath given Himself for us an offering and a sacrifice to God for a sweet smelling savour.

† **Phillippians 2:12 (KJV)** Wherefore, my beloved, as ye have always obeyed, not as in my presence only, but now much more in my absence, work out your own salvation with fear and trembling.

† **Phillippians 2:12 (NASB)** So then, my beloved, just as you have always obeyed, not as in my presence only, but now much more in my absence, work out your salvation with fear and trembling;

† **Colossians 2:12–15 (NASB)** ^{12}having been buried with Him in baptism, in which you were also raised up with Him through faith in the working of God, who raised Him from the dead. When you were dead in your transgressions and the uncircumcision of your flesh, He made you alive together with Him, having forgiven us all our transgressions, having canceled out the certificate of debt consisting of decrees against us, which was hostile to us; and He has taken it out of the way, having nailed it to the cross. When He had disarmed the rulers and authorities, He made a public display of them, having triumphed over them through Him.

† **Colossians 3:12–13 (KJV)** Put on therefore, as the elect of God, holy and beloved, bowels of mercies, kindness, humbleness of mind, meekness, longsuffering; Forbearing one another, and forgiving one another, if any man have a quarrel against any: even as Christ forgave you, so also do ye.

† **Hebrews 1:2 (KJV)** Hath in these last days spoken

unto us by His Son, whom He hath appointed heir of all things, by whom also He made the worlds;

† **Hebrews 10:25 (KJV)** Not forsaking the assembling of ourselves together, as the manner of some is; but exhorting one another: and so much the more, as ye see the day approaching.

† **Hebrews 12:23-25 (AMPC)** And to the church (assembly) of the Firstborn who are registered [as citizens] in heaven, and to the God Who is Judge of all, and to the spirits of the righteous (the redeemed in heaven) who have been made perfect, And to Jesus, the Mediator (Go-between, Agent) of a new covenant, and to the sprinkled blood which speaks [of mercy], a better and nobler and more gracious message than the blood of Abel [which cried out for vengeance]. So see to it that you do not reject Him or refuse to listen to and heed Him Who is speaking [to you now]. For if they [the Israelites] did not escape when they refused to listen and heed Him Who warned and divinely instructed them [here] on earth [revealing with heavenly warnings His will], how much less shall we escape if we reject and turn our backs on Him Who cautions and admonishes [us] from heaven?

† **1 Peter 2:9 (KJV)** But ye are a chosen generation, a royal priesthood, an holy nation, a peculiar people; that ye should shew forth the praises of Him who hath called you out of darkness into His marvellous light;

† **1 Peter 2:21 (NKJV)** For to this you were called,

because Christ also suffered for us, leaving us an example, that you should follow His steps:

† **1 Peter 4:11-13 (KJV)** If any man speak, let him speak as the oracles of God; if any man minister, let him do it as of the ability which God giveth: that God in all things may be glorified through Jesus Christ, to whom be praise and dominion for ever and ever. Amen. Beloved, think it not strange concerning the fiery trial which is to try you, as though some strange thing happened unto you: But rejoice, inasmuch as ye are partakers of Christ's sufferings; that, when his glory shall be revealed, ye may be glad also with exceeding joy.

† **1 John 5:18–20 (KJV)** We know that whosoever is born of God sinneth not; but he that is begotten of God keepeth himself, and that wicked one toucheth him not. And we know that we are of God, and the whole world lieth in wickedness. And we know that the Son of God is come, and hath given us an understanding, that we may know Him that is true, and we are in Him that is true, even in His Son Jesus Christ. This is the true God, and eternal life.

Increasing / Receiving

Increasing and receiving are synonyms with each other. In order to increase in anything, there has to be something received. Likewise, receiving something will give increase to what is already possessed. See Psalms 115:14 right here, as a perfect example.

† **Genesis 47:27 (AMPC)** And Israel dwelt in the land of Egypt, in the country of Goshen; and they gained possessions there and grew and multiplied exceedingly.

† **Leviticus 25:12 (KJV)** For it is the jubile; it shall be holy unto you: ye shall eat the increase thereof out of the field.

† **Deuteronomy 1:11 (NASB)** May the LORD, the God of your fathers, increase you a thousand-fold more than you are and bless you, just as He has promised you!

† **1 Chronicles 4:10 (KJV)** And Jabez called on the God of Israel, saying, "Oh that thou wouldest bless me indeed, and enlarge my coast, and that thine hand might be with me, and that thou wouldest keep me from evil, that it may not grieve me!" And God granted him that which he requested.

- † **Psalm 75:10 Living Bible (TLB)** "I will cut off the strength of evil men," says the Lord, "and increase the power of good men in their place."
- † **Psalm 115:14 (KJV)** The Lord shall increase you more and more, you and your children.
- † **Psalm 126:6 (KJV)** He that goeth forth and weepeth, bearing precious seed, shall doubtless come again with rejoicing, bringing his sheaves with him.
- † **Proverbs 11:24 (NIV)** One person gives freely, yet gains even more; another withholds unduly, but comes to poverty.
- † **Isaiah 55:10 (KJV)** For as the rain cometh down, and the snow from heaven, and returneth not thither, but watereth the earth, and maketh it bring forth and bud, that it may give seed to the sower, and bread to the eater:
- † **Amos 9:13 (KJV)** Behold, the days come, saith the Lord, that the plowman shall overtake the reaper, and the treader of grapes him that soweth seed; and the mountains shall drop sweet wine, and all the hills shall melt.
- † **Zechariah 8:12 (KJV)** For the seed shall be prosperous; the vine shall give her fruit, and the ground shall give her increase, and the heavens shall give their dew; and I will cause the remnant of this people to possess all these things.
- † **Matthew 13:8 (KJV)** But other fell into good ground,

and brought forth fruit, some an hundredfold, some sixtyfold, some thirtyfold.

† **Matthew 13:23-24 (KJV)** But he that received seed into the good ground is he that heareth the word, and understandeth it; which also beareth fruit, and bringeth forth, some an hundredfold, some sixty, some thirty. Another parable put he forth unto them, saying, The kingdom of Heaven is likened unto a man which sowed good seed in his field:

† **Mark 4:15-20 (KJV)** And these are they by the way side, where the word is sown; but when they have heard, Satan cometh immediately, and taketh away the word that was sown in their hearts. And these are they likewise which are sown on stony ground; who, when they have heard the word, immediately receive it with gladness; And have no root in themselves, and so endure but for a time: afterward, when affliction or persecution ariseth for the word's sake, immediately they are offended. And these are they which are sown among thorns; such as hear the word, And the cares of this world, and the deceitfulness of riches, and the lusts of other things entering in, choke the word, and it becometh unfruitful. And these are they which are sown on good ground; such as hear the word, and receive it, and bring forth fruit, some thirtyfold, some sixty, and some an hundred.

† **John 4:36-38 (AMPC)** Already the reaper is getting his wages [he who does the cutting now has his

reward], for he is gathering fruit (crop) unto life eternal, so that he who does the planting and he who does the reaping may rejoice together. For in this the saying holds true, One sows and another reaps. I sent you to reap a crop for which you have not toiled. Other men have labored and you have stepped in to reap the results of their work.

† **Luke 6:38 (KJV)** Give, and it shall be given unto you; good measure, pressed down, and shaken together, and running over, shall men give into your bosom. For with the same measure that ye mete withal it shall be measured to you again.

† **2 Corinthians 8:7 (KJV)** Therefore, as ye abound in every thing, in faith, and utterance, and knowledge, and in all diligence, and in your love to us, see that ye abound in this grace also.

† **2 Corinthians 9:6 (KJV)** But this I say, he which soweth sparingly shall reap also sparingly; and he which soweth bountifully shall reap also bountifully.

† **2 Corinthians 9:8–11 (MSG)** God can pour on the blessings in astonishing ways so that you're ready for anything and everything, more than just ready to do what needs to be done. As one psalmist puts it, He throws caution to the winds, giving to the needy in reckless abandon. His right-living, right- giving ways never run out, never wear out. This most generous God who gives seed to the farmer that becomes bread for your meals is more than extravagant with you. He

gives you something you can then give away, which grows into full-formed lives, robust in God, wealthy in every way, so that you can be generous in every way, producing with us great praise to God.

† **2 Corinthians 9:10–11 (KJV)** Now He that ministereth seed to the sower both minister bread for your food, and multiply your seed sown, and increase the fruits of your righteousness;) Being enriched in every thing to all bountifulness, which causeth through us thanksgiving to God.

† **Philippians 4:19 (KJV)** But my God shall supply all your need according to His riches in glory by Christ Jesus.

† **Hebrews 12:28 (KJV)** Wherefore we receiving a kingdom which cannot be moved, let us have grace, whereby we may serve God acceptably with reverence and godly fear:

Influence

Our pastor teaches us about the Law of Association, which is a great law. We can choose who we associate with, because it determines who we will become or how people would see us. My example: an accomplice to a crime, (Bad example, right? Really, we don't have to be doing anything, but just by being there, we can get in trouble too.) It is our personal choice to stay there. Depending on some situations, such as age, we may not have a choice, but God still hears us and will give us a way of escape.

There are times when we can't prevent what we hear or see. For instance, what we see or what is said by others that is not of God. God gave us a word that separates the good part, which we keep within us, and discard the bad from us. This scripture works on our spirit, from the inside out to manifestation. For whatever we see and hear that is unwanted, "SAY," whether under our breath, but out loud: (see 2 Corinthians 10:5, Isaiah 54:17 and Psalm 34:7 here. Hebrews 4:12 here gives how things are separated.

We have to be aware of who is influencing us. Whether good or bad; draw inward the good, draw away from the bad. God will help us, go to Him, He is our ultimate influencer!

† **Psalm 34:7 (NKJV)** The angel of the LORD encamps all around those who fear Him, and delivers them.

† **Psalm 112:9 (NASB)** He has given freely to the poor, His righteousness endures forever; His horn will be exalted in honor.

† **Isaiah 51:1–3 (KJV)** 1 Hearken to me, ye that follow after righteousness, ye that seek the Lord: look unto the rock whence ye are hewn, and to the hole of the pit whence ye are digged. Look unto Abraham your father, and unto Sarah that bare you: for I called him alone, and blessed him, and increased him. For the Lord shall comfort Zion: he will comfort all her waste places; and he will make her wilderness like Eden, and her desert like the garden of the Lord; joy and gladness shall be found therein, thanksgiving, and the voice of melody.

† **Isaiah 54:17 (NKJV)** No weapon formed against you shall prosper, And every tongue *which* rises against you in judgment You shall condemn. This *is* the heritage of the servants of the LORD, And their righteousness *is* from Me," Says the LORD.

† **2 Corinthians 1:12 (AMPC)** It is a reason for pride and exultation to which our conscience testifies that we have conducted ourselves in the world [generally] and especially toward you, with devout and pure motives and godly sincerity, not in fleshly wisdom but by the grace of God (the unmerited favor and merciful

kindness by which God, exerting His holy influence upon souls, turns them to Christ, and keeps, strengthens, and increases them in Christian virtues).

† **2 Corinthians 10:4-5 (NKJV)** For the weapons of our warfare *are* not carnal but mighty in God for pulling down strongholds, casting down arguments and every high thing that exalts itself against the knowledge of God, bringing every thought into captivity to the obedience of Christ,

† **Hebrews 4:12 (KJV)** For the word of God is quick, and powerful, and sharper than any twoedged sword, piercing even to the dividing asunder of soul and spirit, and of the joints and marrow, and is a discerner of the thoughts and intents of the heart.

† **Hebrews 4:12 (MSG)** His powerful Word is sharp as a surgeon's scalpel, cutting through everything, whether doubt or defense, laying us open to listen and obey. Nothing and no one is impervious to God's Word.

Integrity / Trust

Integrity is one of the most important traits to have. Wouldn't you want someone to do what they say they would do? When they don't, it is hard to believe them. Trust is an asset that should never be lost. This is why I trust in the Lord, He is always faithful to His Word.

When I put my trust in God, I do it by faith. I haven't seen Him (yet) or do I hear His voice audibly (yet expecting), but after meditating and confessing His word, I can discern/sense Him. He speaks to my spirit; it is this knowing on the inside that no one can convince me otherwise of His existence, His character, or especially His love for me. When we trust Him by faith and believe without having to see Him, He will manifest Himself to us. There is this great phrase out "Believing is Seeing" !!! We walk (live) by Faith and not by sight, that's trusting in God the Father, Son and Holy Spirit; the spirit realm.

We as children of God are to imitate Him, in order to have integrity, we must be trustworthy. For as He is in the spirit realm, so are we in this physical world, Amen !!!

† **Psalm 20:6–8 (AMPC)** Now I know that the Lord saves His anointed; He will answer him from His holy

heaven with the saving strength of His right hand. Some trust in and boast of chariots and some of horses, but we will trust in and boast of the name of the Lord our God. They are bowed down and fallen, but we are risen and stand upright.

† **Psalm 56:11 (KJV)** In God have I put my trust: I will not be afraid what man can do unto me.

† **Proverbs 3:5-6 (KJV)** Trust in the LORD with all thine heart; and lean not unto thine own understanding. In all thy ways acknowledge him, and he shall direct thy paths.

† **Proverbs 3:5–6 (AMPC)** Lean on, trust in, and be confident in the Lord with all your heart and mind and do not rely on your own insight or understanding. In all your ways know, recognize, and acknowledge Him, and He will direct and make straight and plain your paths.

† **Proverbs 14:26 (KJV)** In the fear of the Lord is strong confidence: and his children shall have a place of refuge.

† **Psalm 112:5 (KJV)** A good man sheweth favour, and lendeth: he will guide his affairs with discretion.

† **Proverbs 16:20 (KJV)** He that handleth a matter wisely shall find good: and whoso trusteth in the Lord, happy is he.

† **Proverbs 22:1 (KJV)** A good name is rather to be chosen than great riches, and loving favour rather than

silver and gold.

† **Ecclesiastes 5:5 (NASB)** It is better that you should not vow than that you should vow and not pay.

† **Luke 16:10–12 (NASB)** "He who is faithful in a very little thing is faithful also in much; and he who is unrighteous in a very little thing is unrighteous also in much. Therefore if you have not been faithful in the *use of* unrighteous wealth, who will entrust the true *riches* to you? And if you have not been faithful in *the use of* that which is another's, who will give you that which is your own?

† **Hebrews 10:35 (AMPC)** Do not, therefore, fling away your fearless confidence, for it carries a great and glorious compensation of reward.

Giving Is Jesus Christ

J esus Christ is my Lord and Savior, He is the Messiah, He is my Elder Brother, He is my Healer, He is my King, He is my Peace, He is my Joy, He is my Strength, He is my Life, He is my God!

Thank You Jesus for Your Precious Blood !!!

† **Psalm 118:21–23 (AMPC)** I will confess, praise, and give thanks to You, for You have heard and answered me; and You have become my Salvation and Deliverer. The stone which the builders rejected has become the chief cornerstone. This is from the Lord and is His doing; it is marvelous in our eyes.

† **Isaiah 9:6 (AMPC)** For to us a Child is born, to us a Son is given; and the government shall be upon His shoulder, and His name shall be called Wonderful Counselor, Mighty God, Everlasting Father [of Eternity], Prince of Peace.

† **Isaiah 53:5 (AMPC)** But He was wounded for our transgressions, He was bruised for our guilt and iniquities; the chastisement [needful to obtain] peace and well-being for us was upon Him, and with the stripes [that wounded] Him we are healed and made whole.

† **Matthew 1:16 (KJV)** And Jacob begat Joseph the

husband of Mary, of whom was born Jesus, who is called Christ.

† **Matthew 1:18 (KJV)** Now the birth of Jesus Christ was on this wise: When as His mother Mary was espoused to Joseph, before they came together, she was found with child of the Holy Ghost.

† **Luke 23:45–46 (KJV)** And the sun was darkened, and the veil of the temple was rent in the midst. And when Jesus had cried with a loud voice, He said, Father, into Thy hands I commend My spirit: and having said thus, He gave up the ghost.

† **John 1:1–3 (KJV)** In the beginning was the Word, and the Word was with God, and the Word was God. The same was in the beginning with God. All things were made by him; and without him was not any thing made that was made.

† **John 1:13–14 (KJV)** Which were born, not of blood, nor of the will of the flesh, nor of the will of man, but of God. And the Word was made flesh, and dwelt among us, (and we beheld His glory, the glory as of the only begotten of the Father,) full of grace and truth.

† **John 1:41 (AMPC)** He first sought out *and* found his own brother Simon and said to him, We have found (discovered) the Messiah!—which translated is the Christ (the Anointed One).

† **John 3:13–15 (AMPC)** And yet no one has ever gone

up to heaven, but there is One Who has come down from heaven—the Son of Man [Himself], Who is (dwells, has His home) in heaven. And just as Moses lifted up the serpent in the desert [on a pole], so must [so it is necessary that] the Son of Man be lifted up [on the cross], In order that everyone who believes in Him [who cleaves to Him, trusts Him, and relies on Him] may not perish, but have eternal life and [actually] live forever!

† **John 10:10 (AMPC)** The thief comes only in order to steal and kill and destroy. I came that they may have and enjoy life, and have it in abundance (to the full, till it overflows).

† **John 11:27 (AMPC)** She said to Him, Yes, Lord, I have believed [I do believe] that You are the Christ (the Messiah, the Anointed One), the Son of God, [even He] Who was to come into the world. [It is for Your coming that the world has waited.]

† **John 17:3 (AMPC)** And this is eternal life: [it means] to know (to perceive, recognize, become acquainted with, and understand) You, the only true *and* real God, and [likewise] to know Him, Jesus [as the] Christ (the Anointed One, the Messiah), Whom You have sent.

† **John 20:31 (AMPC)** But these are written (recorded) in order that you may believe that Jesus is the Christ (the Anointed One), the Son of God, and that through believing *and* cleaving to *and* trusting *and* relying upon Him you may have life through (in) His name

[through Who He is].

† **Romans 15:29 (KJV)** And I am sure that, when I come unto you, I shall come in the fulness of the blessing of the gospel of Christ.

† **Galatians 2:20 (KJV)** I am crucified with Christ: nevertheless I live; yet not I, but Christ liveth in me: and the life which I now live in the flesh I live by the faith of the Son of God, who loved me, and gave Himself for me.

† **Ephesians 1:20-21 (KJV)** Which He wrought in Christ, when He raised Him from the dead, and set Him at His own right hand in the heavenly places, Far above all principality, and power, and might, and dominion, and every name that is named, not only in this world, but also in that which is to come:

† **Colossians 1:15-18 (NKJV)** He is the image of the invisible God, the firstborn over all creation. For by Him all things were created that are in heaven and that are on earth, visible and invisible, whether thrones or dominions or principalities or powers. All things were created through Him and for Him. And He is before all things, and in Him all things consist. And He is the head of the body, the church, who is the beginning, the firstborn from the dead, that in all things He may have the preeminence.

† **1 John 3:8 (AMPC)** [But] he who commits sin [who practices evildoing] is of the devil [takes his character

from the evil one], for the devil has sinned (violated the divine law) from the beginning. The reason the Son of God was made manifest (visible) was to undo (destroy, loosen, and dissolve) the works the devil [has done].

Joy

Joy is such a little word, but it is full of power. By having joy, it can turn a life of defeat into Heaven on earth. A little ray of hope can ignite the joy in the darkest of hearts. I am happy to be in this frame of mind. Happiness to me is knowing that I am in Christ and Christ is in me. Nothing to the contrary matters. Having the Holy Spirit inside of me, I will grow in learning from Him, so that I can bring more joy to myself, and to share with as many as I am assigned.

It gives me great pleasure in knowing that I have this great opportunity and I will use it to the glory of God. (A Fruit of the Spirit attribute)

† **Nehemiah 8:10 (NKJV)** Then he said to them, "Go your way, eat the fat, drink the sweet, and send portions to those for whom nothing is prepared; for *this* day *is* holy to our Lord. Do not sorrow, for the joy of the LORD is your strength."

† **Psalm 5:11 (KJV)** But let all those that put their trust in Thee rejoice: let them ever shout for joy, because Thou defendest them: let them also that love Thy name be joyful in Thee.

† **Psalm 16:11 (KJV)** Thou wilt shew me the path of life: in Thy presence is fulness of joy; at Thy right

hand there are pleasures for evermore.

✝ **Psalm 35:27 (NKJV)** Let them shout for joy and be glad, Who favor my righteous cause; And let them say continually, "Let the Lord be magnified, Who has pleasure in the prosperity of His servant."

✝ **Psalm 89:14–16 (NASB)** Righteousness and justice are the foundation of Your throne; Lovingkindness and truth go before You. How blessed are the people who know the joyful sound! O Lord, they walk in the light of Your countenance. In Your name they rejoice all the day, And by Your righteousness they are exalted.

✝ **Psalm 118:22–24 (KJV)** The stone which the builders refused is become the head stone of the corner. This is the Lord's doing; it is marvellous in our eyes. This is the day which the Lord hath made; we will rejoice and be glad in it.

✝ **Psalm 144:14–15 (AMPC)** When our oxen are well loaded; when there is no invasion [of hostile armies] and no going forth [against besiegers—when there is no murder or manslaughter] and no outcry in our streets; Happy and blessed are the people who are in such a case; yes, happy (blessed, fortunate, prosperous, to be envied) are the people whose God is the Lord!

✝ **Ecclesiastes 2:26 (KJV)** For God giveth to a man that is good in His sight wisdom, and knowledge, and joy:

but to the sinner He giveth travail, to gather and to heap up, that he may give to him that is good before God.

† **Isaiah 51:3 (KJV)** For the Lord shall comfort Zion: He will comfort all her waste places; and He will make her wilderness like Eden, and her desert like the garden of the Lord; joy and gladness shall be found therein, thanksgiving, and the voice of melody.

† **1 Thessalonians 1:6 (KJV)** And ye became followers of us, and of the Lord, having received the word in much affliction, with joy of the Holy Ghost.

† **1 Thessalonians 2:19-20 (KJV)** For what is our hope, or joy, or crown of rejoicing? Are not even ye in the presence of our Lord Jesus Christ at his coming? For ye are our glory and joy.

† **1 Timothy 6:17 (KJV)** Charge them that are rich in this world, that they be not highminded, nor trust in uncertain riches, but in the living God, who giveth us richly all things to enjoy;

Justice

To be able to see and to contribute to justice—who in their right mind could sit by and let something bad and unjust happen to someone? We the sons of God, the ambassadors for Christ, we bind poverty and injustice in all its forms, we decree and we command them to cease now, in Jesus' Name. We loose the love of God, we loose the blood of the Lamb, we loose joy, peace, and justice on the earth as it is in Heaven, we loose and live by every word the proceed out of the mouth of God. We call it done now, by faith, In the Name of Jesus, Amen! Poverty and injustice have now been warned. God has a plan called vengeance and recompense. Beware !!!

† **Genesis 18:19 (KJV)** For I know him, that he will command his children and his household after him, and they shall keep the way of the LORD, to do justice and judgment; that the LORD may bring upon Abraham that which he hath spoken of him.

† **Deuteronomy 10:17–19 (NASB)** For the LORD your God is the God of gods and the Lord of lords, the great, the mighty, and the awesome God who does not show partiality nor take a bribe. He executes justice for the orphan and the widow, and shows His love for the alien by giving him food and clothing. So show

your love for the alien, for you were aliens in the land of Egypt.

† **Psalm 103:6 (NLT)** The Lord gives righteousness and justice to all who are treated unfairly.

† **Proverbs 8:14-16 (KJV)** Counsel is mine, and sound wisdom: I am understanding; I have strength. By me kings reign, and princes decree justice. By me princes rule, and nobles, even all the judges of the earth.

† **Proverbs 21:3 (KJV)** To do justice and judgment is more acceptable to the LORD than sacrifice.

† **Ecclesiastes 5:8 (GW)** [Corrupt Officials Have Corrupt Officials over Them] Don't be surprised if you see poor people being oppressed, denied justice, or denied their rights in any district. One authority is watching over another, and they both have authorities watching over them.

† **Ecclesiastes 8:11–13 (AMPC)** ¹¹ Because the sentence against an evil work is not executed speedily, the hearts of the sons of men are fully set to do evil. ¹² Though a sinner does evil a hundred times and his days [seemingly] are prolonged [in his wickedness], yet surely I know that it will be well with those who [reverently] fear God, who revere *and* worship Him, realizing His continual presence. ¹³ But it will not be well with the wicked, neither will he prolong his days like a shadow, because he does not [reverently] fear *and* worship God.

† **Isaiah 1:17 (AMPC)** Learn to do right! Seek justice, relieve the oppressed, and correct the oppressor. Defend the fatherless, plead for the widow.

† **Isaiah 9:6-8 (NKJV)** For unto us a Child is born, Unto us a Son is given; And the government will be upon His shoulder. And His name will be called Wonderful, Counselor, Mighty God, Everlasting Father, Prince of Peace. Of the increase of *His* government and peace *There will be* no end, Upon the throne of David and over His kingdom, To order it and establish it with judgment and justice From that time forward, even forever. The zeal of the LORD of hosts will perform this.

† **Isaiah 51:4–5 (NASB)** "Pay attention to Me, O My people, And give ear to Me, O My nation; For a law will go forth from Me, And I will set My justice for a light of the peoples. "My righteousness is near, My salvation has gone forth, And My arms will judge the peoples; The coastlands will wait for Me, And for My arm they will wait expectantly.

† **Romans 2:1-3 (NIV)** [God's Righteous Judgment] You, therefore, have no excuse, you who pass judgment on someone else, for at whatever point you judge another, you are condemning yourself, because you who pass judgment do the same things. Now we know that God's judgment against those who do such things is based on truth. So when you, a mere human being, pass judgment on them and yet do the same

things, do you think you will escape God's judgment?

Kindness

If anyone has never experience kindness, I pray that it manifests. There is a law of kindness, that when kindness is sown, kindness is reaped (not necessarily from the same place, but another place for sure). No matter what our current situations or circumstances are, we are able to turn it around. Example: Give a smile, a genuine act of kindness, and it will be given back multiplied. (A Fruit of the Spirit attribute)

† **Psalm 25:10 (AMPC)** All the paths of the Lord are mercy *and* steadfast love, even truth *and* faithfulness are they for those who keep His covenant and His testimonies.

† **Isaiah 57:14-15 (CEV)** [The LORD Helps the Helpless] The LORD says, "Clear the road! Get it ready for my people." Our holy God lives forever in the highest heavens, and this is what he says: Though I live high above in the holy place, I am here to help those who are humble and depend only on me.

† **Galatians 5:22-23 (NASB)** But the fruit of the Spirit is love, joy, peace, patience, kindness, goodness, faithfulness, gentleness, self-control; against such things there is no law.

† **Philippians 4:8 (KJV)** Finally, brethren, whatsoever

things are true, whatsoever things are honest, whatsoever things are just, whatsoever things are pure, whatsoever things are lovely, whatsoever things are of good report; if there be any virtue, and if there be any praise, think on these things.

† **Colossians 3:12-13 (NASB)** So, as those who have been chosen of God, holy and beloved, put on a heart of compassion, kindness, humility, gentleness and patience; bearing with one another, and forgiving each other, whoever has a complaint against anyone; just as the Lord forgave you, so also should you.

† **Titus 3:3–7 (AMPC)** ³ For we also were once thoughtless *and* senseless, obstinate *and* disobedient, deluded *and* misled; [we too were once] slaves to all sorts of cravings *and* pleasures, wasting our days in malice and jealousy *and* envy, hateful (hated, detestable) and hating one another. ⁴ But when the goodness and loving-kindness of God our Savior to man [as man] appeared, ⁵ He saved us, not because of any works of righteousness that we had done, but because of His own pity *and* mercy, by [the] cleansing [bath] of the new birth (regeneration) and renewing of the Holy Spirit, ⁶ Which He poured out [so] richly upon us through Jesus Christ our Savior. ⁷ [And He did it in order] that we might be justified by His grace (by His favor, wholly undeserved), [that we might be acknowledged and counted as conformed to the divine will in purpose, thought, and action], and that we

might become heirs of eternal life according to [our] hope.

† **1 Peter 2:2-4 (AMPC)** Like newborn babies you should crave (thirst for, earnestly desire) the pure (unadulterated) spiritual milk, that by it you may be nurtured *and* grow unto [completed] salvation, Since you have [already] tasted the goodness *and* kindness of the Lord. Come to Him [then, to that] Living Stone which men tried *and* threw away, but which is chosen [and] precious in God's sight.

Kingdom of God / Kingdom of Heaven

The Kingdom of God is the government of Heaven. This is the government that was announced in Isaiah 9. It is a kingdom of power and authority that governs with fairness and justice. The Kingdom of God is within me and you when we become sons of God.

We, the citizens of the Kingdom of Heaven, must enforce justice on earth as it is in Heaven. In all that we do, we must seek first God's Kingdom and His righteousness.

Our Lord and King Jesus and His Kingdom reigns over all and shall reign forever and ever, Amen !!!

† **Psalm 22:28 (AMPC)** For the kingship and the kingdom are the Lord's, and He is the ruler over the nations.

† **Isaiah 9:7 (AMPC)** Of the increase of His government and of peace there shall be no end, upon the throne of David and over his kingdom, to establish it and to uphold it with justice and with righteousness from the [latter] time forth, even forevermore. The zeal of the Lord of hosts will perform this.

† **Matthew 3:2 (AMPC)** And saying, Repent (think

differently; change your mind, regretting your sins and changing your conduct), for the kingdom of Heaven is at hand.

† **Matthew 4:23 (AMPC)** And He went about all Galilee, teaching in their synagogues and preaching the good news (Gospel) of the kingdom, and healing every disease and every weakness *and* infirmity among the people.

† **Matthew 6:33 (KJV)** But seek ye first the kingdom of God, and His righteousness; and all these things shall be added unto you.

† **Matthew 13:19–23 (AMPC)** While anyone is hearing the Word of the kingdom and does not grasp and comprehend it, the evil one comes and snatches away what was sown in his heart. This is what was sown along the roadside. As for what was sown on thin (rocky) soil, this is he who hears the Word and at once welcomes and accepts it with joy; Yet it has no real root in him, but is temporary (inconstant, lasts but a little while); and when affliction or trouble or persecution comes on account of the Word, at once he is caused to stumble [he is repelled and begins to distrust and desert Him Whom he ought to trust and obey] and he falls away. As for what was sown among thorns, this is he who hears the Word, but the cares of the world and the pleasure and delight and glamour and deceitfulness of riches choke and suffocate the Word, and it yields no fruit. As for what was sown on

good soil, this is he who hears the Word and grasps and comprehends it; he indeed bears fruit and yields in one case a hundred times as much as was sown, in another sixty times as much, and in another thirty.

† **Matthew 13:36-43 (KJV)** Then Jesus sent the multitude away, and went into the house: and His disciples came unto Him, saying, Declare unto us the parable of the tares of the field. He answered and said unto them, He that soweth the good seed is the Son of man; The field is the world; the good seed are the children of the kingdom; but the tares are the children of the wicked one; The enemy that sowed them is the devil; the harvest is the end of the world; and the reapers are the angels. As therefore the tares are gathered and burned in the fire; so shall it be in the end of this world. The Son of man shall send forth his angels, and they shall gather out of His kingdom all things that offend, and them which do iniquity; And shall cast them into a furnace of fire: there shall be wailing and gnashing of teeth. Then shall the righteous shine forth as the sun in the kingdom of their Father. Who hath ears to hear, let him hear.

† **Matthew 13:47-48 (KJV)** Again, the kingdom of heaven is like unto a net, that was cast into the sea, and gathered of every kind: Which, when it was full, they drew to shore, and sat down, and gathered the good into vessels, but cast the bad away.

† **Matthew 25:13 (AMPC)** Watch therefore [give strict

attention and be cautious and active], for you know neither the day nor the hour when the Son of Man will come.

† **Mark 4:26–28 (AMPC)** And He said, The kingdom of God is like a man who scatters seed upon the ground, And then continues sleeping and rising night and day while the seed sprouts and grows and increases—he knows not how. The earth produces [acting] by itself—first the blade, then the ear, then the full grain in the ear.

† **Luke 8:10 (AMPC)** He said to them, To you it has been given to [come progressively to] know (to recognize and understand more strongly and clearly) the mysteries and secrets of the kingdom of God, but for others they are in parables, so that, [though] looking, they may not see; and hearing, they may not comprehend.

† **Luke 12:32 (KJV)** Fear not, little flock; for it is your Father's good pleasure to give you the kingdom.

† **Luke 13:18–19 (NASB)** So He was saying, "What is the kingdom of God like, and to what shall I compare it? It is like a mustard seed, which a man took and threw into his own garden; and it grew and became a tree, and THE BIRDS OF THE AIR NESTED IN ITS BRANCHES."

† **Luke 17:20–21 (NASB)** Now having been questioned by the Pharisees as to when the kingdom of God was

coming, He answered them and said, "The kingdom of God is not coming with signs to be observed; nor will they say, 'Look, here *it is*!' or, 'There *it is*!' For behold, the kingdom of God is in your midst."

† **John 3:5 (NASB)** Jesus answered, "Truly, truly, I say to you, unless one is born of water and the Spirit he cannot enter into the kingdom of God.

† **Acts 1:3 (AMPC)** To them also He showed Himself alive after His passion (His suffering in the garden and on the cross) by [a series of] many convincing demonstrations [unquestionable evidences and infallible proofs], appearing to them during forty days and talking [to them] about the things of the kingdom of God.

† **Acts 14:22 (NASB)** Confirming the souls of the disciples, and exhorting them to continue in the faith, and that we must through much tribulation enter into the kingdom of God.

† **Acts 28:31 (KJV)** Preaching the kingdom of God, and teaching those things which concern the Lord Jesus Christ, with all confidence, no man forbidding him.

† **Revelation 11:15 (KJV)** And the seventh angel sounded; and there were great voices in Heaven, saying, The kingdoms of this world are become the kingdoms of our Lord, and of His Christ; and He shall reign for ever and ever.

Knowledge

When I think of Hosea 4:6, I believe God is saying here, some people think this scripture means to get a good education (which is good, but this is not what God said). I have noticed that some people have heard and understood what God said. This is why I chose to learn from these men and women of God.

I remember not too long after being saved, as I listened to my pastor, I thought, He knows something! To this day, I seek the truth. I have a hunger for the truth. I have learned more in the few years there than all the years of my life. I am able to discern where God is and is not. God talks through him, this is why I follow him as he (and I) follow Christ. The Holy Spirit teaches us all things !!! (Read John 14:26 here.)

† **Hosea 4:6 (KJV)** My people are destroyed for lack of knowledge:

† **Matthew 12:32 (KJV)** And whosoever speaketh a word against the Son of man, it shall be forgiven him: but whosoever speaketh against the Holy Ghost, it shall not be forgiven him, neither in this world, neither in the world to come.

† **Matthew 16:16–17 (KJV)** And Simon Peter answered and said, Thou art the Christ, the Son of the living

God. And Jesus answered and said unto him, Blessed art thou, Simon Barjona: for flesh and blood hath not revealed it unto thee, but My Father which is in Heaven.

† **Luke 10:39, 42 (KJV)** And she had a sister called Mary, which also sat at Jesus' feet, and heard his word. But one thing is needful: and Mary hath chosen that good part, which shall not be taken away from her.

† **Luke 11:34 (NLT)** "Your eye is a lamp that provides light for your body. When your eye is good, your whole body is filled with light. But when it is bad, your body is filled with darkness.

† **John 14:26 (NKJV)** But the Helper, the Holy Spirit, whom the Father will send in My name, He will teach you all things, and bring to your remembrance all things that I said to you.

† **1 Corinthians 2:13 (KJV)** Which things also we speak, not in the words which man's wisdom teacheth, but which the Holy Ghost teacheth; comparing spiritual things with spiritual.

† **2 Corinthians 2:14 (KJV)** Now thanks be unto God, which always causeth us to triumph in Christ, and maketh manifest the savour of his knowledge by us in every place.

† **Ephesians 3:18–20 (KJV)** May be able to comprehend with all saints what is the breadth, and

length, and depth, and height; And to know the love of Christ, which passeth knowledge, that ye might be filled with all the fulness of God. Now unto Him that is able to do exceeding abundantly above all that we ask or think, according to the power that worketh in us,

† **Hebrews 11:6 (KJV)** But without faith it is impossible to please Him: for he that cometh to God must believe that He is, and that He is a rewarder of them that diligently seek Him.

† **2 Peter 1:3-4 (KJV)** According as His divine power hath given unto us all things that pertain unto life and godliness, through the knowledge of Him that hath called us to glory and virtue: Whereby are given unto us exceeding great and precious promises: that by these ye might be partakers of the divine nature, having escaped the corruption that is in the world through lust.

Letting Go

Y ou are probably saying, "If only I knew or could see if I am going the right way, before I give my life to this Jesus." All I can tell you is from my experience, I thank God, that I didn't have to go through so many hardships in order to know and see that Jesus is the only way to Heaven.

I pray that you don't learn the hard way. The hard way is of the devil, who is trying to kill you. I know there are a lot of voices out in the world, really loud ones that force themselves in your ear and mind, which goes down into your heart.

If you would give God a try by listening to the Gospel of Jesus on a device or even going to a Bible-based church and of course, read the Bible for yourself, because the Holy Spirit speaks to us through the Word of God. I know there is someone whom you have noticed, who has a peace about them. This peace of God is available to you.

Letting go means to let go the old worldly way of thinking. If you haven't confessed Jesus as your Lord and Savior, please do and begin to renew your mind with the Word of God. You will never regret it. Let Jesus help you, by letting go.

† **Romans 12:2 (KJV)** And be not conformed to this

world: but be ye transformed by the renewing of your mind, that ye may prove what is that good, and acceptable, and perfect, will of God.

† **2 Corinthians 5:17 (KJV)** Therefore if any man be in Christ, he is a new creature: old things are passed away; behold, all things are become new.

† **Philippians 3:13 (KJV)** Brethren, I count not myself to have apprehended: but this one thing I do, forgetting those things which are behind, and reaching forth unto those things which are before,

† **1 Peter 1:14 (AMPC)** [Live] as children of obedience [to God]; do not conform yourselves to the evil desires [that governed you] in your former ignorance [when you did not know the requirements of the Gospel].

† **Hebrews 12:1–2 (NKJV)** [The Race of Faith] Therefore we also, since we are surrounded by so great a cloud of witnesses, let us lay aside every weight, and the sin which so easily ensnares us, and let us run with endurance the race that is set before us, looking unto Jesus, the author and finisher of our faith, who for the joy that was set before Him endured the cross, despising the shame, and has sat down at the right hand of the throne of God.

Life / Salvation

LIFE

In the Beginning, God created all life. In Genesis Chapter 2, it tells us after God had created and formed man, God breathed into man's nostrils, the breath of life and man became a living soul. The Hebrew translation says man became a speaking spirit.

Life was good, until the serpent, the devil; Satan approached Eve in the Garden of Eden. When Adam & Eve ate the fruit from the tree of knowledge of good and evil, which God told them not to eat of that tree, this is when sin; the curse was allowed to take control over the earth.

Mankind was separated spiritually from God because of the disobedient act of Adam. They were no longer allowed to live in the Garden, which was like Heaven on earth. They were put out of the Garden and had to live in a world controlled by Satan, also known as the world system; a world without God. This world is filled with pain, sorrow and toil.

I believe God told me how sin came in the world, even before He created Adam. I believe Satan [at the time Lucifer] had eaten from the tree of knowledge of good and evil, while he was in Heaven. The Garden of

Eden's tree on earth was a duplicate of Heaven's. Of course, Satan knew the effects of this tree and God's response (Lucifer was thrown out of Heaven, so now man would also be thrown out of the Garden) after he cleverly got Eve and then Adam to eat of the fruit. Some of the angels had to have eaten from the tree also, but obviously not much or they wouldn't have chosen Satan over God as their master (guilt and fear won them over). I am sure God told them that tree was off limits, but they chose to be disobedient also. I was thinking, Lucifer probably ate his fill first and then talked some angels into eating, whether he picked the fruit without them knowing that it came from the ~~forbidden~~ tree of the knowledge of good and evil or Lucifer convinced them that God said it was ok to eat from this tree. Selah.

[Another thought: I didn't want to use the word *forbidden*, because I went back to see if this word was in Genesis and it wasn't. I don't know about the angels, but I believe this may mean that God had given Adam a choice. It was Adam's freewill choice to eat the fruit, because God gave him the condition or alternative of what would happen, if he ate it. Notice in Genesis 2:16, God **commanded** Adam to **freely eat** from all of the other trees. I believe God commanded as his Creator and a loving Father to protect Adam. This could mean that **God's Grace** was **freely** given, ***but*** in Genesis 2:17, the words ***shall not*** was used, which means a *law*. The definition for a law is that something must happen or somebody is forced to do something because of the law was broken. So I believe since Adam and Eve broke this law, they were disconnected from God spiritually and had to be put out of the **Garden of Eden**. I believe the Garden; the environment itself stood for **God's Amazing Grace.** Mankind fell from the Grace of God (see Galatians 5:4 here). This is why I believe God made the tree of knowledge of good and evil, as part of His ultimate redemptive plan; Jesus Christ; His Grace.

Now back to Satan, who wanted to know what God knew or thought that by eating from that tree, it would give him God's knowledge. It was the same lack of knowledge when Jesus was crucified (See 1 Corinthians 2:7-9 here). I believe, Satan can never know all that God knows, because God's knowledge was not in that tree, His knowledge is in Himself. God was using that tree as a part of His plan.

We are all spirits and will never die, but will live for all Eternity, either in Heaven or hell. In Noah days, even after the flood, these spirits were still around in the atmosphere and in the water. Of course, God knew all of that, He just didn't want those evil men to multiply more, and so He destroyed them by the flood. The flesh was destroyed, and maybe God was using the water to wash away their sins, even before Jesus was born in the world. Maybe they were crying out to God for forgiveness, during this time. Only God knows!

Oh right, God did keep Noah and his family. Noah was a just man and he walked with God. Yes, God knew that there was still some evil in the world, but He also knew that there was some good in the earth, so He used Noah as a seed to start again, until Jesus.

I believe God is still separating those who are obedient to Him, and repentant because He wants to share His Glorious Eternity with us (See Revelation 21:1-5 here).

SALVATION

God knew that mankind needed a Savior; we had to be redeemed from Satan. Money wasn't enough for Satan, he wanted Jesus' blood. So he thought when he had Jesus crucified, he had won, but Thanks be to God, Jesus got the victory instead. Salvation is of the Lord (Please read and study, the complete chapter of Giving Is Jesus Christ). Jesus Christ has already defeated Satan, and has the authority to give us everlasting life, if we accept Jesus as our Lord and Savior.

God is waiting for each of us; we have to now let God know that we choose Jesus. We all had the knowledge of good and evil in us, because of Adam (even though, we wasn't physically there, it was pass down to all mankind), so now we each have to **ON PURPOSE** choose Jesus.

God gave us this freewill to decide. God gives us the choice to go with Satan. For those who want to make their own decisions, here is that opportunity. There is only two ways to choose, because of how one choose, everything after that choice would be the effect of that decision. When we really choose Jesus, the Holy Spirit helps us to grow in Christ. If someone chooses Satan, God will allow him or her to go with him, because it was their freewill decision to choose Satan. There is not a third choice. By not choosing Jesus, a person automatically chose Satan (period).

God already knows our thoughts and what we will do, before we think or do anything. He wants us to decide and make up our minds. Who do you want to spend the Eternity with? Heaven with God, or hell with Satan?

† **Genesis 2:7 (KJV)** And the Lord God formed man of the dust of the ground, and breathed into his nostrils the breath of life; and man became a living soul (In Hebrew: speaking spirit).

† **Genesis 2:16-17 (KJV)** And the LORD God commanded the man, saying, Of every tree of the garden thou mayest freely eat: But of the tree of the knowledge of good and evil, thou shalt not eat of it:

for in the day that thou eatest thereof thou shalt surely die.

† **Genesis 6:3 (NLT)** In the future, their normal lifespan will be no more than 120 years."

† **Genesis 6:8-9 (AMPC)** ⁸But Noah found grace (favor) in the eyes of the Lord. ⁹This is the history of the generations of Noah. Noah was a just *and* righteous man, blameless *in* his [evil] generation; Noah walked [in habitual fellowship] with God.

† **Exodus 12:21–23 (NKJV)** Then Moses called for all the elders of Israel and said to them, "Pick out and take lambs for yourselves according to your families, and kill the Passover lamb. And you shall take a bunch of hyssop, dip it in the blood that is in the basin, and strike the lintel and the two doorposts with the blood that is in the basin. And none of you shall go out of the door of his house until morning. For the Lord will pass through to strike the Egyptians; and when He sees the blood on the lintel and on the two doorposts, the Lord will pass over the door and not allow the destroyer to come into your houses to strike you.

† **Deuteronomy 11:21 (KJV)** That your days may be multiplied, and the days of your children, in the land which the Lord sware unto your fathers to give them, as the days of Heaven upon the earth.

† **Joshua 2:12 (AMPC)** Now then, I pray you, swear to me by the Lord, since I have shown you kindness, that

you also will show kindness to my father's house, and give me a sure sign,

† **Joshua 2:18–19 (AMPC)** Behold, when we come into the land, you shall bind this scarlet cord in the window through which you let us down, and you shall bring your father and mother, your brothers, and all your father's household into your house. And if anyone goes out of the doors of your house into the street, his blood shall be upon his head, and we will be guiltless; but if a hand is laid upon anyone who is with you in the house, his blood shall be on our head.

† **Job 1:9–10 (AMPC)** ⁹ Then Satan answered the Lord, Does Job [reverently] fear God for nothing? ¹⁰ Have You not put a hedge about him and his house and all that he has, on every side? You have conferred prosperity *and* happiness upon him in the work of his hands, and his possessions have increased in the land.

† **Psalm 91:10 (KJV)** There shall no evil befall thee, neither shall any plague come nigh thy dwelling.

† **Psalm 91:10 (NLT)** no evil will conquer you; no plague will come near your home.

† **Psalm 91:16 (AMPC)** With long life will I satisfy him and show him My salvation.

† **Psalm 118:17 (AMPC)** I shall not die but live, and shall declare the works and recount the illustrious acts of the Lord.

† **Ecclesiastes 5:15 (NLT)** We all come to the end of

our lives as naked and empty-handed as on the day we were born. We can't take our riches with us.

† **Matthew 10:39 (KJV)** He that findeth his life shall lose it: and he that loseth his life for my sake shall find it.

† **Matthew 27:51–53 (KJV)** And, behold, the veil of the temple was rent in twain from the top to the bottom; and the earth did quake, and the rocks rent; And the graves were opened; and many bodies of the saints which slept arose, And came out of the graves after his resurrection, and went into the holy city, and appeared unto many.

† **Mark 5:39, 41–42 (KJV)** And when He was come in, He saith unto them, Why make ye this ado, and weep? the damsel is not dead, but sleepeth... And He took the damsel by the hand, and said unto her, Talitha cumi; which is, being interpreted, Damsel, I say unto thee, arise. And straightway the damsel arose, and walked; for she was of the age of twelve years. And they were astonished with a great astonishment.

† **Luke 8:9–11 (KJV)** And His disciples asked him, saying, What might this parable be? And He said, Unto you it is given to know the mysteries of the kingdom of God: but to others in parables; that seeing they might not see, and hearing they might not understand. Now the parable is this: The seed is the word of God.

† **John 1:10–13 (NLT)** He came into the very world He created, but the world didn't recognize Him. He came to His own people, and even they rejected Him. But to all who believed Him and accepted Him, He gave the right to become children of God. They are reborn—not with a physical birth resulting from human passion or plan, but a birth that comes from God.

† **John 4:21–23 (NLT)** Jesus replied, "Believe me, dear woman, the time is coming when it will no longer matter whether you worship the Father on this mountain or in Jerusalem. You Samaritans know very little about the One you worship, while we Jews know all about Him, for salvation comes through the Jews. But the time is coming—indeed it's here now—when true worshipers will worship the Father in spirit and in truth. The Father is looking for those who will worship Him that way.

† **John 6:43–45 (KJV)** Jesus therefore answered and said unto them, Murmur not among yourselves. No man can come to Me, except the Father which hath sent Me draw him: and I will raise him up at the last day. It is written in the prophets, And they shall be all taught of God. Every man therefore that hath heard, and hath learned of the Father, cometh unto Me.

† **John 10:27–29 (NLT)** My sheep listen to My voice; I know them, and they follow Me. I give them eternal life, and they will never perish. No one can snatch them away from Me, for My Father has given them to

Me, and He is more powerful than anyone else. No one can snatch them from the Father's hand.

† **John 11:42–44 (AMPC)** Yes, I know You always hear and listen to Me, but I have said this on account of and for the benefit of the people standing around, so that they may believe that You did send Me [that You have made Me Your Messenger]. When He had said this, He shouted with a loud voice, Lazarus, come out! And out walked the man who had been dead, his hands and feet wrapped in burial cloths (linen strips), and with a [burial] napkin bound around his face. Jesus said to them, Free him of the burial wrappings and let him go.

† **Acts 16:30–34 (NLT)** Then he brought them out and asked, "Sirs, what must I do to be saved?" They replied, "Believe in the Lord Jesus and you will be saved, along with everyone in your household." And they shared the word of the Lord with him and with all who lived in his household. Even at that hour of the night, the jailer cared for them and washed their wounds. Then he and everyone in his household were immediately baptized. He brought them into his house and set a meal before them, and he and his entire household rejoiced because they all believed in God.

† **Romans 1:16 (KJV)** For I am not ashamed of the gospel of Christ: for it is the power of God unto salvation to every one that believeth; to the Jew first, and also to the Greek.

† **Romans 6:4 (NLT)** For we died and were buried with Christ by baptism. And just as Christ was raised from the dead by the glorious power of the Father, now we also may live new lives.

† **Romans 10:9–10 (KJV)** That if thou shalt confess with thy mouth the Lord Jesus, and shalt believe in thine heart that God hath raised Him from the dead, thou shalt be saved. For with the heart man believeth unto righteousness; and with the mouth confession is made unto salvation.

† **Romans 11:11 (NLT)** Did God's people stumble and fall beyond recovery? Of course not! They were disobedient, so God made salvation available to the Gentiles. But He wanted His own people to become jealous and claim it for themselves.

† **1 Corinthians 2:7-9 (AMPC)** [7] But rather what we are setting forth is a wisdom of God once hidden [from the human understanding] and now revealed to us by God—[that wisdom] which God devised *and* decreed before the ages for our glorification [to lift us into the glory of His presence]. [8] None of the rulers of this age *or* world perceived *and* recognized *and* understood this, for if they had, they would never have crucified the Lord of glory. [9] But, on the contrary, as the Scripture says, What eye has not seen and ear has not heard and has not entered into the heart of man, [all that] God has prepared (made and keeps ready) for those who love Him [who hold Him in affectionate

reverence, promptly obeying Him and gratefully recognizing the benefits He has bestowed].

† **1 Corinthians 7:14 (KJV)** For the unbelieving husband is sanctified by the wife, and the unbelieving wife is sanctified by the husband: else were your children unclean; but now are they holy.

† **1 Corinthians 15:21–23 (NLT)** So you see, just as death came into the world through a man, now the resurrection from the dead has begun through another Man. Just as everyone dies because we all belong to Adam, everyone who belongs to Christ will be given new life. But there is an order to this resurrection: Christ was raised as the first of the harvest; then all who belong to Christ will be raised when He comes back.

† **1 Corinthians 15:51–58 (KJV)** Behold, I shew you a mystery; We shall not all sleep, but we shall all be changed, In a moment, in the twinkling of an eye, at the last trump: for the trumpet shall sound, and the dead shall be raised incorruptible, and we shall be changed. For this corruptible must put on incorruption, and this mortal must put on immortality. So when this corruptible shall have put on incorruption, and this mortal shall have put on immortality, then shall be brought to pass the saying that is written, Death is swallowed up in victory. O death, where is thy sting? O grave, where is thy victory? The sting of death is sin; and the strength of sin is the law. But thanks be to

God, which giveth us the victory through our Lord Jesus Christ. Therefore, my beloved brethren, be ye stedfast, unmoveable, always abounding in the work of the Lord, forasmuch as ye know that your labour is not in vain in the Lord.

† **2 Corinthians 4:2–4 (NLT)** We reject all shameful deeds and underhanded methods. We don't try to trick anyone or distort the word of God. We tell the truth before God, and all who are honest know this. If the Good News we preach is hidden behind a veil, it is hidden only from people who are perishing. Satan, who is the god of this world, has blinded the minds of those who don't believe. They are unable to see the glorious light of the Good News. They don't understand this message about the glory of Christ, who is the exact likeness of God.

† **2 Corinthians 4:2–4 (AMPC)** We have renounced disgraceful ways (secret thoughts, feelings, desires and underhandedness, the methods and arts that men hide through shame); we refuse to deal craftily (to practice trickery and cunning) or to adulterate or handle dishonestly the Word of God, but we state the truth openly (clearly and candidly). And so we commend ourselves in the sight and presence of God to every man's conscience. But even if our Gospel (the glad tidings) also be hidden (obscured and covered up with a veil that hinders the knowledge of God), it is hidden [only] to those who are perishing and obscured [only]

to those who are spiritually dying and veiled [only] to those who are lost. For the god of this world has blinded the unbelievers' minds [that they should not discern the truth], preventing them from seeing the illuminating light of the Gospel of the glory of Christ (the Messiah), Who is the Image and Likeness of God.

† **Galatians 5:4 (NKJV)** You have become estranged from Christ, you who *attempt to* be justified by law; you have fallen from grace.

† **1 Thessalonians 4:13–18 (KJV)** But I would not have you to be ignorant, brethren, concerning them which are asleep, that ye sorrow not, even as others which have no hope. For if we believe that Jesus died and rose again, even so them also which sleep in Jesus will God bring with him. For this we say unto you by the word of the Lord, that we which are alive and remain unto the coming of the Lord shall not prevent them which are asleep. For the Lord himself shall descend from heaven with a shout, with the voice of the archangel, and with the trump of God: and the dead in Christ shall rise first: Then we which are alive and remain shall be caught up together with them in the clouds, to meet the Lord in the air: and so shall we ever be with the Lord. Wherefore comfort one another with these words.

† **1 Thessalonians 5:23–24 (AMPC)** And may the God of peace Himself sanctify you through and through [separate you from profane things, make you pure and

wholly consecrated to God]; and may your spirit and soul and body be preserved sound and complete [and found] blameless at the coming of our Lord Jesus Christ (the Messiah). Faithful is He Who is calling you [to Himself] and utterly trustworthy, and He will also do it [fulfill His call by hallowing and keeping you].

† **1 Timothy 4:16 (AMPC)** Look well to yourself [to your own personality] and to [your] teaching; persevere in these things [hold to them], for by so doing you will save both yourself and those who hear you.

† **Hebrews 9:27 (NLT)** And just as each person is destined to die once and after that comes judgment,

† **James 4:7–8 (AMPC)** So be subject to God. Resist the devil [stand firm against him], and he will flee from you. Come close to God and He will come close to you. [Recognize that you are] sinners, get your soiled hands clean; [realize that you have been disloyal] wavering individuals with divided interests, and purify your hearts [of your spiritual adultery].

† **1 Peter 1:3–4 (NLT)** "The Hope of Eternal Life" All praise to God, the Father of our Lord Jesus Christ. It is by His great mercy that we have been born again, because God raised Jesus Christ from the dead. Now we live with great expectation, and we have a priceless inheritance—an inheritance that is kept in Heaven for you, pure and undefiled, beyond the reach of change and decay.

† **1 Peter 1:23 (TLB)** For you have a new life. It was not passed on to you from your parents, for the life they gave you will fade away. This new one will last forever, for it comes from Christ, God's ever-living Message to men.

† **2 Peter 1:10–11 (NLT)** So, dear brothers and sisters, work hard to prove that you really are among those God has called and chosen. Do these things, and you will never fall away. Then God will give you a grand entrance into the eternal Kingdom of our Lord and Savior Jesus Christ.

† **2 Peter 1:11 (AMPC)** Thus there will be richly and abundantly provided for you entry into the eternal kingdom of our Lord and Savior Jesus Christ.

† **2 Peter 3:9–14 (KJV)** The Lord is not slack concerning His promise, as some men count slackness; but is longsuffering to us-ward, not willing that any should perish, but that all should come to repentance. But the day of the Lord will come as a thief in the night; in the which the heavens shall pass away with a great noise, and the elements shall melt with fervent heat, the earth also and the works that are therein shall be burned up. Seeing then that all these things shall be dissolved, what manner of persons ought ye to be in all holy conversation and godliness, Looking for and hasting unto the coming of the day of God, wherein the heavens being on fire shall be dissolved, and the elements shall melt with fervent heat? Nevertheless

we, according to His promise, look for new heavens and a new earth, wherein dwelleth righteousness. Wherefore, beloved, seeing that ye look for such things, be diligent that ye may be found of Him in peace, without spot, and blameless.

† **1 John 5:13 (KJV)** These things have I written unto you that believe on the name of the Son of God; that ye may know that ye have eternal life, and that ye may believe on the name of the Son of God.

† **Revelation 14:9–13 (NLT)** Then a third angel followed them, shouting, "Anyone who worships the beast and his statue or who accepts his mark on the forehead or on the hand must drink the wine of God's anger. It has been poured full strength into God's cup of wrath. And they will be tormented with fire and burning sulfur in the presence of the holy angels and the Lamb. The smoke of their torment will rise forever and ever, and they will have no relief day or night, for they have worshiped the beast and his statue and have accepted the mark of his name." This means that God's holy people must endure persecution patiently, obeying His commands and maintaining their faith in Jesus. And I heard a voice from Heaven saying, "Write this down: Blessed are those who die in the Lord from now on. Yes, says the Spirit, they are blessed indeed, for they will rest from their hard work; for their good deeds follow them!"

† **Revelation 21:1–5 (KJV)** And I saw a New Heaven

and a New Earth: for the first heaven and the first earth were passed away; and there was no more sea. And I John saw the Holy City, New Jerusalem, coming down from God out of Heaven, prepared as a bride adorned for her husband. And I heard a great voice out of Heaven saying, Behold, the tabernacle of God is with men, and He will dwell with them, and they shall be His people, and God Himself shall be with them, and be their God. And God shall wipe away all tears from their eyes; and there shall be no more death, neither sorrow, nor crying, neither shall there be any more pain: for the former things are passed away. And He that sat upon the throne said, Behold, I make all things new. And He said unto me, Write: for these words are true and faithful.

Light

For it is written, Jesus is the Light. He has given us the honor to also be the light that sits on a hill (bigger hills; mountains). For as Jesus is, so are we in this world! He said we shall do greater works. We are not to stand by and do nothing, but we are to let our light so shine, before men, so that our Father in Heaven can get all the glory.

Choose which mountain you will take dominion over, and know that our solutions of light always dominates the problems of darkness.

Let us shine our light by demonstrating our problem-solving gifts in a dark world, for the glory of God !!!

† **Genesis 1:2–4 (KJV)** And the earth was without form, and void; and darkness was upon the face of the deep. And the Spirit of God moved upon the face of the waters. And God said, Let there be light: and there was light. And God saw the light, that it was good: and God divided the light from the darknes

† **Isaiah 58:7–8 (AMPC)** ⁷ Is it not to divide your bread with the hungry and bring the homeless poor into your house—when you see the naked, that you cover him, and that you hide not yourself from [the needs of] your own flesh *an* blood? ⁸ Then shall your light break forth

like the morning, and your healing (your restoration and the power of a new life) shall spring forth speedily; your righteousness (your rightness, your justice, and your right relationship with God) shall go before you [conducting you to peace and prosperity], and the glory of the Lord shall be your rear guard.

† **Matthew 5:13–15 (NKJV)** "You are the salt of the earth; but if the salt loses its flavor, how shall it be seasoned? It is then good for nothing but to be thrown out and trampled underfoot by men. "You are the light of the world. A city that is set on a hill cannot be hidden. Nor do they light a lamp and put it under a basket, but on a lampstand, and it gives light to all who are in the house.

† **Matthew 5:16 (KJV)** Let your light so shine before men, that they may see your good works, and glorify your Father which is in heaven.

† **Matthew 6:21–23 (KJV)** For where your treasure is, there will your heart be also. The light of the body is the eye: if therefore thine eye be single, thy whole body shall be full of light. But if thine eye be evil, thy whole body shall be full of darkness. If therefore the light that is in thee be darkness, how great is that darkness!

† **John 1:3–5 (NKJV)** All things were made through Him, and without Him nothing was made that was made. In Him was life, and the life was the light of men. And the light shines in the darkness, and the

darkness did not comprehend it.

† **John 1:6–9 (KJV)** There was a man sent from God, whose name was John. The same came for a witness, to bear witness of the Light, that all men through him might believe. He was not that Light, but was sent to bear witness of that Light. That was the true Light, which lighteth every man that cometh into the world.

† **John 8:12 (AMPC)** Once more Jesus addressed the crowd. He said, I am the Light of the world. He who follows Me will not be walking in the dark, but will have the Light which is Life.

† **1 John 1:7 (KJV)** But if we walk in the light, as he is in the light, we have fellowship one with another, and the blood of Jesus Christ His Son cleanseth us from all sin.

Love

We are commanded to love God and love all people. We can only love this way, if God's love is in our hearts. When we make the decision to love people unconditionally— God's way—then expect to increase in Blessings, because we are using our faith to please God.

God is Jesus Christ, Jesus is Love, everyone wants love and everyone needs love. God loves us so much! (John 3:16). Let us give by demonstration in the sharing of God's love! God not only commanded us to love one another, but He said that love is a debt (see Romans 13:8 under Giving What Is Due) that is never fulfilled, which means we have to continue to love—period. (A Fruit of the Spirit attribute)

† **Proverbs 18:19 (NLT)** An offended friend is harder to win back than a fortified city. Arguments separate friends like a gate locked with bars.

† **Proverbs 25:21 (KJV)** If thine enemy be hungry, give him bread to eat; and if he be thirsty, give him water to drink:

† **Matthew 18:15 (NIV)** "If your brother or sister sins, go and point out their fault, just between the two of you. If they listen to you, you have won them over.

† **Matthew 22:37–39 (KJV)** Jesus said unto him, Thou shalt love the Lord thy God with all thy heart, and with all thy soul, and with all thy mind. This is the first and great commandment. And the second is like unto it, Thou shalt love thy neighbour as thyself.

† **Mark 12:30–31 (KJV)** And thou shalt love the Lord thy God with all thy heart, and with all thy soul, and with all thy mind, and with all thy strength: this is the first commandment. And the second is like, namely this, Thou shalt love thy neighbour as thyself. There is none other commandment greater than these.

† **Luke 17:3–4 (AMPC)** Pay attention and always be on your guard [looking out for one another]. If your brother sins (misses the mark), solemnly tell him so and reprove him, and if he repents (feels sorry for having sinned), forgive him. And even if he sins against you seven times in a day, and turns to you seven times and says, I repent [I am sorry], you must forgive him (give up resentment and consider the offense as recalled and annulled).

† **John 3:16 (KJV)** For God so loved the world, that He gave His only begotten Son, that whosoever believeth in Him should not perish, but have everlasting life.

† **John 15:12–14 (NLT)** This is my commandment: Love each other in the same way I have loved you. There is no greater love than to lay down one's life for one's friends. You are my friends if you do what I command.

† **Romans 13:8 (AMPC)** Keep out of debt *and* owe no man anything, except to love one another; for he who loves his neighbor [who practices loving others] has fulfilled the Law [relating to one's fellowmen, meeting all its requirements].

† **1 Corinthians 13:4–8 (AMPC)** Love endures long and is patient and kind; love never is envious nor boils over with jealousy, is not boastful or vainglorious, does not display itself haughtily. It is not conceited (arrogant and inflated with pride); it is not rude (unmannerly) and does not act unbecomingly. Love (God's love in us) does not insist on its own rights or its own way, for it is not self-seeking; it is not touchy or fretful or resentful; it takes no account of the evil done to it [it pays no attention to a suffered wrong]. It does not rejoice at injustice and unrighteousness, but rejoices when right and truth prevail. Love bears up under anything and everything that comes, is ever ready to believe the best of every person, its hopes are fadeless under all circumstances, and it endures everything [without weakening]. Love never fails [never fades out or becomes obsolete or comes to an end].

† **1 Corinthians 13:13 (AMPC)** And so faith, hope, love abide [faith—conviction and belief respecting man's relation to God and divine things; hope—joyful and confident expectation of eternal salvation; love—true affection for God and man, growing out of God's

love for and in us], these three; but the greatest of these is love.

† **Galatians 5:6 (KJV)** For in Jesus Christ neither circumcision availeth any thing, nor uncircumcision; but faith which worketh by love.

† **Ephesians 2:4–5 (KJV)** But God, who is rich in mercy, for His great love wherewith He loved us, Even when we were dead in sins, hath quickened us together with Christ, (by grace ye are saved;)

† **Ephesians 3:17 (KJV)** That Christ may dwell in your hearts by faith; that ye, being rooted and grounded in love,

† **Ephesians 5:2 (NKJV)** And walk in love, as Christ also has loved us and given Himself for us, an offering and a sacrifice to God for a sweet-smelling aroma.

† **1 John 3:17 (NLT)** If someone has enough money to live well and sees a brother or sister in need but shows no compassion—how can God's love be in that person?

† **1 John 4:8 (KJV)** He that loveth not knoweth not God; for GOD IS LOVE.

† **1 John 4:18 (KJV)** There is no fear in love; but perfect love casteth out fear:

Mercy

Thank God for His mercy. If we really think about it, He didn't have to send His son to save us by dying that terrible way. He could have killed us all—as well as Noah—and we wouldn't have known anything, because we wouldn't be here.

We should be so grateful, but some of us are acting like the children in the wilderness. We are still murmuring and complaining. It would seem like we would know better having the Bible, history, and our own experiences and other resources.

Let us seek God's face by using our faith in all we do to please Him!

† **Deuteronomy 4:30–31 (KJV)** When thou art in tribulation, and all these things are come upon thee, even in the latter days, if thou turn to the Lord thy God, and shalt be obedient unto His voice; (For the Lord thy God is a merciful God;) He will not forsake thee, neither destroy thee, nor forget the covenant of thy fathers which He sware unto them.

† **Psalm 102:13 (KJV)** Thou shalt arise, and have mercy upon Zion: for the time to favour her, yea, the set time, is come.

- **Psalm 107:1 (AMPC)** O give thanks to the Lord, for He is good; for His mercy and loving-kindness endure forever!

- **Proverbs 14:21 (KJV)** He that despiseth his neighbour sinneth: but he that hath mercy on the poor, happy is he.

- **Matthew 5:7 (NKJV)** Blessed *are* the merciful, For they shall obtain mercy.

- **Luke 10:36-37 (AMPC)** Which of these three do you think proved himself a neighbor to him who fell among the robbers? He answered, The one who showed pity *and* mercy to him. And Jesus said to him, Go and do likewise.

- **Romans 9:15–17 (NLT)** For God said to Moses, "I will show mercy to anyone I choose, and I will show compassion to anyone I choose." So it is God who decides to show mercy. We can neither choose it nor work for it.

- **2 Corinthians 4:1 (NLT)** Therefore, since God in His mercy has given us this new way, we never give up.

- **Ephesians 2:4–5 (NKJV)** But God, who is rich in mercy, because of His great love with which He loved us, even when we were dead in trespasses, made us alive together with Christ (by grace you have been saved).

- **1 Peter 1:3 (KJV)** Blessed be the God and Father of our Lord Jesus Christ, which according to His abundant mercy hath begotten us again unto a lively hope by the resurrection of Jesus Christ from the dead,

Giving Is Never Lacking

Wow! "Never lacking any good thing." That sound good !!! Did you know this is possible for anyone who has faith to believe it? What do you want? What do you want to be? What do you want to do? Imagine yourself doing it. Don't try to figure it out by calculating how much it would cost. Just close your eyes and imagine that it is yours now.

You are relaxing and smiling. Start thanking God for it and believe you receive it. Sow something toward that dream/desire. If not money, sow your time, volunteer and help someone. Always act on your faith to keep hope alive for manifestation. Stay away from doubt and fear, and stay positive.

The Lord is our Good Shepherd !!!

† **1 Kings 17:10-14 (KJV)** [10] So he arose and went to Zarephath. And when he came to the gate of the city, behold, the widow woman was there gathering of sticks: and he called to her, and said, Fetch me, I pray thee, a little water in a vessel, that I may drink. [11] And as she was going to fetch it, he called to her, and said, Bring me, I pray thee, a morsel of bread in thine hand. [12] And she said, As the LORD thy God liveth, I have not a cake, but an handful of meal in a barrel, and a

little oil in a cruse: and, behold, I am gathering two sticks, that I may go in and dress it for me and my son, that we may eat it, and die. ¹³ And Elijah said unto her, Fear not; go and do as thou hast said: but make me thereof a little cake first, and bring it unto me, and after make for thee and for thy son. ¹⁴ For thus saith the LORD God of Israel, The barrel of meal shall not waste, neither shall the cruse of oil fail, until the day that the LORD sendeth rain upon the earth.

† **2 Kings 4 (KJV)** ¹ Now there cried a certain woman of the wives of the sons of the prophets unto Elisha, saying, Thy servant my husband is dead; and thou knowest that thy servant did fear the LORD: and the creditor is come to take unto him my two sons to be bondmen. ² And Elisha said unto her, What shall I do for thee? tell me, what hast thou in the house? And she said, Thine handmaid hath not any thing in the house, save a pot of oil. ³ Then he said, Go, borrow thee vessels abroad of all thy neighbours, even empty vessels; borrow not a few. ⁴ And when thou art come in, thou shalt shut the door upon thee and upon thy sons, and shalt pour out into all those vessels, and thou shalt set aside that which is full. ⁵ So she went from him, and shut the door upon her and upon her sons, who brought the vessels to her; and she poured out. ⁶ And it came to pass, when the vessels were full, that she said unto her son, Bring me yet a vessel. And he said unto her, There is not a vessel more. And the oil stayed. ⁷ Then she came and told the man of God. And

he said, Go, sell the oil, and pay thy debt, and live thou and thy children of the rest.

† **Psalm 23 (KJV)** The Lord is my shepherd; I shall not want. He maketh me to lie down in green pastures: He leadeth me beside the still waters. He restoreth my soul: He leadeth me in the paths of righteousness for His name's sake. Yea, though I walk through the valley of the shadow of death, I will fear no evil: for thou art with me; thy rod and thy staff they comfort me. Thou preparest a table before me in the presence of mine enemies: thou anointest my head with oil; my cup runneth over. Surely goodness and mercy shall follow me all the days of my life: and I will dwell in the house of the Lord for ever.

† **Psalm 34:10 (KJV)** The young lions do lack, and suffer hunger: but they that seek the Lord shall not want any good thing.

† **Psalm 37:25 (KJV)** I have been young, and now am old; yet have I not seen the righteous forsaken, nor his seed begging bread.

† **Psalm 37:24-26 (MSG)** Stalwart walks in step with GOD; his path blazed by GOD, he's happy. If he stumbles, he's not down for long; GOD has a grip on his hand. I once was young, now I'm a graybeard — not once have I seen an abandoned believer, or his kids out roaming the streets. Every day he's out giving and lending, his children making him proud.

- † **Psalm 84:11 (KJV)** For the Lord God is a sun and shield: the Lord will give grace and glory: no good thing will he withhold from them that walk uprightly.

- † **Matthew 25:20-23 (KJV)** [20] And so he that had received five talents came and brought other five talents, saying, Lord, thou deliveredst unto me five talents: behold, I have gained beside them five talents more. [21] His lord said unto him, Well done, thou good and faithful servant: thou hast been faithful over a few things, I will make thee ruler over many things: enter thou into the joy of thy lord. [22] He also that had received two talents came and said, Lord, thou deliveredst unto me two talents: behold, I have gained two other talents beside them. [23] His lord said unto him, Well done, good and faithful servant; thou hast been faithful over a few things, I will make thee ruler over many things: enter thou into the joy of thy lord.

- † **Luke 5:3-7 (AMPC)** [3] And getting into one of the boats, [the one] that belonged to Simon (Peter), He requested him to draw away a little from the shore. Then He sat down and continued to teach the crowd [of people] from the boat. [4] When He had stopped speaking, He said to Simon (Peter), Put out into the deep [water], and lower your nets for a haul. [5] And Simon (Peter) answered, Master, we toiled all night [exhaustingly] and caught nothing [in our nets]. But on the ground of Your word, I will lower the nets [again]. [6] And when they had done this, they caught a great number of fish; and as their nets were [at the point of] breaking, ⁷ They signaled to their partners in the other boat to come and take hold with them. And they came and filled both the boats, so that they began to sink.

† **Luke 6:38 (NKJV)** Give, and it will be given to you: good measure, pressed down, shaken together, and running over will be put into your bosom. For with the same measure that you use, it will be measured back to you."

† **John 6:9-13 (KJV)** ⁹ There is a lad here, which hath five barley loaves, and two small fishes: but what are they among so many? ¹⁰ And Jesus said, Make the men sit down. Now there was much grass in the place. So the men sat down, in number about five thousand. ¹¹ And Jesus took the loaves; and when he had given thanks, he distributed to the disciples, and the disciples to them that were set down; and likewise of the fishes as much as they would. ¹² When they were filled, he said unto his disciples, Gather up the fragments that remain, that nothing be lost. ¹³ Therefore they gathered them together, and filled twelve baskets with the fragments of the five barley loaves, which remained over and above unto them that had eaten.

† **John 21:10-11 (AMPC)** Jesus said to them, Bring some of the fish which you have just caught. So Simon Peter went aboard and hauled the net to land, full of large fish, 153 of them; and [though] there were so many of them, the net was not torn.

† **2 Corinthians 9:8 (KJV)** And God is able to make all grace abound toward you; that ye, always having all sufficiency in all things, may abound to every good work:

† **Ephesians 3:20 (AMPC)** Now to Him Who, by (in consequence of) the [action of His] power that is at work within us, is able to [carry out His purpose and] do superabundantly, far over *and* above all that we [dare] ask or think [infinitely beyond our highest prayers, desires, thoughts, hopes, or dreams]—

† **James 1:2-4 (AMPC)** ² Consider it wholly joyful, my brethren, whenever you are enveloped in *or* encounter trials of any sort *or* fall into various temptations. ³ Be assured *and* understand that the trial *and* proving of your faith bring out endurance *and* steadfastness *and* patience. ⁴ But let endurance *and* steadfastness *and* patience have full play *and* do a thorough work, so that you may be [people] perfectly and fully developed [with no defects], lacking in nothing.

Obey / Obedience

God has already given us everything we need in this life. Yes, the devil threw a monkey wrench in our lives at the beginning through Adam and Eve; now this only means that we have to use our faith to believe we can do all things through Christ. We had become separated from God; we couldn't hear Him any longer, because fear was introduced to us through sin. Even though we were not there physically when Adam disobeyed God, we were in him as a seed. The curse came into the world and it affected everyone and everything. This is why God sent His son; Jesus to die for us, so that we can return to Him, through Jesus Christ our Savior.

We all have this great opportunity to accept Jesus as our Lord and Savior; this will allow God to work through us again, but even better than He had through Adam. If we keep our mind stayed on Jesus by doing things according to God's will, we as His manifested sons of God can have Heaven on Earth, for His Kingdom has come. When we obey God by not letting fear (the devil, bad thoughts nor negative actions) have any place in our minds, or hearts, we are building up our faith, as we pray in the Spirit. Obedience to God is having an abundant life (see Isaiah 1:19 here).

† **Genesis 1:28 (KJV)** And God blessed them, and God said unto them, Be fruitful, and multiply, and replenish the earth, and subdue it: and have dominion over the fish of the sea, and over the fowl of the air, and over every living thing that moveth upon the earth.

† **Genesis 3:4–5 (KJV)** And the serpent said unto the woman, Ye shall not surely die: For God doth know that in the day ye eat thereof, then your eyes shall be opened, and ye shall be as gods, knowing good and evil.

† **Deuteronomy 11:25 (KJV)** There shall no man be able to stand before you: for the Lord your God shall lay the fear of you and the dread of you upon all the land that ye shall tread upon, as He hath said unto you.

† **Deuteronomy 12:11 (KJV)** Then there shall be a place which the Lord your God shall choose to cause His name to dwell there; thither shall ye bring all that I command you; your burnt offerings, and your sacrifices, your tithes, and the heave offering of your hand, and all your choice vows which ye vow unto the Lord:

† **Deuteronomy 28:2 (KJV)** And all these blessings shall come on thee, and overtake thee, if thou shalt hearken unto the voice of the Lord thy God.

† **Proverbs 15:10 (AMPC)** There is severe discipline for him who forsakes God's way; and he who hates reproof will die [physically, morally, and spiritually].

† **Isaiah 1:19 (KJV)** If ye be willing and obedient, ye shall eat the good of the land:

† **John 10:27–28 (KJV)** My sheep hear My voice, and I know them, and they follow Me: And I give unto them eternal life; and they shall never perish, neither shall any man pluck them out of My hand.

† **John 15:5–8 (NLT)** "Yes, I am the vine; you are the branches. Those who remain in me, and I in them, will produce much fruit. For apart from me you can do nothing. Anyone who does not remain in me is thrown away like a useless branch and withers. Such branches are gathered into a pile to be burned. But if you remain in me and my words remain in you, you may ask for anything you want, and it will be granted! When you produce much fruit, you are my true disciples. This brings great glory to my Father.

† **1 Corinthians 15:22 (KJV)** For as in Adam all die, even so in Christ shall all be made alive.

† **1 John 5:3 (KJV)** For this is the love of God, that we keep his commandments: and his commandments are not grievous.

† **Jude 20 (NKJV)** [Maintain Your Life with God] But you, beloved, building yourselves up on your most holy faith, praying in the Holy Spirit,

Opportunity

O pportunity is an open door to the favor of God. When we seek God, be obedient to what He tells us, then expect opportunity to be an open door for us!

† **Malachi 3:8 (MSG)** "Begin by being honest. Do honest people rob God? But you rob me day after day. "You ask, 'How have we robbed you?' "The tithe and the offering — that's how!

† **Luke 11:10 (KJV)** For every one that asketh receiveth; and he that seeketh findeth; and to him that knocketh it shall be opened.

† **1 Corinthians 16:9-10 (AMPC)** ^{9} For a wide door of opportunity for effectual [service] has opened to me [there, a great and promising one], and [there are] many adversaries. ^{10} When Timothy arrives, see to it that [you put him at ease, so that] he may be fearless among you, for he is [devotedly] doing the Lord's work, just as I am.

† **Galatians 6:10 (KJV)** As we have therefore opportunity, let us do good unto all men, especially unto them who are of the household of faith.

† **Colossians 4:2-4 (NLT)** Devote yourselves to prayer with an alert mind and a thankful heart. Pray for us,

too, that God will give us many opportunities to speak about his mysterious plan concerning Christ.

† **Colossians 4:5–6 (NIV)** Be wise in the way you act toward outsiders; make the most of every opportunity. Let your conversation be always full of grace, seasoned with salt, so that you may know how to answer everyone.

† **2 Timothy 4:2 (NLT)** Preach the word of God. Be prepared, whether the time is favorable or not. Patiently correct, rebuke, and encourage your people with good teaching.

Patience

I have discovered that patience is our friend. Don't rush into anything and don't be anxious about anything; all this does is grant the devil an open door in your situation. This is the entrance of fear. Please don't give place to the devil through fear. Whenever a situation arises that may stir up negative emotions, just stop in your tracks, take a deep breath, and calm down. If an answer has to be given, wait with patience and love, and then give an answer. (A Fruit of the Spirit attribute)

† **Luke 8:15 (KJV)** But that on the good ground are they, which in an honest and good heart, having heard the word, keep it, and bring forth fruit with patience.

† **Romans 8:25 (AMPC)** But if we hope for what is still unseen by us, we wait for it with patience *and* composure.

† **Romans 15:4-6 (KJV)** For whatsoever things were written aforetime were written for our learning, that we through patience and comfort of the scriptures might have hope. Now the God of patience and consolation grant you to be likeminded one toward another according to Christ Jesus: That ye may with one mind and one mouth glorify God, even the Father of our Lord Jesus Christ.

† **Romans 15:4-6 (AMPC)** For whatever was thus written in former days was written for our instruction, that by [our steadfast and patient] endurance and the encouragement [drawn] from the Scriptures we might hold fast to *and* cherish hope. Now may the God Who gives the power of patient endurance (steadfastness) and Who supplies encouragement, grant you to live in such mutual harmony *and* such full sympathy with one another, in accord with Christ Jesus, That together you may [unanimously] with united hearts *and* one voice, praise and glorify the God and Father of our Lord Jesus Christ (the Messiah).

† **Colossians 1:11-12 (AMPC)** [We pray] that you may be invigorated *and* strengthened with all power according to the might of His glory, [to exercise] every kind of endurance and patience (perseverance and forbearance) with joy, Giving thanks to the Father, Who has qualified *and* made us fit to share the portion which is the inheritance of the saints (God's holy people) in the Light.

† **1 Thessalonians 1:3 (KJV)** Remembering without ceasing your work of faith, and labour of love, and patience of hope in our Lord Jesus Christ, in the sight of God and our Father;

† **2 Thessalonians 3:5 (AMPC)** May the Lord direct your hearts into [realizing and showing] the love of God and into the steadfastness *and* patience of Christ *and* in waiting for His return.

† **Hebrews 12:1 (KJV)** Wherefore seeing we also are compassed about with so great a cloud of witnesses, let us lay aside every weight, and the sin which doth so easily beset us, and let us run with patience the race that is set before us,

† **James 1:2–4 (KJV)** My brethren, count it all joy when ye fall into divers temptations; Knowing this, that the trying of your faith worketh patience. But let patience have her perfect work, that ye may be perfect and entire, wanting nothing.

Peace

Peace is a world full of Love. Peace is knowing that God loves us for God is Love. Peace is not worrying about anything. When we walk in Love, there is peace (a supernatural peace), because we are allowing Jesus to be on our mind, so don't worry (see Isaiah 26:3 here).

When we are calm, we can hear the solution that He is giving us. Jesus is the Prince of Peace and He wants us to come to Him, if there is a lack of peace in our lives. (A Fruit of the Spirit attribute)

† **Psalm 122:6–7 (NLT)** Pray for peace in Jerusalem. May all who love this city prosper. O Jerusalem, may there be peace within your walls and prosperity in your palaces.

† **Proverbs 14:30 (AMPC)** A calm *and* undisturbed mind *and* heart are the life *and* health of the body, but envy, jealousy, *and* wrath are like rottenness of the bones.

† **Proverbs 16:7 (AMPC)** When a man's ways please the Lord, He makes even his enemies to be at peace with him.

† **Isaiah 9:6–7 (KJV)** For unto us a child is born, unto us a Son is given: and the government shall be upon His shoulder: and His name shall be called Wonderful,

Counsellor, The mighty God, The everlasting Father, The Prince of Peace. Of the increase of His government and peace there shall be no end, upon the throne of David, and upon His kingdom, to order it, and to establish it with judgment and with justice from henceforth even for ever. The zeal of the Lord of hosts will perform this.

† **Isaiah 26:3 (KJV)** Thou wilt keep him in perfect peace, whose mind is stayed on Thee: because he trusteth in Thee.

† **Isaiah 32:16–18 (NLT)** Justice will rule in the wilderness and righteousness in the fertile field. And this righteousness will bring peace. Yes, it will bring quietness and confidence forever. My people will live in safety, quietly at home. They will be at rest.

† **Isaiah 32:17–18 (KJV)** And the work of righteousness shall be peace; and the effect of righteousness quietness and assurance for ever. And my people shall dwell in a peaceable habitation, and in sure dwellings, and in quiet resting places;

† **John 14:1 (KJV)** Let not your heart be troubled: ye believe in God, believe also in me.

† **Philippians 4:6–7 (KJV)** Be careful for nothing; but in every thing by prayer and supplication with thanksgiving let your requests be made known unto God. And the peace of God, which passeth all understanding, shall keep your hearts and minds

through Christ Jesus.

Power / Reigning

To the sons of God who have made the decision to answer the call of the great commission, It Is Time For Greater Manifestation !!!

Go into all the world and preach the gospel to all creation and this is also to the sons of God who are like Aaron and Hur, who held up the hands of Moses.

Let us go forth to use the gifts and talents God has given us for the advancement of the Kingdom of God.

We as born-again believers have to really take time out, to go somewhere quiet to meditate and study Romans 5:17 see here. Ask the Holy Spirit to help give understanding, because God points out who we are and what type of life we should be living. Have we indeed accepted Jesus Christ as our Lord and Savior? By accepting, did we know we have these precious gifts? Jesus' death, burial, and resurrection purpose was to give us this power, to reign as kings through Jesus Christ.

† **Exodus 17:10–12 (KJV)** So Joshua did as Moses said to him, and fought with Amalek. And Moses, Aaron, and Hur went up to the top of the hill. And so it was, when Moses held up his hand, that Israel prevailed; and when he let down his hand, Amalek prevailed. But

Moses' hands became heavy; so they took a stone and put it under him, and he sat on it. And Aaron and Hur supported his hands, one on one side, and the other on the other side; and his hands were steady until the going down of the sun.

† **Psalm 103:19 (KJV)** The Lord hath prepared His throne in the heavens; and His kingdom ruleth over all

† **Isaiah 13:1–3 (NLT)** A Message about Babylon Isaiah son of Amoz received this message concerning the destruction of Babylon: "Raise a signal flag on a bare hilltop. Call up an army against Babylon. Wave your hand to encourage them as they march into the palaces of the high and mighty. I, the Lord, have dedicated these soldiers for this task. Yes, I have called mighty warriors to express My anger, and they will rejoice when I am exalted."

† **Jeremiah 1:9–10 (KJV)** Then the Lord put forth his hand, and touched my mouth. And the Lord said unto me, Behold, I have put my words in thy mouth. See, I have this day set thee over the nations and over the kingdoms, to root out, and to pull down, and to destroy, and to throw down, to build, and to plant.

† **Mark 16:15 (NIV)** He said to them, "Go into all the world and preach the gospel to all creation.

† **Luke 10:19 (KJV)** Behold, I give unto you power to tread on serpents and scorpions, and over all the power of the enemy: and nothing shall by any means hurt

you.

† **Acts 1:8 (KJV)** But ye shall receive power, after that the Holy Ghost is come upon you: and ye shall be witnesses unto me both in Jerusalem, and in all Judaea, and in Samaria, and unto the uttermost part of the earth.

† **Romans 5:17 (AMPC)** For if because of one man's trespass (lapse, offense) death reigned through that one, much more surely will those who receive [God's] overflowing grace (unmerited favor) and the free gift of righteousness [putting them into right standing with Himself] reign as kings in life through the one Man Jesus Christ (the Messiah, the Anointed One).

† **1 Corinthians 10:26 (KJV)** For the earth is the Lord's, and the fulness thereof.

† **Ephesians 1:11, 18–23 (AMPC)** In Him we also were made [God's] heritage (portion) and we obtained an inheritance; for we had been foreordained (chosen and appointed beforehand) in accordance with His purpose, Who works out everything in agreement with the counsel and design of His [own] will, ... By having the eyes of your heart flooded with light, so that you can know and understand the hope to which He has called you, and how rich is His glorious inheritance in the saints (His set-apart ones), And [so that you can know and understand] what is the immeasurable and unlimited and surpassing greatness of His power in and for us who believe, as demonstrated in the

working of His mighty strength, Which He exerted in Christ when He raised Him from the dead and seated Him at His [own] right hand in the heavenly [places], Far above all rule and authority and power and dominion and every name that is named [above every title that can be conferred], not only in this age and in this world, but also in the age and the world which are to come. And He has put all things under His feet and has appointed Him the universal and supreme Head of the church [a headship exercised throughout the church], Which is His body, the fullness of Him Who fills all in all [for in that body lives the full measure of Him Who makes everything complete, and Who fills everything everywhere with Himself].

† **Ephesians 3:16 (KJV)** That He would grant you, according to the riches of His glory, to be strengthened with might by His Spirit in the inner man.

† **Revelation 5:10 (AMPC)** And You have made them a kingdom (royal race) and priests to our God, and they shall reign [as kings] over the earth!

† **Revelation 22:5 (AMPC)** And there shall be no more night; they have no need for lamplight or sunlight, for the Lord God will illuminate them and be their light, and they shall reign [as kings] forever and ever (through the eternities of the eternities).

Praise and Worship

God deserves all of our praise and all of the worship. Let us give what is due Him; by praising God and worshipping Him only. Let the walls and all obstruction fall like in Jericho, as we sing and shout praises to the Lord for we are the advancing the Kingdom of God.

I thank You, Father God, in all that I do, I give You all of my praise and I worship You only, in Jesus' Name. Amen !!!

† **Joshua 6:8-9, 20 (NASB)** ⁸ And it was *so*, that when Joshua had spoken to the people, the seven priests carrying the seven trumpets of rams' horns before the LORD went forward and blew the trumpets; and the ark of the covenant of the LORD followed them. ⁹ The armed men went before the priests who blew the trumpets, and the rear guard came after the ark, while they continued to blow the trumpets. ²⁰ So the people shouted, and *priests* blew the trumpets; and when the people heard the sound of the trumpet, the people shouted with a great shout and the wall fell down flat, so that the people went up into the city, every man straight ahead, and they took the city.

† **Psalm 27:6 (NLT)** Then I will hold my head high above my enemies who surround me. At His sanctuary

I will offer sacrifices with shouts of joy, singing and praising the Lord with music.

† **Psalm 71:7–8 (NLT)** My life is an example to many, because You have been my strength and protection.

† **Psalm 92:1 (KJV)** It is a good thing to give thanks unto the Lord, and to sing praises unto Thy name, O Most High:

† **Psalm 109:29–31 (AMPC)** Let my adversaries be clothed with shame and dishonor, and let them cover themselves with their own disgrace and confusion as with a robe. I will give great praise and thanks to the Lord with my mouth; yes, and I will praise Him among the multitude. For He will stand at the right hand of the poor and needy, to save him from those who condemn his life.

† **Psalm 138:2 (NLT)** I bow before Your Holy Temple as I worship. I praise Your name for Your unfailing love and faithfulness; for Your promises are backed by all the honor of Your Name. That is why I can never stop praising You; I declare Your glory all day long.

† **Psalm 140:12–13 (NLT)** But I know the Lord will help those they persecute; He will give justice to the poor. Surely righteous people are praising Your name; the godly will live in Your presence.

† **Psalm 150:6 (KJV)** Let every thing that hath breath praise the Lord. Praise ye the Lord!

† **Matthew 2:1-2 (NKJV)** Now after Jesus was born in

Bethlehem of Judea in the days of Herod the king, behold, wise men from the East came to Jerusalem, saying, "Where is He who has been born King of the Jews? For we have seen His star in the East and have come to worship Him."

† **Matthew 2:11 (AMPC)** And on going into the house, they saw the Child with Mary His mother, and they fell down and worshiped Him. Then opening their treasure bags, they presented to Him gifts—gold and frankincense and myrrh.

† **Matthew 21:16 (NKJV)** and said to Him, "Do You hear what these are saying?" And Jesus said to them, "Yes. Have you never read, 'Out of the mouth of babes and nursing infants You have perfected praise'?"

† **John 4:23 (AMPC)** A time will come, however, indeed it is already here, when the true (genuine) worshipers will worship the Father in spirit and in truth (reality); for the Father is seeking just such people as these as His worshipers.

† **John 4:23-24 (MSG)** "It's who you are and the way you live that count before God. Your worship must engage your spirit in the pursuit of truth. That's the kind of people the Father is out looking for: those who are simply and honestly *themselves* before him in their worship. God is sheer being itself—Spirit. Those who worship him must do it out of their very being, their spirits, their true selves, in adoration."

† **Acts 2:46–47 (AMPC)** And day after day they regularly assembled in the temple with united purpose, and in their homes they broke bread [including the Lord's Supper]. They partook of their food with gladness and simplicity and generous hearts, Constantly praising God and being in favor and goodwill with all the people; and the Lord kept adding [to their number] daily those who were being saved [from spiritual death].

† **Acts 10:45–47 (NLT)** The Jewish believers who came with Peter were amazed that the gift of the Holy Spirit had been poured out on the Gentiles, too. For they heard them speaking in other tongues and praising God.

† **1 Timothy 2:8 (NLT)** In every place of worship, I want men to pray with holy hands lifted up to God, free from anger and controversy.

Pray / Prayer / Praying

Prayer time for me is usually at twelve midnight. I enjoy talking to God first thing in the morning; I enjoy talking to Jesus and thanking Him throughout the day as the Holy Spirit talks to my spirit. Yes, a big part of prayer is "listening." We must stop talking long enough to hear what the Lord is saying to us. How else would we know what to do?

God doesn't talk to our mind, He talks to our spirit; the real us. We are spirit; we have a mind and we live in a body; spirit, soul (mind) and body (See Romans 8:15-16 and 1 Thessalonians 5:23 here). When our spirit is in control over our mind and body, we will be able to hear God clearer to respond to what He is telling us to do. That's being a doer of the word of God, by taking action! Action is needed for manifestation. Whether it is speaking it out, which is mandatory (not silent prayers) !!! God speaks, so likewise we speak (see Voice). God may want us to go here or go there, so let us be mindful and attentive to Him.

Journaling is very important, so have available, a pencil and paper or whatever to jot down what He is saying. I usually use the memo pad on your phone and it helps me when I include the date and time, because it is important to know when God said certain things. Don't rely on the mind to store it, because it may get tares and weeds in it.

I enjoy praying in the Spirit more than my language, because I desire to pray according to His will. I may pray a quick prayer for someone or something in passing, when I see or hear something that requires immediate attention. Whatever we do, we must pray first !!!

† **Genesis 26:4-6 (AMPC)** And I will make your descendants to multiply as the stars of the heavens, and will give to your posterity all these lands (kingdoms); and by your Offspring shall all the nations of the earth be blessed, *or* by Him bless themselves, ⁵ For Abraham listened to *and* obeyed My voice and kept My charge, My commands, My statutes, and My laws. ⁶ So Isaac stayed in Gerar.

† **Job 42:10 (KJV)** And the Lord turned the captivity of Job, when he prayed for his friends: also the Lord gave Job twice as much as he had before.

† **Matthew 6:9–13 (KJV)** After this manner therefore pray ye: Our Father which art in heaven, Hallowed be thy name. Thy kingdom come, Thy will be done in earth, as it is in heaven. Give us this day our daily bread. And forgive us our debts, as we forgive our debtors. And lead us not into temptation, but deliver us from evil: For thine is the kingdom, and the power,

and the glory, for ever. Amen.

† **Matthew 18:18 (KJV)** Verily I say unto you, Whatsoever ye shall bind on earth shall be bound in heaven: and whatsoever ye shall loose on earth shall be loosed in heaven.

† **Matthew 18:19 (KJV)** Again I say unto you, That if two of you shall agree on earth as touching any thing that they shall ask, it shall be done for them of my Father which is in heaven.

† **Mark 11:17 (NLT)** He said to them, "The Scriptures declare, 'My Temple will be called a house of prayer for all nations,' but you have turned it into a den of thieves."

† **Luke 18:1 (KJV)** And he spake a parable unto them to this end, that men ought always to pray, and not to faint;

† **Luke 18:1 (AMPC)** Also [Jesus] told them a parable to the effect that they ought always to pray and not to turn coward (faint, lose heart, and give up).

† **John 14:10–11 (KJV)** Believest thou not that I am in the Father, and the Father in Me? the words that I speak unto you I speak not of Myself: but the Father that dwelleth in Me, He doeth the works. Believe Me that I am in the Father, and the Father in Me: or else believe Me for the very works' sake.

† **John 16:23 (KJV)** And in that day ye shall ask Me

nothing. Verily, verily, I say unto you, Whatsoever ye shall ask the Father in My name, He will give it you.

† **Acts 1:14 (KJV)** These all continued with one accord in prayer and supplication, with the women, and Mary the mother of Jesus, and with His brethren.

† **Acts 4:31 (KJV)** And when they had prayed, the place was shaken where they were assembled together; and they were all filled with the Holy Ghost, and they spake the word of God with boldness.

† **Acts 6:4 (KJV)** But we will give ourselves continually to prayer, and to the ministry of the word.

† **Acts 12:12 (KJV)** And when he had considered the thing, he came to the house of Mary the mother of John, whose surname was Mark; where many were gathered together praying.

† **Acts 28:8 (KJV)** And it came to pass, that the father of Publius lay sick of a fever and of a bloody flux: to whom Paul entered in, and prayed, and laid his hands on him, and healed him.

† **Romans 8:15-16 (AMPC)** For [the Spirit which] you have now received [is] not a spirit of slavery to put you once more in bondage to fear, but you have received the Spirit of adoption [the Spirit producing sonship] in [the bliss of] which we cry, Abba (Father)! Father! The Spirit Himself [thus] testifies together with our own spirit, [assuring us] that we are children of God.

- † **Romans 8:26 (KJV)** Likewise the Spirit also helpeth our infirmities: for we know not what we should pray for as we ought: but the Spirit itself maketh intercession for us with groanings which cannot be uttered.

- † **Romans 12:12 (KJV)** Rejoicing in hope; patient in tribulation; continuing instant in prayer;

- † **Ephesians 1:15-20 (KJV)** Wherefore I also, after I heard of your faith in the Lord Jesus, and love unto all the saints, Cease not to give thanks for you, making mention of you in my prayers; That the God of our Lord Jesus Christ, the Father of glory, may give unto you the spirit of wisdom and revelation in the knowledge of him: The eyes of your understanding being enlightened; that ye may know what is the hope of his calling, and what the riches of the glory of his inheritance in the saints, And what is the exceeding greatness of his power to us-ward who believe, according to the working of his mighty power, Which he wrought in Christ, when he raised him from the dead, and set him at his own right hand in the heavenly places,

- † **Colossians 4:2 (KJV)** Continue in prayer, and watch in the same with thanksgiving;

- † **1 Thessalonians 5:17 (KJV)** Pray without ceasing.

- † **1 Thessalonians 5:23 (AMPC)** And may the God of peace Himself sanctify you through and through [separate you from profane things, make you pure and wholly consecrated to God]; and may your spirit and soul and body be preserved sound *and* complete [and found] blameless at the coming of our Lord Jesus Christ (the Messiah).

† **1 Timothy 2:1–3 (KJV)** I exhort therefore, that, first of all, supplications, prayers, intercessions, and giving of thanks, be made for all men; For kings, and for all that are in authority; that we may lead a quiet and peaceable life in all godliness and honesty. For this is good and acceptable in the sight of God our Saviour;

† **Hebrews 7:23–25 (NLT)** There were many priests under the old system, for death prevented them from remaining in office. But because Jesus lives forever, His priesthood lasts forever. Therefore He is able, once and forever, to save those who come to God through Him. He lives forever to intercede with God on their behalf.

† **James 5:16 (KJV)** Confess your faults one to another, and pray one for another, that ye may be healed. The effectual fervent prayer of a righteous man availeth much.

† **1 John 5:14–15 (KJV)** And this is the confidence that we have in Him, that, if we ask any thing according to His will, He heareth us: And if we know that He hear us, whatsoever we ask, we know that we have the petitions that we desired of Him.

† **3 John 2 (AMPC)** Beloved, I pray that in every way you may succeed *and* prosper and be in good health [physically], just as [I know] your soul prospers [spiritually].

Prepare / Preparing

Every day as we go through life, let us prepare for the second coming of our Lord Jesus Christ. What a glorious time that will be for those, who have accepted Jesus as their Lord and Savior. No one, but the Father knows the day, so let us make the decision to be ready, Amen !!!

† **Isaiah 62:10–11 (AMPC)** Go through, go through the gates! Prepare the way for the people. Cast up, cast up the highway! Gather out the stones. Lift up a standard or ensign over and for the peoples. Behold, the Lord has proclaimed to the end of the earth: Say to the Daughter of Zion, Behold, your salvation comes [in the person of the Lord]; behold, His reward is with Him, and His work and recompense before Him.

† **Hosea 6:2–3 (AMPC)** After two days He will revive us (quicken us, give us life); on the third day He will raise us up that we may live before Him. Yes, let us know (recognize, be acquainted with, and understand) Him; let us be zealous to know the Lord [to appreciate, give heed to, and cherish Him]. His going forth is prepared and certain as the dawn, and He will come to us as the [heavy] rain, as the latter rain that waters the earth.

† **Habakkuk 2:2–3 (KJV)** And the Lord answered me, and said, Write the vision, and make it plain upon tables, that he may run that readeth it. For the vision is yet for an appointed time, but at the end it shall speak, and not lie: though it tarry, wait for it; because it will surely come, it will not tarry.

† **Matthew 15:13 (KJV)** But He answered and said, Every plant, which My heavenly Father hath not planted, shall be rooted up.

† **Matthew 25:33–35 (NLT)** He will place the sheep at His right hand and the goats at His left. "Then the King will say to those on His right, 'Come, you who are blessed by My Father, inherit the Kingdom prepared for you from the creation of the world. For I was hungry, and you fed me. I was thirsty, and you gave me a drink. I was a stranger, and you invited me into your home.

† **Hebrews 12:7–9 (NLT)** As you endure this divine discipline, remember that God is treating you as His own children. Who ever heard of a child who is never disciplined by its father? If God doesn't discipline you as He does all of His children, it means that you are illegitimate and are not really His children at all. Since we respected our earthly fathers who disciplined us, shouldn't we submit even more to the discipline of the Father of our spirits, and live forever?

† **Revelation 21:1–3 (KJV)** And I saw a new heaven and a new earth: for the first heaven and the first earth

were passed away; and there was no more sea. And I John saw the holy city, new Jerusalem, coming down from God out of heaven, prepared as a bride adorned for her husband. And I heard a great voice out of heaven saying, Behold, the tabernacle of God is with men, and He will dwell with them, and they shall be His people, and God Himself shall be with them, and be their God.

His Presence

The knowing that the Lord is always with me is like Heaven on Earth. Thank You, my Lord, for Your Presence, for Your Presence is always welcome here !!!

† **Exodus 33:13–14 (AMPC)** Now therefore, I pray You, if I have found favor in Your sight, show me now Your way, that I may know You [progressively become more deeply and intimately acquainted with You, perceiving and recognizing and understanding more strongly and clearly] and that I may find favor in Your sight. And [Lord, do] consider that this nation is Your people. And the Lord said, My Presence shall go with you, and I will give you rest.

† **Exodus 33:15 (KJV)** And he said unto Him, If Thy presence go not with me, carry us not up hence.

† **1 Chronicles 16:27 (KJV)** Glory and honour are in His presence; strength and gladness are in His place.

† **Psalm 100:1–3 (KJV)** Make a joyful noise unto the Lord, all ye lands. Serve the Lord with gladness: come before His presence with singing. Know ye that the Lord He is God: it is He that hath made us, and not we ourselves; we are His people, and the sheep of His pasture.

† **1 Corinthians 1:29 (KJV)** That no flesh should glory in His presence.

† **2 Corinthians 4:17–18 (AMPC)** For our light, momentary affliction (this slight distress of the passing hour) is ever more and more abundantly preparing and producing and achieving for us an everlasting weight of glory [beyond all measure, excessively surpassing all comparisons and all calculations, a vast and transcendent glory and blessedness never to cease!], Since we consider and look not to the things that are seen but to the things that are unseen; for the things that are visible are temporal (brief and fleeting), but the things that are invisible are deathless and everlasting.

† **Hebrews 13:5 (AMPC)** Let your character or moral disposition be free from love of money [including greed, avarice, lust, and craving for earthly possessions] and be satisfied with your present [circumstances and with what you have]; for He [God] Himself has said, I will not in any way fail you nor give you up nor leave you without support. [I will] not, [I will] not, [I will] not in any degree leave you helpless nor forsake nor let [you] down (relax My hold on you)! [Assuredly not!]

† **Hebrews 13:6 (KJV)** So that we may boldly say, The Lord is my helper, and I will not fear what man shall do unto me.

Protection / Safety

Before giving my life to Jesus and even before I had learned about renewing my mind with the Word of God, there was always something that made me feel protected. Now I know the truth; my Lord said He will never leave me nor forsake me. Someone prayed for me !!!

I now pray Psalms 91 (see here), and I confess I am a son of God. I am the righteousness of God in Christ Jesus. I have been equipped with the word of God to plead the blood of Jesus and know I can call upon the Name of Jesus. The Holy Spirit lives within me and He leads and guides me. I acknowledge my angels, who are camped around about me to keep me safe from all harm. I cast down imaginations in my mind that doesn't line up with the Word of God, for I have a sound mind. I am eternally grateful that I can cast my cares upon the Lord for He cares me. I AM COVERED, IN JESUS' NAME !!!

† **Exodus 8:22 (KJV)** And I will sever in that day the land of Goshen, in which my people dwell, that no swarms of flies shall be there; to the end thou mayest know that I am the Lord in the midst of the earth.

† **2 Kings 6:15–17 (AMPC)** [15] When the servant of the

man of God rose early and went out, behold, an army with horses and chariots was around the city. Elisha's servant said to him, Alas, my master! What shall we do? ¹⁶ [Elisha] answered, Fear not; for those with us are more than those with them. ¹⁷ Then Elisha prayed, Lord, I pray You, open his eyes that he may see. And the Lord opened the young man's eyes, and he saw, and behold, the mountain was full of horses and chariots of fire round about Elisha.

† **2 Kings 6:16 (KJV)** And he answered, Fear not: for they that be with us are more than they that be with them.

† **Psalm 3:3–4 (KJV)** But thou, O Lord, art a shield for me; my glory, and the lifter up of mine head. I cried unto the Lord with my voice, and he heard me out of his holy hill. Selah.

† **Psalm 12:5-6 (AMPC)** Now will I arise, says the Lord, because the poor are oppressed, because of the groans of the needy; I will set him in safety *and* in the salvation for which he pants. The words *and* promises of the Lord are pure words, like silver refined in an earthen furnace, purified seven times over.

† **Psalm 32:7 (KJV)** Thou art my hiding place; thou shalt preserve me from trouble; thou shalt compass me about with songs of deliverance. Selah.

† **Psalm 91:1-16 (KJV)** ¹ He that dwelleth in the secret place of the most High shall abide under the shadow

of the Almighty. ² I will say of the Lord, He is my refuge and my fortress: my God; in him will I trust. ³ Surely he shall deliver thee from the snare of the fowler, and from the noisome pestilence. ⁴ He shall cover thee with his feathers, and under his wings shalt thou trust: his truth shall be thy shield and buckler. ⁵ Thou shalt not be afraid for the terror by night; nor for the arrow that flieth by day; ⁶ Nor for the pestilence that walketh in darkness; nor for the destruction that wasteth at noonday. ⁷ A thousand shall fall at thy side, and ten thousand at thy right hand; but it shall not come nigh thee. ⁸ Only with thine eyes shalt thou behold and see the reward of the wicked. ⁹ Because thou hast made the Lord, which is my refuge, even the most High, thy habitation; ¹⁰ There shall no evil befall thee, neither shall any plague come nigh thy dwelling. ¹¹ For he shall give his angels charge over thee, to keep thee in all thy ways. ¹² They shall bear thee up in their hands, lest thou dash thy foot against a stone. ¹³ Thou shalt tread upon the lion and adder: the young lion and the dragon shalt thou trample under feet. ¹⁴ Because he hath set his love upon me, therefore will I deliver him: I will set him on high, because he hath known my name. ¹⁵ He shall call upon me, and I will answer him: I will be with him in trouble; I will deliver him, and honour him. ¹⁶ With long life will I satisfy him, and shew him my salvation.]

† **Psalm 121:1–3 (KJV)** I will lift up mine eyes unto the hills, from whence cometh my help. My help cometh

from the Lord, which made heaven and earth. He will not suffer thy foot to be moved: he that keepeth thee will not slumber.

† **Proverbs 1:33 (NKJV)** But whoever listens to me will dwell safely, And will be secure, without fear of evil."

† **Proverbs 3:22-24 (KJV)** So shall they be life unto thy soul, and grace to thy neck. Then shalt thou walk in thy way safely, and thy foot shall not stumble. When thou liest down, thou shalt not be afraid: yea, thou shalt lie down, and thy sleep shall be sweet.

† **Proverbs 11:14 (KJV)** Where no counsel is, the people fall: but in the multitude of counsellors there is safety.

† **Proverbs 19:23 (KJV)** The fear of the LORD tendeth to life: and he that hath it shall abide satisfied; he shall not be visited with evil.

† **Isaiah 33:21–22 (NLT)** But there the glorious LORD will be unto us a place of broad rivers and streams; wherein shall go no galley with oars, neither shall gallant ship pass thereby. For the LORD is our judge, the LORD is our lawgiver, the LORD is our king; he will save us.

† **Isaiah 54:17 (KJV)** No weapon that is formed against thee shall prosper; and every tongue that shall rise against thee in judgment thou shalt condemn. This is the heritage of the servants of the Lord, and their

righteousness is of me, saith the Lord.

- † **Nahum 1:7 (AMPC)** The Lord is good, a Strength *and* Stronghold in the day of trouble; He knows (recognizes, has knowledge of, and understands) those who take refuge *and* trust in Him.

- † **Zechariah 9:11–12 (AMPC)** ¹¹ As for you also, because of *and* for the sake of the [covenant of the Lord with His people, which was sealed with sprinkled] covenant blood, I have released *and* sent forth your imprisoned people out of the waterless pit. ¹² Return to the stronghold [of security and prosperity], you prisoners of hope; even today do I declare that I will restore double your former prosperity to you.

- † **Luke 18:7-8 (AMPC)** And will not [our just] God defend *and* protect *and* avenge His elect (His chosen ones), who cry to Him day and night? Will He defer them *and* delay help on their behalf? I tell you, He will defend *and* protect *and* avenge them speedily. However, when the Son of Man comes, will He find [persistence in] faith on the earth?

Purpose

Purpose? This word purpose was foreign to me. I don't recall ever thinking, What is my purpose in life? I really truly don't remember. Probably because I didn't have a purpose, I was just going through life, day by day, waiting for life to just happen to me.

I thank God that I now don't just let things happen to me. I have a purpose! I have a purpose! Wow, that sounds and feels good!

My overall purpose in life is to do God's will. I enjoy my family, and now that I know my purpose, I can be a better wife, daughter, mother, sister, friend and all. Thank You, Jesus !!!

Purpose definition is the reason for existence; the reason for which things exists or why things has been done a certain way or why things were made.

Discover your purpose in God !!!

† **Esther 4:14 (KJV)** For if thou altogether holdest thy peace at this time, then shall there enlargement and deliverance arise to the Jews from another place; but thou and thy father's house shall be destroyed: and who knoweth whether thou art come to the kingdom for such a time as this?

† **Matthew 28:18–20 (KJV)** And Jesus came and spake

unto them, saying, All power is given unto Me in heaven and in earth. Go ye therefore, and teach all nations, baptizing them in the name of the Father, and of the Son, and of the Holy Ghost: Teaching them to observe all things whatsoever I have commanded you: and, lo, I am with you always, even unto the end of the world. Amen.

† **Luke 2:49 (NKJV)** And He said to them, "Why did you seek Me? Did you not know that I must be about My Father's business?"

† **Acts 26:15–18 (AMPC)** ^{15} And I said, Who are You, Lord? And the Lord said, I am Jesus, Whom you are persecuting. ^{16} But arise and stand upon your feet; for I have appeared to you for this purpose, that I might appoint you to serve as [My] minister and to bear witness both to what you have seen of Me and to that in which I will appear to you, ^{17} Choosing you out [selecting you for Myself] *and* delivering you from among this [Jewish] people and the Gentiles to whom I am sending you ^{18} To open their eyes that they may turn from darkness to light and from the power of Satan to God, so that they may thus receive forgiveness *and* release from their sins and a place *and* portion among those who are consecrated *and* purified by faith in Me.

† **Romans 8:28 (KJV)** And we know that all things work together for good to them that love God, to them who are the called according to His purpose.

† **Ephesians 1:8–10 (AMPC)** ⁸ Which He lavished upon us in every kind of wisdom and understanding (practical insight and prudence), ⁹ Making known to us the mystery (secret) of His will (of His plan, of His purpose). [And it is this:] In accordance with His good pleasure (His merciful intention) which He had previously purposed *and* set forth in Him, ¹⁰ [He planned] for the maturity of the times *and* the climax of the ages to unify all things *and* head them up *and* consummate them in Christ, [both] things in heaven and things on the earth.

† **Ephesians 1:11 (KJV)** In whom also we have obtained an inheritance, being predestinated according to the purpose of Him Who worketh all things after the counsel of His own will:

† **Ephesians 3:9–11 (KJV)** And to make all men see what is the fellowship of the mystery, which from the beginning of the world hath been hid in God, who created all things by Jesus Christ: To the intent that now unto the principalities and powers in heavenly places might be known by the church the manifold wisdom of God, According to the eternal purpose which he purposed in Christ Jesus our Lord:

† **1 Corinthians 1:25–27 (KJV)** ²⁵ Because the foolishness of God is wiser than men; and the weakness of God is stronger than men. ²⁶ For ye see your calling, brethren, how that not many wise men after the flesh, not many mighty, not many noble, are

called: ²⁷ But God hath chosen the foolish things of the world to confound the wise; and God hath chosen the weak things of the world to confound the things which are mighty;

† **2 Peter 1:10–11 (KJV)** Wherefore the rather, brethren, give diligence to make your calling and election sure: for if ye do these things, ye shall never fall: For so an entrance shall be ministered unto you abundantly into the everlasting kingdom of our Lord and Saviour Jesus Christ.

† **1 John 3:8 (NKJV)** He who sins is of the devil, for the devil has sinned from the beginning. For this purpose the Son of God was manifested, that He might destroy the works of the devil.

Reconcile

Being born-again has given me a new outlook on life. There is hope for anything we desire to reach for. Being reconciled with God is like coming back home—actually, it is. Now I know how the prodigal son must have felt when he came to himself and went back to his father (see Luke 15:21–24 here). The unconditional love that was waiting for him was unexplainably wonderful.

† **Luke 15:21–24 (AMPC)** And the son said to him, Father, I have sinned against heaven and in your sight; I am no longer worthy to be called your son [I no longer deserve to be recognized as a son of yours]! But the father said to his bond servants, Bring quickly the best robe (the festive robe of honor) and put it on him; and give him a ring for his hand and sandals for his feet. And bring out that [wheat-] fattened calf and kill it; and let us revel and feast and be happy and make merry, Because this my son was dead and is alive again; he was lost and is found! And they began to revel and feast and make merry,

† **2 Corinthians 5:18-20 (KJV)** ^{18} And all things are of God, who hath reconciled us to himself by Jesus Christ, and hath given to us the ministry of

reconciliation; ¹⁹ To wit, that God was in Christ, reconciling the world unto himself, not imputing their trespasses unto them; and hath committed unto us the word of reconciliation. ²⁰ Now then we are ambassadors for Christ, as though God did beseech you by us: we pray you in Christ's stead, be ye reconciled to God.

† **2 Corinthians 5:20 (KJV)** Now then we are ambassadors for Christ, as though God did beseech you by us: we pray you in Christ's stead, be ye reconciled to God.

† **Ephesians 2:14–16 (AMPC)** ¹⁴ For He is [Himself] our peace (our bond of unity and harmony). He has made us both [Jew and Gentile] one [body], and has broken down (destroyed, abolished) the hostile dividing wall between us, ¹⁵ By abolishing in His [own crucified] flesh the enmity [caused by] the Law with its decrees and ordinances [which He annulled]; that He from the two might create in Himself one new man [one new quality of humanity out of the two], so making peace. ¹⁶ And [He designed] to reconcile to God both [Jew and Gentile, united] in a single body by means of His cross, thereby killing the mutual enmity *and* bringing the feud to an end.

† **Philippians 3:20–21 (AMPC)** But we are citizens of the state (commonwealth, homeland) which is in heaven, and from it also we earnestly *and* patiently await [the coming of] the Lord Jesus Christ (the

Messiah) [as] Savior, Who will transform *and* fashion anew the body of our humiliation to conform to *and* be like the body of His glory *and* majesty, by exerting that power which enables Him even to subject everything to Himself.

† **Colossians 1:20 (AMPC)** And God purposed that through (by the service, the intervention of) Him [the Son] all things should be completely reconciled back to Himself, whether on earth or in heaven, as through Him, [the Father] made peace by means of the blood of His cross.

† **Hebrews 2:17 (KJV)** Wherefore in all things it behoved him to be made like unto his brethren, that he might be a merciful and faithful high priest in things pertaining to God, to make reconciliation for the sins of the people.

† **Hebrews 2:17 (AMPC)** So it is evident that it was essential that He be made like His brethren in every respect, in order that He might become a merciful (sympathetic) and faithful High Priest in the things related to God, to make atonement *and* propitiation for the people's sins.

† **Hebrews 2:17-18 (MSG)** It's obvious, of course, that he didn't go to all this trouble for angels. It was for people like us, children of Abraham. That's why he had to enter into every detail of human life. Then, when he came before God as high priest to get rid of the people's sins, he would have already experienced

it all himself—all the pain, all the testing—and would be able to help where help was needed.

Redemption

After Adam sinned, the rulership of the earth was now Satan's. Adam's spirit was no longer with God; the devil now controlled him through fear. But God had a plan, to get us back, which He made before the foundation of the world. The solution was to send His one and only Son, Jesus, to redeem us with His precious blood.

Jesus had to get us back with His blood, because money wasn't worth anything in comparison to what we are worth. We are a part of God, even in our fallen state. God wanted us back, because He loved us that much to leave us with Satan. We have to remember that we are spirit, so money, gold, silver, and precious stones are physical and would not ever be enough. Only Jesus could redeem us, so He willingly went and died on the cross at Calvary. He was buried and God raise Him back to life. Redemption is ours !!!

† **Job 19:25 (KJV)** For I know that my Redeemer liveth, and that He shall stand at the latter day upon the earth:

† **Job 19:25 (NKJV)** For I know *that* my Redeemer lives, And He shall stand at last on the earth;

† **Psalm 103:19 (KJV)** The Lord hath prepared His

throne in the heavens; and His kingdom ruleth over all.

† **<u>Psalm 107:2 (KJV)</u>** Let the redeemed of the Lord say so, whom He hath redeemed from the hand of the enemy;

† **<u>Romans 3:23–24 (KJV)</u>** For all have sinned, and come short of the glory of God; Being justified freely by his grace through the redemption that is in Christ Jesus:

† **<u>1 Corinthians 1:29–31 (KJV)</u>** That no flesh should glory in His presence. But of Him are ye in Christ Jesus, who of God is made unto us wisdom, and righteousness, and sanctification, and redemption: That, according as it is written, He that glorieth, let him glory in the Lord.

† **<u>Galatians 3:13–14 (KJV)</u>** Christ hath redeemed us from the curse of the law, being made a curse for us: for it is written, Cursed is every one that hangeth on a tree: That the blessing of Abraham might come on the Gentiles through Jesus Christ; that we might receive the promise of the Spirit through faith.

† **<u>Ephesians 1:6–8 (KJV)</u>** To the praise of the glory of His grace, wherein He hath made us accepted in the beloved. In whom we have redemption through His blood, the forgiveness of sins, according to the riches of His grace; Wherein He hath abounded toward us in all wisdom and prudence;

† **Revelation 5:9 (NKJV)** And they sang a new song, saying: "You are worthy to take the scroll, And to open its seals; For You were slain, And have redeemed us to God by Your blood Out of every tribe and tongue and people and nation,

Relationship(s)

A relationship is a connection to someone or something. I believe a relationship is much more than a physical connection, it is also spiritual. We have to know this! God, our Creator made one man; Adam. We were all inside of Adam as a seed, so since the fall of Adam, our spirit went under submission to the lordship of the god of this world; Satan. Our spirit had died, which means we; our spirit could no longer hear the voice of God. There was only fear & doubt that blinded the mind, which made us to be controlled only by Satan. Our body and mind were always to be directed by our spirit. Satan uses the mind (disconnected from God) that is not in a relationship with God. He tells the mind what to do, so of course, the body and the spirit has to go along. Thank God for Jesus, Who shed His precious blood for us, so that we can have this great opportunity to be re-connected; be in right standing (reconciled back) to God. Our spirit has to be born-again, and the only way to have this opportunity is by accepting Jesus as our Lord and Savior. There are only two decisions, God or the devil and by not openly confessing/choosing Jesus, by default, Satan is the choice.

Now, a friend is someone to go to confide in. My

true friend is Jesus; I can walk and talk with Him at anytime. What a great relationship to have! I don't need to call to set up an appointment, for the Holy Spirit is always with me.

If there is anyone who wants a friend like Jesus, He is available, just ask Him into your heart. You will never be alone, or lonely again.

Once our spirit is reconnected with God, we have to renew our mind with the Word of God, so that we will learn to know God's Will for our lives, then our other relationships can be healed, delivered and made whole.

† **Genesis 22:17-18 (AMPC)** In blessing I will bless you and in multiplying I will multiply your descendants like the stars of the heavens and like the sand on the seashore. And your Seed (Heir) will possess the gate of His enemies, And in your Seed [Christ] shall all the nations of the earth be blessed *and* [by Him] bless themselves, because you have heard *and* obeyed My voice.

† **Esther 8:1-2 (MSG)** That same day King Xerxes gave Queen Esther the estate of Haman, archenemy of the Jews. And Mordecai came before the king because Esther had explained their relationship. The king took off his signet ring, which he had taken back from Haman, and gave it to Mordecai. Esther appointed Mordecai over Haman's estate.

† **Esther 8:1-3 (AMPC)** On that day King Ahasuerus gave the house of Haman, the Jews' enemy, to Queen

Esther. And Mordecai came before the king, for Esther had told what he was to her. And the king took off his [signet] ring, which he had taken from Haman, and gave it to Mordecai. And Esther set Mordecai over the house of Haman. And Esther spoke yet again to the king and fell down at his feet and besought him with tears to avert the evil plot of Haman the Agagite and his scheme that he had devised against the Jews.

† **Proverbs 5:15-16 (AMPC)** Drink waters out of your own cistern [of a pure marriage relationship], and fresh running waters out of your own well. Should your offspring be dispersed abroad as water brooks in the streets?

† **Isaiah 26:7-8 (AMPC)** The way of the [consistently] righteous (those living in moral and spiritual rectitude in every area and relationship of their lives) is level *and* straight; You, O [Lord], Who are upright, direct aright *and* make level the path of the [uncompromisingly] just *and* righteous. Yes, in the path of Your judgments, O Lord, we wait [expectantly] for You; our heartfelt desire is for Your name and for the remembrance of You.

† **Isaiah 58:7-9 (AMPC)** Is it not to divide your bread with the hungry and bring the homeless poor into your house—when you see the naked, that you cover him, and that you hide not yourself from [the needs of] your own flesh *and* blood? Then shall your light break forth like the morning, and your healing (your restoration

and the power of a new life) shall spring forth speedily; your righteousness (your rightness, your justice, and your right relationship with God) shall go before you [conducting you to peace and prosperity], and the glory of the Lord shall be your rear guard. Then you shall call, and the Lord will answer; you shall cry, and He will say, Here I am. If you take away from your midst yokes of oppression [wherever you find them], the finger pointed in scorn [toward the oppressed or the godly], and every form of false, harsh, unjust, *and* wicked speaking,

† **Luke 20:37-39 (AMPC)** ^{37} But that the dead are raised [from death]—even Moses made known *and* showed in the passage concerning the [burning] bush, where he calls the Lord, The God of Abraham, the God of Isaac, and the God of Jacob. ^{38} Now He is not the God of the dead, but of the living, for to Him all men are alive [whether in the body or out of it] *and* they are alive [not dead] unto Him [in definite relationship to Him]. ^{39} And some of the scribes replied, Teacher, you have spoken well *and* expertly [so that there is no room for blame].

† **Romans 1:25 (MSG)** And all this because they traded the true God for a fake god, and worshiped the god they made instead of the God who made them—the God we bless, the God who blesses *us*. Oh, yes!

† **Romans 1:24-25 (AMPC)** ^{24} Therefore God gave them up in the lusts of their [own] hearts to sexual

impurity, to the dishonoring of their bodies among themselves [abandoning them to the degrading power of sin], ²⁵ Because they exchanged the truth of God for a lie and worshiped and served the creature rather than the Creator, Who is blessed forever! Amen (so be it).

† **Romans 5:14-16 (AMPC)** ¹⁴ Yet death held sway from Adam to Moses [the Lawgiver], even over those who did not themselves transgress [a positive command] as Adam did. Adam was a type (prefigure) of the One Who was to come [in reverse, the former destructive, the Latter saving]. ¹⁵ But God's free gift is not at all to be compared to the trespass [His grace is out of all proportion to the fall of man]. For if many died through one man's falling away (his lapse, his offense), much more profusely did God's grace and the free gift [that comes] through the undeserved favor of the one Man Jesus Christ abound *and* overflow to *and* for [the benefit of] many. ¹⁶ Nor is the free gift at all to be compared to the effect of that one [man's] sin. For the sentence [following the trespass] of one [man] brought condemnation, whereas the free gift [following] many transgressions brings justification (an act of righteousness).

† **Romans 14:1 (MSG)** Welcome with open arms fellow believers who don't see things the way you do. And don't jump all over them every time they do or say something you don't agree with — even when it seems that they are strong on opinions but weak in the

faith department. Remember, they have their own history to deal with. Treat them gently.

† **Romans 14:1-2 (AMPC)** As for the man who is a weak believer, welcome him [into your fellowship], but not to criticize his opinions *or* pass judgment on his scruples *or* perplex him with discussions. One [man's faith permits him to] believe he may eat anything, while a weaker one [limits his] eating to vegetables.

† **Romans 14:22-23 (MSG)** Cultivate your own relationship with God, but don't impose it on others. You're fortunate if your behavior and your belief are coherent. But if you're not sure, if you notice that you are acting in ways inconsistent with what you believe — some days trying to impose your opinions on others, other days just trying to please them—then you know that you're out of line. If the way you live isn't consistent with what you believe, then it's wrong.

† **Galatians 5:14-16 (AMPC)** For the whole Law [concerning human relationships] is complied with in the one precept, You shall love your neighbor as [you do] yourself. But if you bite and devour one another [in partisan strife], be careful that you [and your whole fellowship] are not consumed by one another. But I say, walk *and* live [habitually] in the [Holy] Spirit [responsive to *and* controlled *and* guided by the Spirit]; then you will certainly not gratify the cravings *and* desires of the flesh (of human nature without

God).

† **Acts 3:24-26 (AMPC)** ²⁴ Indeed, all the prophets from Samuel and those who came afterwards, as many as have spoken, also promised *and* foretold *and* proclaimed these days. ²⁵ You are the descendants (sons) of the prophets and the heirs of the covenant which God made *and* gave to your forefathers, saying to Abraham, And in your Seed (Heir) shall all the families of the earth be blessed *and* benefited. ²⁶ It was to you first that God sent His Servant *and* Son *Jesus*, when He raised Him up [provided and gave Him for us], to bless you in turning every one of you from your wickedness *and* evil ways.

† **2 Corinthians 5:17-19 (AMPC)** ¹⁷ Therefore if any person is [ingrafted] in Christ (the Messiah) he is a new creation (a new creature altogether); the old [previous moral and spiritual condition] has passed away. Behold, the fresh *and* new has come! ¹⁸ But all things are from God, Who through *Jesus* Christ reconciled us to Himself [received us into favor, brought us into harmony with Himself] and gave to us the ministry of reconciliation [that by word and deed we might aim to bring others into harmony with Him]. ¹⁹ It was God [personally present] in Christ, reconciling *and* restoring the world to favor with Himself, not counting up *and* holding against [men] their trespasses [but cancelling them], and committing to us the message of reconciliation (of the restoration

to favor).

† **2 Corinthians 5:21 (AMPC)** For our sake He made Christ [virtually] to be sin Who knew no sin, so that in *and* through Him we might become [endued with, viewed as being in, and examples of] the righteousness of God [what we ought to be, approved and acceptable and in right relationship with Him, by His goodness].

† **Galatians 3:26-29 (AMPC)** For in Christ Jesus you are all sons of God through faith. For as many [of you] as were baptized into Christ [into a spiritual union and communion with Christ, the Anointed One, the Messiah] have put on (clothed yourselves with) Christ. There is [now no distinction] neither Jew nor Greek, there is neither slave nor free, there is not male and female; for you are all one in Christ Jesus. And if you belong to Christ [are in Him Who is Abraham's Seed], then you are Abraham's offspring and [spiritual] heirs according to promise.

† **1 Thessalonians 2:19-20 (KJV)** For what is our hope, or joy, or crown of rejoicing? Are not even ye in the presence of our Lord Jesus Christ at his coming? For ye are our glory and joy.

† **1 Thessalonians 5:23-24 (KJV)** And the very God of peace sanctify you wholly; and I pray God your whole spirit and soul and body be preserved blameless unto the coming of our Lord Jesus Christ. Faithful is he that calleth you, who also will do it.

† **1 Thessalonians 5:23-24 (MSG)** May God himself, the God who makes everything holy and whole, make you holy and whole, put you together—spirit, soul, and body—and keep you fit for the coming of our Master, Jesus Christ. The One who called you is completely dependable. If he said it, he'll do it!

Remember / Remembrance

Remember, we as the righteousness of God are Blessed, because we have the mind of Christ. Remember, Jesus only listened to the Father. We are now in Christ and Christ is in us. Remember, God has given us the power to get wealth (Deuteronomy 18:8 see here). Let us now use our wealth, resources, gifts, and talents for the glory of God.

Remembrance is the act or process of remembering Someone, a state of being remembered, and the act of honoring Someone.

LET US BE MINDFUL, JESUS IS WORTHY !!!

† **Deuteronomy 6:10–12 (AMPC)** And when the Lord your God brings you into the land which He swore to your fathers, to Abraham, Isaac, and Jacob, to give you, with great and goodly cities which you did not build, And houses full of all good things which you did not fill, and cisterns hewn out which you did not hew, and vineyards and olive trees which you did not plant, and when you eat and are full, Then beware lest you forget the Lord, Who brought you out of the land of Egypt, out of the house of bondage.

† **Deuteronomy 8:18 (KJV)** But thou shalt remember the Lord thy God: for it is He that giveth thee power to

get wealth, that He may establish His covenant which He sware unto thy fathers, as it is this day.

† **Psalm 34:15-17 (KJV)** The eyes of the LORD are upon the righteous, and his ears are open unto their cry. The face of the LORD is against them that do evil, to cut off the remembrance of them from the earth. The righteous cry, and the LORD heareth, and delivereth them out of all their troubles.

† **Proverbs 10:7 (NKJV)** The memory of the righteous *is* blessed, But the name of the wicked will rot.

† **Lamentations 3:19-24 (MSG)** [It's a Good Thing to Hope for Help from God] I'll never forget the trouble, the utter lostness, the taste of ashes, the poison I've swallowed. I remember it all—oh, how well I remember—the feeling of hitting the bottom. But there's one other thing I remember, and remembering, I keep a grip on hope: GOD's loyal love couldn't have run out, his merciful love couldn't have dried up. They're created new every morning.

† **Luke 22:18-20 (AMPC)** For I say to you that from now on I shall not drink of the fruit of the vine at all until the kingdom of God comes. Then He took a loaf [of bread], and when He had given thanks, He broke [it] and gave it to them saying, This is My body which is given for you; do this in remembrance of Me. And in like manner, He took the cup after supper, saying, This cup is the new testament *or* covenant [ratified] in My blood, which is shed (poured out) for you.

† **Ephesians 2:11-13 (AMPC)** ¹¹ Therefore, remember that at one time you were Gentiles (heathens) in the flesh, called Uncircumcision by those who called themselves Circumcision, [itself a mere mark] in the flesh made by human hands. ¹² [Remember] that you were at that time separated (living apart) from Christ [excluded from all part in Him], utterly estranged *and* outlawed from the rights of Israel as a nation, and strangers with no share in the sacred compacts of the [Messianic] promise [with no knowledge of or right in God's agreements, His covenants]. And you had no hope (no promise); you were in the world without God. ¹³ But now in Christ Jesus, you who once were [so] far away, through (by, in) the blood of Christ have been brought near.

† **Ephesians 2:11-13 (MSG)** But don't take any of this for granted. It was only yesterday that you outsiders to God's ways had no idea of any of this, didn't know the first thing about the way God works, hadn't the faintest idea of Christ. You knew nothing of that rich history of God's covenants and promises in Israel, hadn't a clue about what God was doing in the world at large. Now because of Christ—dying that death, shedding that blood—you who were once out of it altogether are in on everything.

Repent

The word repent is not such a bad word. It is actually a good word. Repent means to think differently and to change our mind, along with regretting our sins and changing our conduct.

Even though we sinned, God has called us to come back to Him, because He loves us. Some may be saying that they have never sinned or don't believe in God.

Well, first let us clear up something. God created us all. The real us is not our bodies. We are a three-part being. We are a spirit, we possess a soul and we live in a body. God created our entire being.

Once we were all children of God, then Adam sinned by disobeying God, by doing what the devil wanted him to do. After Adam sinned, the nature of his spirit automatically converted from God's spirit to the devil's spirit. Because of Adam, we all became children of the devil, we obtained his nature. This is how we got the title of sinner. Now, Thanks be to God, we are no longer sinners, if we confess Jesus as our Lord and Savior, according to Romans 10:9-10, see under Life/Salvation). We are saved by His grace (See Ephesians 2:5-6, under Image ...). "We" are spirit, it is our mind and body that still has to be renewed and transformed. (See Romans 12:1-2 under Transformation)

† **Numbers 23:19 (KJV)** God is not a man, that He should lie; neither the son of man, that He should repent: hath He said, and shall He not do it? or hath He spoken, and shall He not make it good?

† **Matthew 3:2 (AMPC)** And saying, Repent (think differently; change your mind, regretting your sins and changing your conduct), for the kingdom of heaven is at hand.

† **Matthew 9:13 (AMPC)** Go and learn what this means: I desire mercy [that is, readiness to help those in trouble] and not sacrifice and sacrificial victims. For I came not to call and invite [to repentance] the righteous (those who are upright and in right standing with God), but sinners (the erring ones and all those not free from sin).

† **Luke 15:10 (KJV)** Likewise, I say unto you, there is joy in the presence of the angels of God over one sinner that repenteth.

† **Acts 17:28–30 (KJV)** [28] For in him we live, and move, and have our being; as certain also of your own poets have said, For we are also his offspring. [29] Forasmuch then as we are the offspring of God, we ought not to think that the Godhead is like unto gold, or silver, or stone, graven by art and man's device. [30] And the times

of this ignorance God winked at; but now commandeth all men every where to repent:

† **Romans 11:29 (KJV)** For the gifts and calling of God are without repentance.

GIVING IS GOD

His Rest

When I finally realized that I had Someone who really truly cares for me, unconditionally loves me, I was and still am so very grateful, yet still amazed. It is a great feeling and knowing to be allowed to rest in Jesus' arms, to tell Him my secrets, even though He knows them already, but He would let me tell Him anyway. His love comforts and vindicates me. I believe I have entered into God's rest.

† **Psalm 9:9-11 (AMPC)** ⁹The Lord also will be a refuge *and* a high tower for the oppressed, a refuge *and* a stronghold in times of trouble (high cost, destitution, and desperation). ¹⁰And they who know Your name [who have experience and acquaintance with Your mercy] will lean on *and* confidently put their trust in You, for You, Lord, have not forsaken those who seek (inquire of and for) You [on the authority of God's Word and the right of their necessity]. ¹¹Sing praises to the Lord, Who dwells in Zion! Declare among the peoples His doings!

† **Psalm 25:1-3 (AMPC)** [A Psalm] of David. ¹Unto You, O Lord, do I bring my life. ²O my God, I trust, lean on, rely on, *and* am confident in You. Let me not be put to shame *or* [my hope in You] be disappointed;

let not my enemies triumph over me. ³ Yes, let none who trust *and* wait hopefully *and* look for You be put to shame *or* be disappointed; let them be ashamed who forsake the right *or* deal treacherously without cause.

† **Psalm 37:3 (AMPC)** Trust (lean on, rely on, and be confident) in the Lord and do good; so shall you dwell in the land and feed surely on His faithfulness, *and* truly you shall be fed.

† **Psalm 37:4-5 (AMPC)** Delight yourself also in the Lord, and He will give you the desires *and* secret petitions of your heart. Commit your way to the Lord [roll and repose each care of your load on Him]; trust (lean on, rely on, and be confident) also in Him and He will bring it to pass.

† **Matthew 11:28–30 (KJV)** Come unto Me, all ye that labour and are heavy laden, and I will give you rest. Take My yoke upon you, and learn of Me; for I am meek and lowly in heart: and ye shall find rest unto your souls. For My yoke is easy, and My burden is light.

† **2 Corinthians 1:3–4 (KJV)** Blessed be God, even the Father of our Lord Jesus Christ, the Father of mercies, and the God of all comfort; Who comforteth us in all our tribulation, that we may be able to comfort them which are in any trouble, by the comfort wherewith we ourselves are comforted of God.

† **Hebrews 4:1 (KJV)** Let us therefore fear, lest, a

promise being left us of entering into his rest, any of you should seem to come short of it.

† **Hebrews 4:9–11 (KJV)** [9] There remaineth therefore a rest to the people of God. [10] For he that is entered into his rest, he also hath ceased from his own works, as God did from his. [11] Let us labour therefore to enter into that rest, lest any man fall after the same example of unbelief.

Restoration

I thank God, I look forward to restoration in my life. It is not that I've lost a lot of personal possessions, but I believe God will restore everything that my ancestors had been without, going back to ten generations on all sides of my family. My children and my children's children will never have to lack any good thing, ever again. By faith, I have complete restoration in my life, in Jesus' Name, Amen !!!

† **Deuteronomy 30:1-5 (MSG)** Here's what will happen. While you're out among the nations where GOD has dispersed you and the blessings and curses come in just the way I have set them before you, and you and your children take them seriously and come back to GOD, your God, and obey him with your whole heart and soul according to everything that I command you today, GOD, your God, will restore everything you lost; he'll have compassion on you; he'll come back and pick up the pieces from all the places where you were scattered. No matter how far away you end up, GOD, your God, will get you out of there and bring you back to the land your ancestors once possessed. It will be yours again. He will give you a good life and make you more numerous than

your ancestors.

† **Psalm 23:3 (KJV)** He restoreth my soul: he leadeth me in the paths of righteousness for his name's sake.

† **Proverbs 6:30-31 (NKJV)** *People* do not despise a thief If he steals to satisfy himself when he is starving. Yet *when* he is found, he must restore sevenfold; He may have to give up all the substance of his house.

† **Proverbs 6:30-31 (AMPC)** Men do not despise a thief if he steals to satisfy himself when he is hungry; But if he is found out, he must restore seven times [what he stole]; he must give the whole substance of his house [if necessary—to meet his fine].

† **Isaiah 58:11-12 (AMPC)** And the Lord shall guide you continually and satisfy you in drought *and* in dry places and make strong your bones. And you shall be like a watered garden and like a spring of water whose waters fail not. And your ancient ruins shall be rebuilt; you shall raise up the foundations of [buildings that have laid waste for] many generations; and you shall be called Repairer of the Breach, Restorer of Streets to Dwell In.

† **Jeremiah 30:16-18 (KJV)** Therefore all they that devour thee shall be devoured; and all thine adversaries, every one of them, shall go into captivity; and they that spoil thee shall be a spoil, and all that prey upon thee will I give for a prey. For I will restore health unto thee, and I will heal thee of thy wounds,

saith the LORD; because they called thee an Outcast, saying, This is Zion, whom no man seeketh after. Thus saith the LORD; Behold, I will bring again the captivity of Jacob's tents, and have mercy on his dwelling places; and the city shall be builded upon her own heap, and the palace shall remain after the manner thereof.

† **Joel 2:25–26 (KJV)** And I will restore to you the years that the locust hath eaten, the cankerworm, and the caterpiller, and the palmerworm, My great army which I sent among you. And ye shall eat in plenty, and be satisfied, and praise the name of the Lord your God, that hath dealt wondrously with you: and My people shall never be ashamed.

† **Acts 3:20-22 (AMPC)** [20] And that He may send [to you] the Christ (the Messiah), Who before was designated *and* appointed for you—even Jesus, [21] Whom heaven must receive [and retain] until the time for the complete restoration of all that God spoke by the mouth of all His holy prophets for ages past [from the most ancient time in the memory of man]. [22] Thus Moses said *to the forefathers*, The Lord God will raise up for you a Prophet from among your brethren as [He raised up] me; Him you shall listen to *and* understand by hearing *and* heed in all things whatever He tells you.

† **Galatians 6:1 (AMPC)** Brethren, if any person is overtaken in misconduct or sin of any sort, you who

are spiritual [who are responsive to and controlled by the Spirit] should set him right and restore and reinstate him, without any sense of superiority and with all gentleness, keeping an attentive eye on yourself, lest you should be tempted also.

Right / Righteousness

I am the righteousness of God in Christ. To know that I am in right standing with God is so wonderful, because I know that it was nothing that I had done. I only made the right decision to say "Yes" to accept Jesus as my Lord and Savior. There has never been a person or place, nor will there ever be for me, than right here with my Lord. Yes, I owe it all to Jesus, I boast on Him only !!!

† **Psalm 112:2–4 (KJV)** His seed shall be mighty upon earth: the generation of the upright shall be blessed. Wealth and riches shall be in his house: and his righteousness endureth for ever. Unto the upright there ariseth light in the darkness: he is gracious, and full of compassion, and righteous.

† **Proverbs 8:18 (KJV)** Riches and honour are with me; yea, durable riches and righteousness.

† **Matthew 5:6 (KJV)** Blessed are they which do hunger and thirst after righteousness: for they shall be filled.

† **John 15:18–20 (AMPC)** ¹⁸ If the world hates you, know that it hated Me before it hated you. ¹⁹ If you belonged to the world, the world would treat you with affection *and* would love you as its own. But because you are not of the world [no longer one with it], but I

have chosen (selected) you out of the world, the world hates (detests) you. ²⁰ Remember that I told you, A servant is not greater than his master [is not superior to him]. If they persecuted Me, they will also persecute you; if they kept My word *and* obeyed My teachings, they will also keep *and* obey yours.

† **Romans 3:23 (KJV)** For all have sinned, and come short of the glory of God;

† **Romans 3:20-26 (AMPC)** ²⁰ For no person will be justified (made righteous, acquitted, and judged acceptable) in His sight by observing the works prescribed by the Law. For [the real function of] the Law is to make men recognize *and* be conscious of sin [not mere perception, but an acquaintance with sin which works toward repentance, faith, and holy character]. ²¹ But now the righteousness of God has been revealed independently *and* altogether apart from the Law, although actually it is attested by the Law and the Prophets, ²² Namely, the righteousness of God which comes by believing *with* personal trust *and* confident reliance on Jesus Christ (the Messiah). [And it is meant] for all who believe. For there is no distinction, ²³ Since all have sinned and are falling short of the honor *and* glory which God bestows *and* receives. ²⁴ [All] are justified *and* made upright *and* in right standing with God, freely *and* gratuitously by His grace (His unmerited favor and mercy), through the redemption which is [provided] in Christ Jesus,

⁲⁵ Whom God put forward [before the eyes of all] as a mercy seat *and* propitiation by His blood [the cleansing and life-giving sacrifice of atonement and reconciliation, to be received] through faith. This was to show God's righteousness, because in His divine forbearance He had passed over *and* ignored former sins without punishment. ²⁶ It was to demonstrate *and* prove at the present time (in the now season) that He Himself is righteous and that He justifies *and* accepts as righteous him who has [true] faith in Jesus.

† **Romans 3:25 (AMPC)** Whom God put forward [before the eyes of all] as a mercy seat *and* propitiation by His blood [the cleansing and life-giving sacrifice of atonement and reconciliation, to be received] through faith. This was to show God's righteousness, because in His divine forbearance He had passed over *and* ignored former sins without punishment.

† **Romans 5:18 (AMPC)** Well then, as one man's trespass [one man's false step and falling away led] to condemnation for all men, so one Man's act of righteousness [leads] to acquittal *and* right standing with God and life for all men.

† **2 Corinthians 5:21 (AMPC)** For our sake He made Christ [virtually] to be sin Who knew no sin, so that in *and* through Him we might become [endued with, viewed as being in, and examples of] the righteousness of God [what we ought to be, approved and acceptable

and in right relationship with Him, by His goodness].

† **2 Corinthians 5:21 (KJV)** For He hath made Him to be sin for us, Who knew no sin; that we might be made the righteousness of God in Him.

† **2 Ephesians 2:9 (AMPC)** Not because of works [not the fulfillment of the Law's demands], lest any man should boast. [It is not the result of what anyone can possibly do, so no one can pride himself in it or take glory to himself.]

† **Philippians 3:9 (KJV)** And be found in him, not having mine own righteousness, which is of the law, but that which is through the faith of Christ, the righteousness which is of God by faith:

† **Philippians 3:7-9 (NASB)** ⁷But whatever things were gain to me, those things I have counted as loss for the sake of Christ. ⁸More than that, I count all things to be loss in view of the surpassing value of knowing Christ Jesus my Lord, for whom I have suffered the loss of all things, and count them but rubbish so that I may gain Christ,⁹ and may be found in Him, not having a righteousness of my own derived from *the* Law, but that which is through faith in Christ, the righteousness which *comes* from God on the basis of faith,

† **Philippians 3:7-9 (AMPC)** ⁷But whatever former things I had that might have been gains to me, I have come to consider as [one combined] loss for Christ's sake. ⁸Yes, furthermore, I count everything as loss

compared to the possession of the priceless privilege (the overwhelming preciousness, the surpassing worth, and supreme advantage) of knowing Christ Jesus my Lord *and* of progressively becoming more deeply *and* intimately acquainted with Him [of perceiving and recognizing and understanding Him more fully and clearly]. For His sake I have lost everything and consider it all to be mere rubbish (refuse, dregs), in order that I may win (gain) Christ (the Anointed One), [9] And that I may [actually] be found *and* known as in Him, not having any [self-achieved] righteousness that can be called my own, based on my obedience to the Law's demands (ritualistic uprightness and supposed right standing with God thus acquired), but possessing that [genuine righteousness] which comes through faith in Christ (the Anointed One), the [truly] right standing with God, which comes from God by [saving] faith.

† **1 Peter 3:12 (KJV)** For the eyes of the Lord are over the righteous, and His ears are open unto their prayers: but the face of the Lord is against them that do evil.

† **2 Peter 2:20-21 (KJV)** [20] For if after they have escaped the pollutions of the world through the knowledge of the Lord and Saviour Jesus Christ, they are again entangled therein, and overcome, the latter end is worse with them than the beginning. [21] For it had been better for them not to have known the way of righteousness, than, after they have known it, to turn

from the holy commandment delivered unto them.

† **<u>Revelation 19:6–8 (KJV)</u>** And I heard as it were the voice of a great multitude, and as the voice of many waters, and as the voice of mighty thunderings, saying, Alleluia: for the Lord God omnipotent reigneth. Let us be glad and rejoice, and give honour to Him: for the marriage of the Lamb is come, and His wife hath made herself ready. And to her was granted that she should be arrayed in fine linen, clean and white: for the fine linen is the righteousness of saints.

Sacrifice

Sacrifice to me means giving something that I want or even need in order that someone else can have what he or she wants or needs. In the world, people say that is crazy, but I know that I am not missing out; I may have to wait or maybe not. I know that God will supply the need or want. I would either receive a guaranteed return and possibly a multiplied return back, depending on the kind of giving it is.

† **1 Samuel 15:22 (NASB)** Samuel said, "Has the LORD as much delight in burnt offerings and sacrifices As in obeying the voice of the LORD? Behold, to obey is better than sacrifice, *And* to heed than the fat of rams.

† **Psalm 54:6 (KJV)** I will freely sacrifice unto Thee: I will praise Thy name, O Lord; for it is good.

† **Matthew 26:38–39 (KJV)** Then saith He unto them, My soul is exceeding sorrowful, even unto death: tarry ye here, and watch with Me. And He went a little farther, and fell on His face, and prayed, saying, O my Father, if it be possible, let this cup pass from Me: nevertheless not as I will, but as Thou wilt.

† **Romans 12:1 (KJV)** I beseech you therefore, brethren, by the mercies of God, that ye present your bodies a living sacrifice, holy, acceptable unto God,

which is your reasonable service.

† **Ephesians 5:1–3 (KJV)** Be ye therefore followers of God, as dear children; And walk in love, as Christ also hath loved us, and hath given Himself for us an offering and a sacrifice to God for a sweetsmelling savour.

† **Hebrews 9:22-24 (AMPC)** [In fact] under the Law almost everything is purified by means of blood, and without the shedding of blood there is neither release from sin *and* its guilt *nor* the remission of the due *and* merited punishment for sins. By such means, therefore, it was necessary for the [earthly] copies of the heavenly things to be purified, but the actual heavenly things themselves [required far] better *and* nobler sacrifices than these. For Christ (the Messiah) has not entered into a sanctuary made with [human] hands, only a copy *and* pattern *and* type of the true one, but [He has entered] into heaven itself, now to appear in the [very] presence of God on our behalf.

† **Hebrews 10:12–14 (NASB)** but He, having offered one sacrifice for sins for all time, SAT DOWN AT THE RIGHT HAND OF GOD, waiting from that time onward UNTIL HIS ENEMIES BE MADE A FOOTSTOOL FOR HIS FEET. For by one offering He has perfected for all time those who are sanctified.

† **Hebrews 13:15 (KJV)** By Him therefore let us offer the sacrifice of praise to God continually, that is, the fruit of our lips giving thanks to His name.

† **Hebrews 13:15 (AMPC)** Through Him, therefore, let us constantly *and* at all times offer up to God a sacrifice of praise, which is the fruit of lips that thankfully acknowledge *and* confess *and* glorify His name.

Self-Control

Having self-control is being able to speak to someone with unconditional love, even though the situation makes you want to scream out. We have to be slow to speak; this gives us the opportunity to hear what the Holy Spirit is saying. As we are listening to Him, He is comforting us and giving us the words to say. (A Fruit of the Spirit attribute)

† **Proverbs 14:29 (NASB)** He who is slow to anger has great understanding, But he who is quick-tempered exalts folly.

† **Proverbs 21:23 (NKJV)** Whoever guards his mouth and tongue Keeps his soul from troubles.

† **Matthew 5:5 (KJV)** Blessed are the meek: for they shall inherit the earth.

† **2 Timothy 1:7 (AMPC)** For God did not give us a spirit of timidity (of cowardice, of craven and cringing and fawning fear), but [He has given us a spirit] of power and of love and of calm *and* well-balanced mind *and* discipline *and* self-control.

† **James 3:7–10 (AMPC)** ⁷ For every kind of beast and bird, of reptile and sea animal, can be tamed and has been tamed by human genius (nature). ⁸ But the human tongue can be tamed by no man. It is a restless

(undisciplined, irreconcilable) evil, full of deadly poison. ⁹ With it we bless the Lord and Father, and with it we curse men who were made in God's likeness! ¹⁰ Out of the same mouth come forth blessing and cursing. These things, my brethren, ought not to be so.

Selflessness

I remember when the kids were at home, how when I cooked breakfast or any meal, I would make sure they had their fill and then I would eat. My husband would usually ask for more meat, so I would give what was left. I believe this is why now, it doesn't matter if I have meat on my plate or not. I would always enjoy the food that I have, and I was happy because they were happy.

† **Proverbs 11:25 (NIV)** A generous person will prosper; whoever refreshes others will be refreshed.

† **Isaiah 32:8 (NIV)** But the noble, openhearted, *and* liberal man devises noble things; and he stands for what is noble, openhearted, *and* generous.

† **John 5:30 (AMPC)** I am able to do nothing from Myself [independently, of My own accord—but only as I am taught by God and as I get His orders]. Even as I hear, I judge [I decide as I am bidden to decide. As the voice comes to Me, so I give a decision], and My judgment is right (just, righteous), because I do not seek or consult My own will [I have no desire to do what is pleasing to Myself, My own aim, My own purpose] but only the will and pleasure of the Father Who sent Me.

† **2 Corinthians 9:7 (NIV)** Each of you should give

what you have decided in your heart to give, not reluctantly or under compulsion, for God loves a cheerful giver.

† **2 Corinthians 9:11 (AMPC)** Thus you will be enriched in all things and in every way, so that you can be generous, and [your generosity as it is] administered by us will bring forth thanksgiving to God.

† **1 Thessalonians 5:14 (AMPC)** And we earnestly beseech you, brethren, admonish (warn and seriously advise) those who are out of line [the loafers, the disorderly, and the unruly]; encourage the timid and fainthearted, help and give your support to the weak souls, [and] be very patient with everybody [always keeping your temper].

† **Hebrews 13:16 (AMPC)** Do not forget or neglect to do kindness and good, to be generous and distribute and contribute to the needy [of the church as embodiment and proof of fellowship], for such sacrifices are pleasing to God.

Serving

The law of association is so important, especially in volunteering (serving). This is actually on-the-job training, and don't worry about not getting paid; God will promote us in due season, plus we are gaining experience. Our time is currency, we should use it wisely.

On day, I met a young man named Thomas on public transportation. I had just come from serving at the Joseph Business School. I don't know who spoke first. I believe I nodded and smiled as a gesture as I passed him. We hit it off well; he was sharing with me that his mom died when he was eight years old. As we were talking, I was led to give him my business card, two flyers of our youth events that were coming up. I also felt led to give him my autographed copy of Deena Marie Carr's latest book.

I thanked God for revealing to me that He is confirming the Word preached along with our pastor's teaching on the law of confession. The next day another man of God talked about how good it is to maintain your convictions. He talked about, as a youth, how his friends on the street corner seemed disappointed in him, because he was being more influenced by them. That was the same subject I was talking to Thomas about, how I pointed out to my son that there are some people I went to school with who are still on the corner, now over thirty years later. I told Thomas like I told my son to stay focused on doing better and watch whom you associate with, not that you are better than they are (see Romans 12:3 here). It was surely God confirming that I did the right thing by investing that time with Thomas and my son. I thank God for using me!

Always remember we serve as unto the Lord, now that we are children of God; we are in His service.

† **Matthew 20:28 (KJV)** For even the Son of Man came not to be served but to serve others and to give his life as a ransom for many."

† **Romans 12:1 (NKJV)** [Living Sacrifices to God] I beseech you therefore, brethren, by the mercies of God, that you present your bodies a living sacrifice, holy, acceptable to God, *which is* your reasonable service.

† **Romans 12:3 (KJV)** For I say, through the grace given unto me, to every man that is among you, not to think of himself more highly than he ought to think; but to think soberly, according as God hath dealt to every man the measure of faith.

† **1 Corinthians 6:19 (KJV)** What? know ye not that your body is the Temple of the Holy Ghost which is in you, which ye have of God, and ye are not your own?

† **Galatians 4:7-9 (NKJV)** Therefore you are no longer a slave but a son, and if a son, then an heir of God through Christ. But then, indeed, when you did not know God, you served those which by nature are not gods. But now after you have known God, or rather are known by God, how *is it that* you turn again to the weak and beggarly elements, to which you desire again to be in bondage?

† **Ephesians 6:6-8 (KJV)** Not with eyeservice, as menpleasers; but as the servants of Christ, doing the will of God from the heart; With good will doing service, as to the Lord, and not to men: Knowing that whatsoever good thing any man doeth, the same shall he receive of the Lord, whether he be bond or free.

† **Colossians 3:23–25 (NIV)** ^{23} Whatever you do, work at it with all your heart, as working for the Lord, not for human masters, ^{24} since you know that you will receive an inheritance from the Lord as a reward. It is the Lord Christ you are serving. ^{25} Anyone who does wrong will be repaid for their wrongs, and there is no favoritism.

† **1 Peter 4:10 (NIV)** Each of you should use whatever gift you have received to serve others, as faithful stewards of God's grace in its various forms.

Souls

God made man. He made the body out of the dust, but the spirit, He breathe into Him, Life. Man is a spirit; he/she possess a soul/mind and lives in a body. (See Genesis 2:7 here) Both the soul/mind became alive when the spirit did. The spirit is always to control the mind and the body, which is God's plan for us.

Adam and Eve sinned against God by their disobedience. When they sinned, their spirit died and had to be separated from God (God is Life). I don't believe that the spirit literally died, because a spirit can't die, but their mind/soul was replaced with fear. Fear blinds the mind so that the voice of God can't be heard by humans. Satan knows this! Fear is his tactic. God wants us to wake up to this fact & open up our minds to the Truth.

The Truth is the only way to Free us; by renewing our minds with the Word of God (See John 8:32 and Romans 12:2 here) !!!

God allowed them to eat from all the trees in the Garden of Eden, except one; the tree of the knowledge of good and evil. Because Adam and Eve decided to eat from this tree, God had to put them out of the Garden, for the sake of mankind, in order to be redeemed. Outside of the Garden was nothing but dry ground. It is like in our lives, when we are outside the will of God, there is dryness; a confused wilderness. They had to learn how to feed themselves by growing their own food.

The soul is the mind of the spirit. We are used by God to save our siblings. Not necessarily our natural siblings, but our divine being siblings; the spirit. I believe by us saving and helping the human body (physical people); we are also helping the soul/mind of their spirit. In the physical world where we can see things, it is really the way or condition of the minds of people of how the spirit is doing. Read Psalm 82 (see here), not as being a body, but as a spirit. The strong has to help the weak soul/mind.

God always talks about the fatherless. God is the Father, only to those who accepts Jesus as their Lord and Savior, who becomes a Believer. God even talks about the widows; He would become the husbandman to the Believer. So even if/when in the natural, we are without parents or a husband, God is willing and able to take this role, if we accept Jesus as our Lord and Savior. God is Omnipotent, Omnipresence and Omniscience!

I believe this is the kind of soul in the spirit of a person that we see in the natural: After Adam fell and since Christ, for those who hasn't accepted Jesus, but also the Believers who have not renewed the minds with the word of God.

The needy people, really needs someone to help them. They are hungry, naked, homeless and sick, but there are also needy spirits filled with hatred, unforgiveness and ignorance (lack of who they are or can be in Christ). Their spirits can't help themselves, without them hearing the Gospel of Jesus and/or their minds being renewed with the word of God. Some even think they know the word of God, but if their thoughts are contrary to God's word or mixed with the worldly way (and are not cast down, in Jesus' name), they can't know God's will. The scriptures that they have read or memorized is just words (they made them void of power). God's word is power, but it has to be spoken by the Believer and mixed with the faith of Jesus.

Their spirit is helpless, it is without hope, because their mind, which is its soul is without hope. I believe this is what Jesus meant, when He said, poor in spirit. The spirit is poor, because the soul/mind is poor, without nourishment; the word of God is our food. We need our daily bread!

God is reconciling our soul (the mind of our spirit) back to Him. We are gods (See Psalm 82 right here); our spirits are gods, our body is just along for the ride, but is very important and are needed while we are in this earth. Our body is acting out in the physical world, the condition of the soul (the mind of the spirit).

We must stop looking at our physical body, but attend to our spirit, which will heal our bodies also, by the renewing our mind with the word of God. God has always been talking about our spirit.

We now need to read the whole Bible again, without the body as primary. In 1 Thessalonians 5:23 (see here also), the spirit is first. Selah!

† **Genesis 2:7 (AMPC)** Then the Lord God formed man from the dust of the ground and breathed into his nostrils the breath *or* spirit of life, and man became a living being.

† **Genesis 2:7 (KJV)** And the Lord God formed man of the dust of the ground, and breathed into his nostrils the breath of life; and man became a living soul.

† **Psalm 19:7 (KJV)** The law of the Lord is perfect, converting the soul: the testimony of the Lord is sure, making wise the simple.

† **Psalm 23:3 (KJV)** He restoreth my soul: He leadeth me in the paths of righteousness for His name's sake.

† **Psalm 34:1–3 (KJV)** I will bless the Lord at all times: His praise shall continually be in my mouth. My soul shall make her boast in the Lord: the humble shall hear thereof, and be glad. O magnify the Lord with me, and let us exalt His name together.

† **Psalm 42:1 (KJV)** As the hart panteth after the water brooks, so panteth my soul after thee, O God.

† **Psalm 62:1-5 (KJV)** Truly my soul waiteth upon God: from him cometh my salvation. He only is my rock and my salvation; he is my defence; I shall not be greatly moved. How long will ye imagine mischief against a man? ye shall be slain all of you: as a bowing wall shall ye be, and as a tottering fence. They only consult to cast him down from his excellency: they delight in lies: they bless with their mouth, but they curse inwardly. Selah. My soul, wait thou only upon God; for my expectation is from him.

† **Psalm 62:1-5 (NIV)** Truly my soul finds rest in God; my salvation comes from him. Truly he is my rock and my salvation; he is my fortress, I will never be shaken. How long will you assault me? Would all of you throw me down—this leaning wall, this tottering fence? Surely they intend to topple me from my lofty place; they take delight in lies. With their mouths they bless, but in their hearts they curse. Yes, my soul, find rest in God; my hope comes from him.

† **Psalm 82:1–8 (NIV)** [1] God presides in the great assembly; he renders judgment among the "gods": [2] "How long will you defend the unjust and show partiality to the wicked? [3] Defend the weak and the fatherless; uphold the cause of the poor and the oppressed. [4] Rescue the weak and the needy; deliver them from the hand of the wicked. [5] "The 'gods' know nothing, they understand nothing. They walk about in darkness; all the foundations of the earth are shaken.

⁶ "I said, 'You are "gods"; you are all sons of the Most High.' ⁷ But you will die like mere mortals; you will fall like every other ruler." ⁸ Rise up, O God, judge the earth, for all the nations are your inheritance.

† **Psalm 103:1–2, 22 (KJV)** Bless the Lord, O my soul: and all that is within me, bless His holy name. Bless the Lord, O my soul, and forget not all His benefits: Bless the Lord, all His works in all places of His dominion: bless the Lord, O my soul.

† **Proverbs 10:3 (KJV)** The Lord will not suffer the soul of the righteous to famish: but He casteth away the substance of the wicked.

† **Proverbs 11:17 (KJV)** The merciful man doeth good to his own soul: but he that is cruel troubleth his own flesh.

† **Proverbs 11:25 (KJV)** The liberal soul shall be made fat: and he that watereth shall be watered also himself.

† **Ezekiel 18:4–5 (AMPC)** Behold, all souls are Mine; as the soul of the father, so also the soul of the son is Mine; the soul that sins, it shall die. But if a man is [uncompromisingly] righteous (upright and in right standing with God) and does what is lawful and right,

† **Jonah 2:7 (KJV)** When my soul fainted within me I remembered the Lord: and my prayer came in unto Thee, into Thine holy temple.

† **Matthew 16:25–27 (KJV)** For whosoever will save his life shall lose it: and whosoever will lose his life

for My sake shall find it. For what is a man profited, if he shall gain the whole world, and lose his own soul? or what shall a man give in exchange for his soul? For the Son of man shall come in the glory of His Father with His angels; and then He shall reward every man according to his works.

† **John 14:6 (KJV)** Jesus saith unto him, I am the way, the truth, and the life: no man cometh unto the Father, but by me.

† **John 14:6-7 (MSG)** Jesus said, "I am the Road, also the Truth, also the Life. No one gets to the Father apart from me. If you really knew me, you would know my Father as well. From now on, you do know him. You've even seen him!"

† **John 8:32 (NKJV)** And you shall know the truth, and the truth shall make you free.

† **Acts 2:40–42 (AMPC)** [40] And [Peter] solemnly *and* earnestly witnessed (testified) and admonished (exhorted) with much more continuous speaking *and* warned (reproved, advised, encouraged) them, saying, Be saved from this crooked (perverse, wicked, unjust) generation. [41] Therefore those who accepted *and* welcomed his message were baptized, and there were added that day about 3,000 souls. [42] And they steadfastly persevered, devoting themselves constantly to the instruction and fellowship of the apostles, to the breaking of bread [including the Lord's Supper] and prayers.

† **Romans 8:15–17 (KJV)** For ye have not received the spirit of bondage again to fear; but ye have received the Spirit of adoption, whereby we cry, Abba, Father. The Spirit itself beareth witness with our spirit, that we are the children of God: And if children, then heirs; heirs of God, and joint-heirs with Christ; if so be that we suffer with him, that we may be also glorified together.

† **Romans 12:2 (AMPC)** ² Do not be conformed to this world (this age), [fashioned after and adapted to its external, superficial customs], but be transformed (changed) by the [entire] renewal of your mind [by its new ideals and its new attitude], so that you may prove [for yourselves] what is the good and acceptable and perfect will of God, *even* the thing which is good and acceptable and perfect [in His sight for you].

† **Romans 13:1 (KJV)** Let every soul be subject unto the higher powers. For there is no power but of God: the powers that be are ordained of God.

† **1 Thessalonians 5:23 (NIV)** May God himself, the God of peace, sanctify you through and through. May your whole spirit, soul and body be kept blameless at the coming of our Lord Jesus Christ.

† **Hebrews 4:12 (KJV)** For the word of God is quick, and powerful, and sharper than any twoedged sword, piercing even to the dividing asunder of soul and spirit, and of the joints and marrow, and is a discerner of the thoughts and intents of the heart.

† **Hebrews 10:37–39 (AMPC)** ³⁷ For still a little while (a very little while), and the Coming One will come and He will not delay. ³⁸ But the just shall live by faith [My righteous servant shall live by his conviction respecting man's relationship to God and divine things, and holy fervor born of faith and conjoined with it]; and if he draws back *and* shrinks in fear, My soul has no delight *or* pleasure in him. ³⁹ But our way is not that of those who draw back to eternal misery (perdition) and are utterly destroyed, but we are of those who believe [who cleave to and trust in and rely on God through Jesus Christ, the Messiah] *and* by faith preserve the soul.

† **Hebrews 13:16–17 (NIV)** And do not forget to do good and to share with others, for with such sacrifices God is pleased. Have confidence in your leaders and submit to their authority, because they keep watch over you as those who must give an account. Do this so that their work will be a joy, not a burden, for that would be of no benefit to you.

† **James 5:20 (KJV)** Let him know, that he which converteth the sinner from the error of his way shall save a soul from death, and shall hide a multitude of sins.

† **2 Peter 3:9–14 (KJV)** The Lord is not slack concerning His promise, as some men count slackness; but is longsuffering to us-ward, not willing that any should perish, but that all should come to repentance.

But the day of the Lord will come as a thief in the night; in the which the heavens shall pass away with a great noise, and the elements shall melt with fervent heat, the earth also and the works that are therein shall be burned up. Seeing then that all these things shall be dissolved, what manner of persons ought ye to be in all holy conversation and godliness, Looking for and hasting unto the coming of the day of God, wherein the heavens being on fire shall be dissolved, and the elements shall melt with fervent heat? Nevertheless we, according to His promise, look for new heavens and a new earth, wherein dwelleth righteousness. Wherefore, beloved, seeing that ye look for such things, be diligent that ye may be found of Him in peace, without spot, and blameless.

† **3 John 1:2 (KJV)** Beloved, I wish above all things that thou mayest prosper and be in health, even as thy soul prospereth.

Sow / Sower / Sowed / Sowing

God has given us the ultimate gift of freewill, where we can make the decision to "sow or give" His way. Sowing into someone's life is a privilege and an opportunity. The privilege is the pleasure of knowing that we have changed someone's life for the better by giving to meet a need for them. This also shows if we are good or bad stewards of what God has entrusted to us. The opportunity is that we can reap a multiplied harvest, when we sow in good ground (soil, person, place, company, or ministry). If we didn't hear God on how and when to give/sow, we may not reap anything.

† **Genesis 26:12 (KJV)** Then Isaac sowed in that land, and received in the same year an hundredfold: and the Lord blessed him.

† **Psalm 37:26 (KJV)** He is ever merciful, and lendeth; and his seed is blessed.

† **Psalm 126:5–6 (KJV)** They that sow in tears shall reap in joy. He that goeth forth and weepeth, bearing precious seed, shall doubtless come again with rejoicing, bringing his sheaves with him.

† **Ecclesiastes 11:1–2 (NLT)** Send your grain across the seas, and in time, profits will flow back to you. But divide your investments among many places, for you

do not know what risks might lie ahead.

† **Ecclesiastes 11:4–6 (KJV)** He that observeth the wind shall not sow; and he that regardeth the clouds shall not reap. As thou knowest not what is the way of the spirit, nor how the bones do grow in the womb of her that is with child: even so thou knowest not the works of God who maketh all. In the morning sow thy seed, and in the evening withhold not thine hand: for thou knowest not whether shall prosper, either this or that, or whether they both shall be alike good.

† **Amos 9:13 (KJV)** Behold, the days come, saith the Lord, that the plowman shall overtake the reaper, and the treader of grapes him that soweth seed; and the mountains shall drop sweet wine, and all the hills shall melt.

† **Matthew 6:19–21 (AMPC)** Do not gather and heap up and store up for yourselves treasures on earth, where moth and rust and worm consume and destroy, and where thieves break through and steal. But gather and heap up and store for yourselves treasures in heaven, where neither moth nor rust nor worm consume and destroy, and where thieves do not break through and steal; For where your treasure is, there will your heart be also.

† **Mark 4:14 (KJV)** The sower soweth the word.

† **Mark 4:15–20 (NKJV)** And these are the ones by the wayside where the word is sown. When they hear,

Satan comes immediately and takes away the word that was sown in their hearts. These likewise are the ones sown on stony ground who, when they hear the word, immediately receive it with gladness; and they have no root in themselves, and so endure only for a time. Afterward, when tribulation or persecution arises for the word's sake, immediately they stumble. Now these are the ones sown among thorns; they are the ones who hear the word, and the cares of this world, the deceitfulness of riches, and the desires for other things entering in choke the word, and it becomes unfruitful. But these are the ones sown on good ground, those who hear the word, accept it, and bear fruit: some thirtyfold, some sixty, and some a hundred."

† **1 Corinthians 12:22–24 (AMPC)** But instead, there is [absolute] necessity for the parts of the body that are considered the more weak. And those [parts] of the body which we consider rather ignoble are [the very parts] which we invest with additional honor, and our unseemly parts and those unsuitable for exposure are treated with seemliness (modesty and decorum), Which our more presentable parts do not require. But God has so adjusted (mingled, harmonized, and subtly proportioned the parts of) the whole body, giving the greater honor and richer endowment to the inferior parts which lack [apparent importance],

Spiritual Warfare

Spiritual warfare is an everyday occurrence when born-again. We are not fighting people, but the devil and his cohort in the spirit, the invisible realm. We fight the good fight of faith by confessing God's word to the situation. If we are not born-again, we basically have given up, there is really nothing to fight for, and because we don't know that it is the devil that is hurting us. We think it is people, but it is Satan controlling the mind and actions of those people. His nature is only to kill, steal, and destroy us. Some people believe that they are doing well, without God, but the devil is only using them for his purposes. They will not last long, and if they do have a long life, and has not confessed Jesus is their Lord and Savior, they will live for all eternity in hell with the devil.

When you use God's word, He is the One who fights for us. Get your mind and life back; God will help you, if you ask Him.

† **<u>Isaiah 54:17 (KJV)</u>** No weapon that is formed against thee shall prosper; and every tongue that shall rise against thee in judgment thou shalt condemn. This is the heritage of the servants of the Lord, and their righteousness is of me, saith the Lord.

† **Matthew 5:44 (KJV)** But I say unto you, Love your enemies, bless them that curse you, do good to them that hate you, and pray for them which despitefully use you, and persecute you;

† **Mark 16:17–18 (KJV)** And these signs shall follow them that believe; In my name shall they cast out devils; they shall speak with new tongues; They shall take up serpents; and if they drink any deadly thing, it shall not hurt them; they shall lay hands on the sick, and they shall recover.

† **1 Corinthians 14:2 (KJV)** For he that speaketh in an unknown tongue speaketh not unto men, but unto God: for no man understandeth him; howbeit in the spirit he speaketh mysteries.

† **2 Corinthians 10:5 (KJV)** Casting down imaginations, and every high thing that exalteth itself against the knowledge of God, and bringing into captivity every thought to the obedience of Christ;

† **Ephesians 4:27 (KJV)** Neither give place to the devil.

† **Ephesians 6:10–18 (KJV)** Finally, my brethren, be strong in the Lord, and in the power of his might. Put on the whole armour of God, that ye may be able to stand against the wiles of the devil. For we wrestle not against flesh and blood, but against principalities, against powers, against the rulers of the darkness of this world, against spiritual wickedness in high places. Wherefore take unto you the whole armour of God,

that ye may be able to withstand in the evil day, and having done all, to stand. Stand therefore, having your loins girt about with truth, and having on the breastplate of righteousness; And your feet shod with the preparation of the gospel of peace; Above all, taking the shield of faith, wherewith ye shall be able to quench all the fiery darts of the wicked. And take the helmet of salvation, and the sword of the Spirit, which is the word of God: Praying always with all prayer and supplication in the Spirit, and watching thereunto with all perseverance and supplication for all saints;

† **Ephesians 6:10–18 (AMPC)** [10] In conclusion, be strong in the Lord [be empowered through your union with Him]; draw your strength from Him [that strength which His boundless might provides]. [11] Put on God's whole armor [the armor of a heavy-armed soldier which God supplies], that you may be able successfully to stand up against [all] the strategies *and* the deceits of the devil. [12] For we are not wrestling with flesh and blood [contending only with physical opponents], but against the despotisms, against the powers, against [the master spirits who are] the world rulers of this present darkness, against the spirit forces of wickedness in the heavenly (supernatural) sphere. [13] Therefore put on God's complete armor, that you may be able to resist *and* stand your ground on the evil day [of danger], and, having done all [the crisis demands], to stand [firmly in your place]. [14] Stand therefore [hold your ground], having tightened the belt

of truth around your loins and having put on the breastplate of integrity *and* of moral rectitude *and* right standing with God, ^{15} And having shod your feet in preparation [to face the enemy with the firm-footed stability, the promptness, and the readiness produced by the good news] of the Gospel of peace. ^{16} Lift up over all the [covering] shield of saving faith, upon which you can quench all the flaming missiles of the wicked [one]. ^{17} And take the helmet of salvation and the sword that the Spirit wields, which is the Word of God. ^{18} Pray at all times (on every occasion, in every season) in the Spirit, with all [manner of] prayer and entreaty. To that end keep alert and watch with strong purpose *and* perseverance, interceding in behalf of all the saints (God's consecrated people).

† **Hebrews 10:30 (KJV)** For we know Him that hath said, Vengeance belongeth unto Me, I will recompense, saith the Lord. And again, The Lord shall judge His people.

† **1 Timothy 6:12 (NIV)** Fight the good fight of the faith. Take hold of the eternal life to which you were called when you made your good confession in the presence of many witnesses.

† **James 4:7 (KJV)** Submit yourselves therefore to God. Resist the devil, and he will flee from you.

† **James 5:14 (KJV)** ... anointing him with oil in the name of the Lord:

† **<u>1 John 4:4 (KJV)</u>** Ye are of God, little children, and have overcome them: because greater is He that is in you, than he that is in the world.

Surrender

I surrender all to God, because I know that if I don't, I am defeated to death by Satan. The devil will use our mind that will control our bodies to do his will. It is either God or the devil in control. This should not be a hard decision, but the reason that it may be for some is because the devil, which is the god of the world, has blinded the minds of those who don't or won't believe in God. When you don't choose Jesus, by default, you have automatically have chosen Satan. There is no other way to Heaven, only through Jesus. For Eternity, we are going up (Heaven) or down (hell). Each individual has to make their own choice. **Surrender to Jesus !!!**

† **Deuteronomy 30:19 (NASB)** I call heaven and earth to witness against you today, that I have set before you life and death, the blessing and the curse. So choose life in order that you may live, you and your descendants,

† **Isaiah 55:1-3 (AMPC)** Wait *and* listen, everyone who is thirsty! Come to the waters; and he who has no money, come, buy and eat! Yes, come, buy [priceless, spiritual] wine and milk without money and without price [simply for the self-surrender that accepts the blessing]. Why do you spend your money for that

which is not bread, and your earnings for what does not satisfy? Hearken diligently to Me, and eat what is good, and let your soul delight itself in fatness [the profuseness of spiritual joy]. Incline your ear [submit and consent to the divine will] and come to Me; hear, and your soul will revive; and I will make an everlasting covenant *or* league with you, even the sure mercy (kindness, goodwill, and compassion) promised to David.

† **Romans 1:16–17 (AMPC)** For I am not ashamed of the Gospel (good news) of Christ, for it is God's power working unto salvation [for deliverance from eternal death] to everyone who believes with a personal trust and a confident surrender and firm reliance, to the Jew first and also to the Greek, For in the Gospel a righteousness which God ascribes is revealed, both springing from faith and leading to faith [disclosed through the way of faith that arouses to more faith]. As it is written, The man who through faith is just and upright shall live and shall live by faith.

† **Romans 6:16 (AMPC)** Do you not know that if you continually surrender yourselves to anyone to do his will, you are the slaves of him whom you obey, whether that be to sin, which leads to death, or to obedience which leads to righteousness (right doing and right standing with God)?

† **Galatians 3:7–9 (AMPC)** Know and understand that

it is [really] the people [who live] by faith who are [the true] sons of Abraham. And the Scripture, foreseeing that God would justify (declare righteous, put in right standing with Himself) the Gentiles in consequence of faith, proclaimed the Gospel [foretelling the glad tidings of a Savior long beforehand] to Abraham in the promise, saying, In you shall all the nations [of the earth] be blessed. So then, those who are people of faith are blessed and made happy and favored by God [as partners in fellowship] with the believing and trusting Abraham.

† **Titus 2:12–14 (AMPC)** It has trained us to reject and renounce all ungodliness (irreligion) and worldly (passionate) desires, to live discreet (temperate, self-controlled), upright, devout (spiritually whole) lives in this present world, Awaiting and looking for the [fulfillment, the realization of our] blessed hope, even the glorious appearing of our great God and Savior Christ Jesus (the Messiah, the Anointed One), Who gave Himself on our behalf that He might redeem us (purchase our freedom) from all iniquity and purify for Himself a people [to be peculiarly His own, people who are] eager and enthusiastic about [living a life that is good and filled with] beneficial deeds.

Testimony

My testimony is that I began to realize that God has been trying to wake me up. I began to see how many of my family and love ones were no longer in the living, they died too young. I wish that we had gotten this revelation together that God loves us so much that He sent His Son to die to save us from this false life.

I love God because He first loved me, but I also love God because He chose me to be able to learn and keep learning, Who He is and what He have for me to do for Him. This one truth I have learned shall make someone free …

The Church is Not a building, the Church is the body of Christ !!!

This isn't a time to play church. People go to a church building for a meeting/service, not realizing that we (people) are the Church. It is time for us to wake up and get real about who we are in Christ and what He would have us to do. The Church is the ones responsible for the way things are in the world. God through our Lord Jesus has given us authority to eradicate injustice in all its forms. The Holy Spirit is here to lead us.

Sons of God in the Church, let us rise up to not only tell our testimony, but let our lives demonstrate our testimonies !!!

† **Psalm 19:14 (KJV)** Let the words of my mouth, and the meditation of my heart, be acceptable in thy sight, O Lord, my strength, and my redeemer.

† **John 1:6–9 (NIV)** ⁶There was a man sent from God whose name was John. ⁷He came as a witness to testify concerning that light, so that through him all might believe. ⁸He himself was not the light; he came only as a witness to the light. ⁹The true light that gives light to everyone was coming into the world.

† **John 15:25–27 (AMPC)** But [this is so] that the word written in their Law might be fulfilled, They hated Me without a cause. But when the Comforter (Counselor, Helper, Advocate, Intercessor, Strengthener, Standby) comes, Whom I will send to you from the Father, the Spirit of Truth Who comes (proceeds) from the Father, He [Himself] will testify regarding Me. But you also will testify and be My witnesses, because you have been with Me from the beginning.

† **Acts 10:41–43 (AMPC)** Not by all the people but to us who were chosen (designated) beforehand by God as witnesses, who ate and drank with Him after He arose from the dead. And He charged us to preach to the people and to bear solemn testimony that He is the God-appointed and God-ordained Judge of the living and the dead. To Him all the prophets testify (bear

witness) that everyone who believes in Him [who adheres to, trusts in, and relies on Him, giving himself up to Him] receives forgiveness of sins through His name.

† **1 Thessalonians 1:9–10 (AMPC)** For they themselves volunteer testimony concerning us, telling what an entrance we had among you, and how you turned to God from [your] idols to serve a God Who is alive and true and genuine, And [how you] look forward to and await the coming of His Son from heaven, Whom He raised from the dead—Jesus, Who personally rescues and delivers us out of and from the wrath [bringing punishment] which is coming [upon the impenitent] and draws us to Himself investing us with all the privileges and rewards of the new life in Christ, the Messiah].

† **1 John 5:5–13 (NIV)** [5] Who is it that overcomes the world? Only the one who believes that Jesus is the Son of God. [6] This is the one who came by water and blood—Jesus Christ. He did not come by water only, but by water and blood. And it is the Spirit who testifies, because the Spirit is the truth. [7] For there are three that testify: [8] the Spirit, the water and the blood; and the three are in agreement. [9] We accept human testimony, but God's testimony is greater because it is the testimony of God, which he has given about his Son. [10] Whoever believes in the Son of God accepts this testimony. Whoever does not believe God has

made him out to be a liar, because they have not believed the testimony God has given about his Son. [11] And this is the testimony: God has given us eternal life, and this life is in his Son. [12] Whoever has the Son has life; whoever does not have the Son of God does not have life. [Concluding Affirmations] [13] I write these things to you who believe in the name of the Son of God so that you may know that you have eternal life.

Thankful / Thanksgiving

I am thankful for who God is. I am thankful that He heard my cry and delivered me out of darkness and translated me into the kingdom of His dear Son. Thanksgiving to God for me is not only once a year on Thanksgiving Day—but every day. Thank You, Father God, for Your love for me! Thank You, my Lord Jesus, for Your precious blood! Thank You, my sweet Holy Spirit, for always being with me!

Being thankful is being grateful. Being grateful to me is an automatic response. I didn't realize by accepting Jesus as my Lord and Savior, how my life would change. I have said to many people, "I am really enjoying the second half of my life." The first forty years of my life is nothing compared to the last twenty years in Christ. I know how wonderful the rest of my remaining years will be (up to 120), here on earth and for all Eternity. I am so grateful to be a son of God, for that old man is dead and is no longer here. I am so thankful to be loved by God.

Thanksgiving to God is all year round !!!

† **Psalm 28:6–8 (KJV)** ⁶ Blessed be the LORD, because he hath heard the voice of my supplications. ⁷ The LORD is my strength and my shield; my heart trusted

in him, and I am helped: therefore my heart greatly rejoiceth; and with my song will I praise him. ⁸ The LORD is their strength, and he is the saving strength of his anointed.

† **Psalm 66:8 (AMPC)** Bless our God, O peoples, give Him grateful thanks *and* make the voice of His praise be heard,

† **Psalm 100:4 (KJV)** Enter into His gates with thanksgiving, and into His courts with praise: be thankful unto Him, and bless His name.

† **Psalm 118:23–25 (KJV)** This is the Lord's doing; it is marvellous in our eyes. This is the day which the Lord hath made; we will rejoice and be glad in it. Save now, I beseech thee, O Lord: O Lord, I beseech thee, send now prosperity.

† **Matthew 22:14 (KJV)** For many are called, but few are chosen.

† **1 Corinthians 2:9 (NIV)** However, as it is written: "What no eye has seen, what no ear has heard, and what no human mind has conceived" — the things God has prepared for those who love him—

† **1 Corinthians 8:3 (AMPC)** But if one loves God truly [with affectionate reverence, prompt obedience, and grateful recognition of His blessing], he is known by God [recognized as worthy of His intimacy and love, and he is owned by Him].

† **Colossians 1:12-13 (KJV)** Giving thanks unto the

Father, which hath made us meet to be partakers of the inheritance of the saints in light: Who hath delivered us from the power of darkness, and hath translated us into the kingdom of his dear Son:

† **Colossians 3:15 (NIV)** Let the peace of Christ rule in your hearts, since as members of one body you were called to peace. And be thankful.

† **Colossians 3:17 (KJV)** And whatsoever ye do in word or deed, do all in the name of the Lord Jesus, giving thanks to God and the Father by him.

† **1 Thessalonians 5:18 (KJV)** In every thing give thanks: for this is the will of God in Christ Jesus concerning you.

† **2 Timothy 2:21 (KJV)** If a man therefore purge himself from these, he shall be a vessel unto honour, sanctified, and meet for the master's use, and prepared unto every good work.

† **Hebrews 13:15 (AMPC)** Through Him, therefore, let us constantly and at all times offer up to God a sacrifice of praise, which is the fruit of lips that thankfully acknowledge and confess and glorify His name.

Tithe and Offerings

I thank God that I didn't second guess tithe and offerings. I didn't grow up in a church building. I joined a ministry for a while, as a teenager, but I was one who would go when someone invited me on Easter, Christmas or to an event. I was one who had even said the word hypocrite. Now I know the reason I said it; it was what people around me was saying. We say things without having proof. People stay defeated in life (the past for me), because of the things that are said and done by others to them and eventually we say and believe them.

Life for me is so much better, things are so much clearer. When I feel the pressures of life, by faith, I cast my cares over unto the Lord. The issue may be still there, but I am at peace, and God always works them out.

If I even sense some confusion (sometimes there is no one around that hears me), but I would say something like this, in the name of Jesus, "Shut up, Satan, I know that is you." I become calm, because I chose God over the devil.

Likewise, in paying my tithe and giving my offerings, they are for my benefit. Yes, it does help a lot to do mission work and help in the upkeep of our church buildings, but when we don't pay our tithe and give our offerings, it is we who have lost a great benefit. It is not too late to begin, I am happy that I did.

† **Genesis 14:18–20 (KJV)** And Melchizedek king of Salem brought forth bread and wine: and he was the priest of the most high God. And he blessed him, and said, Blessed be Abram of the most high God, possessor of heaven and earth: And blessed be the most high God, which hath delivered thine enemies into thy hand. And he gave him tithes of all.

† **Genesis 14:17-20 (MSG)** After Abram returned from defeating Kedorlaomer and his allied kings, the king of Sodom came out to greet him in the Valley of Shaveh, the King's Valley. Melchizedek, king of Salem, brought out bread and wine—he was priest of The High God—and blessed him: Blessed be Abram by The High God, Creator of Heaven and Earth. And blessed be The High God, who handed your enemies over to you. Abram gave him a tenth of all the recovered plunder.

† **Leviticus 27:30-31 (AMPC)** And all the tithe of the land, whether of the seed of the land or of the fruit of the tree, is the Lord's; it is holy to the Lord. And if a man wants to redeem any of his tithe, he shall add a fifth to it.

† **2 Kings 12:4–5 (KJV)** And Jehoash said to the priests, All the money of the dedicated things that is brought into the house of the Lord, even the money of every one that passeth the account, the money that every man is set at, and all the money that cometh into any man's heart to bring into the house of the Lord, Let the priests take it to them, every man of his acquaintance: and let them repair the breaches of the house, wheresoever any breach shall be found.

† **Malachi 3:10 (KJV)** Bring ye all the tithes into the storehouse, that there may be meat in mine house, and prove me now herewith, saith the Lord of hosts, if I will not open you the windows of heaven, and pour you out a blessing, that there shall not be room enough to receive it.

† **Hebrews 13:16 (AMPC)** Do not forget or neglect to do kindness and good, to be generous and distribute and contribute to the needy [of the church as embodiment and proof of fellowship], for such sacrifices are pleasing to God.

Transformation

Some Christians wonders why their pastor and/or church leaders doesn't tell/show them how to have God work mightily in their lives, as seen in theirs. Actually I have learned that they are telling and showing us in what they say and do; all the time. We have to be sensitive to the Holy Spirit to have discernment that gives us the ear to hear and the eye to see.

Our studying of the Word of God is renewing our minds to allow us to receive revelation from God; that is to meditate His word day and night as in Joshua 1:8. By not continuing to renew our minds with the Word of God, this allows Satan to slip in and blind our minds. It is like the sunlight shining through the window of your house, and someone pulled the shade down.

Meditating is thinking over and over on His word, why not, the devil replays doubt and unbelief, if we let him by worrying.

As we renew our minds with the Word of God, we are being transformed into the image of God. By reading and meditating on the Word of God, we will begin replacing fear-based thinking with great mountain moving faith. We can see and hear clearly.

God's transformation is done from the inside out, as we keep hearing the Word and obeying Him.

† **Romans 12:1–2 (NIV)** Therefore, I urge you, brothers and sisters, in view of God's mercy, to offer your bodies as a living sacrifice, holy and pleasing to God—this is your true and proper worship. Do not conform to the pattern of this world, but be transformed by the renewing of your mind. Then you will be able to test and approve what God's will is—his good, pleasing and perfect will.

† **Romans 12:1-2 (MSG)** So here's what I want you to do, God helping you: Take your everyday, ordinary life—your sleeping, eating, going-to-work, and walking-around life—and place it before God as an offering. Embracing what God does for you is the best thing you can do for him. Don't become so well-adjusted to your culture that you fit into it without even thinking. Instead, fix your attention on God. You'll be changed from the inside out. Readily recognize what he wants from you, and quickly respond to it. Unlike the culture around you, always dragging you down to its level of immaturity, God brings the best out of you, develops well-formed maturity in you.

† **2 Corinthians 5:1-4 (KJV)** For we know that if our earthly house of this tabernacle were dissolved, we have a building of God, an house not made with hands, eternal in the heavens. For in this we groan,

earnestly desiring to be clothed upon with our house which is from heaven: If so be that being clothed we shall not be found naked. For we that are in this tabernacle do groan, being burdened: not for that we would be unclothed, but clothed upon, that mortality might be swallowed up of life.

† **2 Corinthians 5:1-4 (MSG)** For instance, we know that when these bodies of ours are taken down like tents and folded away, they will be replaced by resurrection bodies in heaven—God-made, not handmade—and we'll never have to relocate our "tents" again. Sometimes we can hardly wait to move—and so we cry out in frustration. Compared to what's coming, living conditions around here seem like a stopover in an unfurnished shack, and we're tired of it! We've been given a glimpse of the real thing, our true home, our resurrection bodies! The Spirit of God whets our appetite by giving us a taste of what's ahead. He puts a little of heaven in our hearts so that we'll never settle for less.

† **Colossians 3:10 (KJV)** And have put on the new man, which is renewed in knowledge after the image of him that created him:

† **Colossians 3:1–10 (NKJV)** If then you were raised with Christ, seek those things which are above, where Christ is, sitting at the right hand of God. Set your mind on things above, not on things on the earth. For you died, and your life is hidden with Christ in God.

When Christ who is our life appears, then you also will appear with Him in glory. Therefore put to death your members which are on the earth: fornication, uncleanness, passion, evil desire, and covetousness, which is idolatry. Because of these things the wrath of God is coming upon the sons of disobedience, in which you yourselves once walked when you lived in them. But now you yourselves are to put off all these: anger, wrath, malice, blasphemy, filthy language out of your mouth. Do not lie to one another, since you have put off the old man with his deeds, and have put on the new man who is renewed in knowledge according to the image of Him who created him,

† **Hebrews 5:12-14 (MSG)** I have a lot more to say about this, but it is hard to get it across to you since you've picked up this bad habit of not listening. By this time you ought to be teachers yourselves, yet here I find you need someone to sit down with you and go over the basics on God again, starting from square one—baby's milk, when you should have been on solid food long ago! Milk is for beginners, inexperienced in God's ways; solid food is for the mature, who have some practice in telling right from wrong.

† **Hebrews 12:26–28 (AMPC)** Then [at Mount Sinai] His voice shook the earth, but now He has given a promise: Yet once more I will shake and make tremble not only the earth but also the [starry] heavens. Now

this expression, Yet once more, indicates the final removal and transformation of all [that can be] shaken—that is, of that which has been created—in order that what cannot be shaken may remain and continue. Let us therefore, receiving a kingdom that is firm and stable and cannot be shaken, offer to God pleasing service and acceptable worship, with modesty and pious care and godly fear and awe;

Trinity

I know you have heard the question, "How can God be three persons in One, which is called the Trinity?" The Trinity is God the Father, God the Son, God the Holy Spirit. It is the same for us, being created by God in His image and after His likeness. We are a three-part being: spirit, soul, and body. We all have been given the capability to become in the natural, a father or mother, a brother or sister, for we are someone's son or daughter. Life in the world may have caused us to not function in some of these positions. But God is faithful, always! (See 1 Thessalonians 5:23 under "Promise.")

† **1 John 5:7–8 (KJV)** For there are three that bear record in heaven, the Father, the Word, and the Holy Ghost: and these three are one. And there are three that bear witness in earth, the Spirit, and the water, and the blood: and these three agree in one.

† **1 John 5:7–8 (AMPC)** So there are three witnesses in heaven: the Father, the Word and the Holy Spirit, and these three are One; and there are three witnesses on the earth: the Spirit, the water, and the blood; and these three agree [are in unison; their testimony coincides].

† **John 14:8–10 (KJV)** Philip saith unto Him, Lord,

show us the Father, and it sufficeth us. Jesus saith unto him, Have I been so long time with you, and yet hast thou not known Me, Philip? he that hath seen Me hath seen the Father; and how sayest thou then, Show us the Father? Believest thou not that I am in the Father, and the Father in Me? the words that I speak unto you I speak not of Myself: but the Father that dwelleth in Me, He doeth the works.

† **John 14:16 (KJV)** And I will pray the Father, and He shall give you another Comforter, that He may abide with you for ever;

† **John 14:26 (KJV)** But the Comforter, which is the Holy Ghost, whom the Father will send in My name, He shall teach you all things, and bring all things to your remembrance, whatsoever I have said unto you.

† **John 15:25–27 (KJV)** But this cometh to pass, that the word might be fulfilled that is written in their law, They hated Me without a cause. But when the Comforter is come, whom I will send unto you from the Father, even the Spirit of truth, which proceedeth from the Father, He shall testify of Me: And ye also shall bear witness, because ye have been with Me from the beginning.

True / Truth

The world is looking for the truth. We as children of God are the ones God wants to use in order to show the world through us, what is truth. He is the true and living God. The proof is manifested works done by the Father in Heaven, but is seen through our good works in helping people in need—by loving one another and by living by faith. If this is not our purpose in life, then the only other alternative is that we have let the devil lie to us.

The Truth is = Jesus is Lord !!!

† **Deuteronomy 18:21–22 (AMPC)** ²¹ And if you say in your [minds and] hearts, How shall we know which words the Lord has not spoken? ²² When a prophet speaks in the name of the Lord, if the word does not come to pass or prove true, that is a word which the Lord has not spoken. The prophet has spoken it presumptuously; you shall not be afraid of him.

† **Psalm 19:8–10 (KJV)** The statutes of the Lord are right, rejoicing the heart: the commandment of the Lord is pure, enlightening the eyes. The fear of the Lord is clean, enduring for ever: the judgments of the Lord are true and righteous altogether. More to be desired are they than gold, yea, than much fine gold: sweeter also than honey and the honeycomb.

† **Psalm 33:4 (KJV)** For the word of the Lord is right, and all his works are done in truth. Thy word is true from the beginning: and every one of thy righteous judgments endureth for ever.

† **Psalm 119:160 (KJV)** Thy word is true from the beginning: and every one of thy righteous judgments endureth for ever.

† **Isaiah 45:22–24 (AMPC)** Look to Me and be saved, all the ends of the earth! For I am God, and there is no other. I have sworn by Myself, the word is gone out of My mouth in righteousness and shall not return, that unto Me every knee shall bow, every tongue shall swear [allegiance]. Only in the Lord shall one say, I have righteousness (salvation and victory) and strength [to achieve]. To Him shall all come who were incensed against Him, and they shall be ashamed.

† **Jeremiah 10:10 (KJV)** But the LORD is the true God, he is the living God, and an everlasting king: at his wrath the earth shall tremble, and the nations shall not be able to abide his indignation.

† **Jeremiah 10:10 (AMPC)** But the LORD is the true God, he is the living God, and an everlasting king: at his wrath the earth shall tremble, and the nations shall not be able to abide his indignation.

† **Zechariah 7:8–10 (KJV)** And the word of the Lord came unto Zechariah, saying, Thus speaketh the Lord of hosts, saying, Execute true judgment, and shew

mercy and compassions every man to his brother: And oppress not the widow, nor the fatherless, the stranger, nor the poor; and let none of you imagine evil against his brother in your heart.

† **Matthew 7:15–16 (AMPC)** Beware of false prophets, who come to you dressed as sheep, but inside they are devouring wolves. You will fully recognize them by their fruits. Do people pick grapes from thorns, or figs from thistles?

† **Matthew 11:6 (AMPC)** And blessed (happy, fortunate, and to be envied) is he who takes no offense at Me and finds no cause for stumbling in or through Me and is not hindered from seeing the Truth.

† **John 4:23–24 (AMPC)** A time will come, however, indeed it is already here, when the true (genuine) worshipers will worship the Father in spirit and in truth (reality); for the Father is seeking just such people as these as His worshipers. God is a Spirit (a spiritual Being) and those who worship Him must worship Him in spirit and in truth (reality).

† **John 8:43–45 (AMPC)** [43] Why do you misunderstand what I say? It is because you are unable to hear what I am saying. [You cannot bear to listen to My message; your ears are shut to My teaching.] [44] You are of your father, the devil, and it is your will to practice the lusts *and* gratify the desires [which are characteristic] of your father. He was a murderer from the beginning and does not stand in the truth, because there is no

truth in him. When he speaks a falsehood, he speaks what is natural to him, for he is a liar [himself] and the father of lies *and* of all that is false. ⁴⁵ But because I speak the truth, you do not believe Me [do not trust Me, do not rely on Me, or adhere to Me].

† **John 8:43-45 (NIV)** ⁴³ Why is my language not clear to you? Because you are unable to hear what I say. ⁴⁴ You belong to your father, the devil, and you want to carry out your father's desires. He was a murderer from the beginning, not holding to the truth, for there is no truth in him. When he lies, he speaks his native language, for he is a liar and the father of lies. ⁴⁵ Yet because I tell the truth, you do not believe me!

† **John 15:1–3 (AMPC)** I am the True Vine, and My Father is the Vinedresser. Any branch in Me that does not bear fruit [that stops bearing] He cuts away (trims off, takes away); and He cleanses and repeatedly prunes every branch that continues to bear fruit, to make it bear more and richer and more excellent fruit. You are cleansed and pruned already, because of the word which I have given you [the teachings I have discussed with you].

† **John 17:2–8 (AMPC)** [Just as] You have granted Him power and authority over all flesh (all humankind), [now glorify Him] so that He may give eternal life to all whom You have given Him. And this is eternal life: [it means] to know (to perceive,

recognize, become acquainted with, and understand) You, the only true and real God, and [likewise] to know Him, Jesus [as the] Christ (the Anointed One, the Messiah), Whom You have sent. I have glorified You down here on the earth by completing the work that You gave Me to do. And now, Father, glorify Me along with Yourself and restore Me to such majesty and honor in Your presence as I had with You before the world existed. I have manifested Your Name [I have revealed Your very Self, Your real Self] to the people whom You have given Me out of the world. They were Yours, and You gave them to Me, and they have obeyed and kept Your word. Now [at last] they know and understand that all You have given Me belongs to You [is really and truly Yours]. For the [uttered] words that You gave Me I have given them; and they have received and accepted [them] and have come to know positively and in reality [to believe with absolute assurance] that I came forth from Your presence, and they have believed and are convinced that You did send Me.

† **John 17:17–19 (KJV)** Sanctify them through Thy truth: Thy word is truth. As Thou hast sent Me into the world, even so have I also sent them into the world. And for their sakes I sanctify Myself, that they also might be sanctified through the truth.

† **Acts 5:38–39 (KJV)** And now I say unto you, Refrain from these men, and let them alone: for if this counsel

or this work be of men, it will come to nought: But if it be of God, ye cannot overthrow it; lest haply ye be found even to fight against God.

† **Romans 3:3–4 (KJV)** For what if some did not believe? shall their unbelief make the faith of God without effect? God forbid: yea, let God be true, but every man a liar; as it is written, That thou mightiest be justified in thy sayings, and mightest overcome when thou art judged.

† **2 Corinthians 6:7–8 (AMPC)** By [speaking] the word of truth, in the power of God, with the weapons of righteousness for the right hand [to attack] and for the left hand [to defend]; Amid honor and dishonor; in defaming and evil report and in praise and good report. [We are branded] as deceivers (impostors), and [yet vindicated as] truthful and honest.

† **1 Thessalonians 2:13 (AMPC)** And we also [especially] thank God continually for this, that when you received the message of God [which you heard] from us, you welcomed it not as the word of [mere] men, but as it truly is, the Word of God, which is effectually at work in you who believe [exercising its superhuman power in those who adhere to and trust in and rely on it].

† **1 Thessalonians 5:21 (AMPC)** But test and prove all things [until you can recognize] what is good; [to that] hold fast.

† **Hebrews 8:1–3 (AMPC)** Now the main point of what we have to say is this: We have such a High Priest, One Who is seated at the right hand of the majestic [God] in heaven, As officiating Priest, a Minister in the holy places and in the true tabernacle which is erected not by man but by the Lord. For every high priest is appointed to offer up gifts and sacrifices; so it is essential for this [High Priest] to have some offering to make also.

† **James 1:12–18 (KJV)** ¹²Blessed is the man that endureth temptation: for when he is tried, he shall receive the crown of life, which the Lord hath promised to them that love him. ¹³Let no man say when he is tempted, I am tempted of God: for God cannot be tempted with evil, neither tempteth he any man: ¹⁴But every man is tempted, when he is drawn away of his own lust, and enticed. ¹⁵Then when lust hath conceived, it bringeth forth sin: and sin, when it is finished, bringeth forth death. ¹⁶Do not err, my beloved brethren. ¹⁷Every good gift and every perfect gift is from above, and cometh down from the Father of lights, with whom is no variableness, neither shadow of turning. ¹⁸Of his own will begat he us with the word of truth, that we should be a kind of firstfruits of his creatures.

† **1 John 2:22 (KJV)** Who is a liar but he that denieth that Jesus is the Christ? He is antichrist, that denieth the Father and the Son.

† **1 John 5:20 (KJV)** And we know that the Son of God is come, and hath given us an understanding, that we may know Him that is true, and we are in Him that is true, even in His Son Jesus Christ. This is the true God, and eternal life.

† **Revelation 19:11–12 (AMPC)** After that I saw heaven opened, and behold, a white horse [appeared]! The One Who was riding it is called Faithful (Trustworthy, Loyal, Incorruptible, Steady) and True, and He passes judgment and wages war in righteousness (holiness, justice, and uprightness). His eyes [blaze] like a flame of fire, and on His head are many kingly crowns (diadems); and He has a title (name) inscribed which He alone knows or can understand.

Understanding

Thank You, Father. In the name of Jesus, I pray for the eyes of our understanding be enlightened to Your will and to Your way and that we shall perform in the way You created us, and that the whole world will be affected by the manifested fruit of our labor of love to You and all mankind. In Jesus' name, Amen.

† **Leviticus 19:31 (AMPC)** Turn not to those [mediums] who have familiar spirits or to wizards; do not seek them out to be defiled by them. I am the Lord your God.

† **Job 32:8 (AMPC)** But there is [a vital force] a spirit [of intelligence] in man, and the breath of the Almighty gives men understanding.

† **Proverbs 3:13 (KJV)** Happy is the man that findeth wisdom, and the man that getteth understanding.

† **Isaiah 11:2-4 (AMPC)** And the Spirit of the Lord shall rest upon Him—the Spirit of wisdom and understanding, the Spirit of counsel and might, the Spirit of knowledge and of the reverential *and* obedient fear of the Lord—And shall make Him of quick understanding, *and* His delight shall be in the reverential *and* obedient fear of the Lord. And He shall not judge by the sight of His eyes, neither decide

by the hearing of His ears; But with righteousness *and* justice shall He judge the poor and decide with fairness for the meek, the poor, *and* the downtrodden of the earth; and He shall smite the earth *and* the oppressor with the rod of His mouth, and with the breath of His lips He shall slay the wicked.

† **Ephesians 1:16–21 (AMPC)** I do not cease to give thanks for you, making mention of you in my prayers. [For I always pray to] the God of our Lord Jesus Christ, the Father of glory, that He may grant you a spirit of wisdom and revelation [of insight into mysteries and secrets] in the [deep and intimate] knowledge of Him, By having the eyes of your heart flooded with light, so that you can know and understand the hope to which He has called you, and how rich is His glorious inheritance in the saints (His set-apart ones), And [so that you can know and understand] what is the immeasurable and unlimited and surpassing greatness of His power in and for us who believe, as demonstrated in the working of His mighty strength, Which He exerted in Christ when He raised Him from the dead and seated Him at His [own] right hand in the heavenly [places], Far above all rule and authority and power and dominion and every name that is named [above every title that can be conferred], not only in this age and in this world, but also in the age and the world which are to come.

† **Ephesians 1:19–22 (KJV)** [19] And what is the

exceeding greatness of his power to us-ward who believe, according to the working of his mighty power, ²⁰ Which he wrought in Christ, when he raised him from the dead, and set him at his own right hand in the heavenly places, ²¹ Far above all principality, and power, and might, and dominion, and every name that is named, not only in this world, but also in that which is to come: ²² And hath put all things under his feet, and gave him to be the head over all things to the church,

† **Ephesians 3:9-12 (AMPC)** ⁹ Also to enlighten all men *and* make plain to them what is the plan [regarding the Gentiles and providing for the salvation of all men] of the mystery kept hidden through the ages *and* concealed until now in [the mind of] God Who created all things *by Christ Jesus*. ¹⁰ [The purpose is] that through the church the complicated, many-sided wisdom of God in all its infinite variety *and* innumerable aspects might now be made known to the angelic rulers and authorities (principalities and powers) in the heavenly sphere. ¹¹ This is in accordance with the terms of the eternal *and* timeless purpose which He has realized *and* carried into effect in [the person of] Christ Jesus our Lord, ¹² In Whom, because of our faith in Him, we dare to have the boldness (courage and confidence) of free access (an unreserved approach to God with freedom and without fear).

† **Ephesians 3:14-21 (NIV)** ¹⁴ For this reason I kneel before the Father, ¹⁵ from whom every family in heaven and on earth derives its name. ¹⁶ I pray that out of his glorious riches he may strengthen you with power through his Spirit in your inner being, ¹⁷ so that Christ may dwell in your hearts through faith. And I pray that you, being rooted and established in love, ¹⁸ may have power, together with all the Lord's holy people, to grasp how wide and long and high and deep is the love of Christ, ¹⁹ and to know this love that surpasses knowledge—that you may be filled to the measure of all the fullness of God. ²⁰ Now to him who is able to do immeasurably more than all we ask or imagine, according to his power that is at work within us, ²¹ to him be glory in the church and in Christ Jesus throughout all generations, for ever and ever! Amen.

† **Colossians 1:9–11 (KJV)** For this cause we also, since the day we heard it, do not cease to pray for you, and to desire that ye might be filled with the knowledge of His will in all wisdom and spiritual understanding; That ye might walk worthy of the Lord unto all pleasing, being fruitful in every good work, and increasing in the knowledge of God; Strengthened with all might, according to His glorious power, unto all patience and longsuffering with joyfulness;

† **Hebrews 5:12-14 (AMPC)** For even though by this time you ought to be teaching others, you actually need someone to teach you over again the very first

principles of God's Word. You have come to need milk, not solid food. For everyone who continues to feed on milk is obviously inexperienced *and* unskilled in the doctrine of righteousness (of conformity to the divine will in purpose, thought, and action), for he is a mere infant [not able to talk yet]! But solid food is for full-grown men, for those whose senses *and* mental faculties are trained by practice to discriminate *and* distinguish between what is morally good *and* noble and what is evil *and* contrary either to divine or human law.

† **Hebrews 11:3 (KJV)** Through faith we understand that the worlds were framed by the word of God, so that things which are seen were not made of things which do appear.

Unity

Let us all, brothers and sisters in Christ, come together in the unity of the faith, and of the knowledge of our Lord and Savior; Jesus Christ to a perfect man, for God has made us to be like Christ in our love, faith, and actions. Yes, God made us and has given us freewill to do good.

We decree unity in the Church and for all division to cease now, in Jesus' name !!!

† **Genesis 2:23–24 (MSG)** The Man said, "... Bone of my bone, flesh of my flesh! Name her Woman for she was made from Man." Therefore a man leaves his father and mother and embraces his wife. They become one flesh.

† **Genesis 2:24 (KJV)** Therefore shall a man leave his father and his mother, and shall cleave unto his wife: and they shall be one flesh.

† **Deuteronomy 6:6–7 (AMPC)** And these words which I am commanding you this day shall be [first] in your [own] minds and hearts; [then] You shall whet and sharpen them so as to make them penetrate, and teach and impress them diligently upon the [minds and] hearts of your children, and shall talk of them when you sit in your house and when you walk by the way,

and when you lie down and when you rise up.

† **Psalm 133:1 (KJV)** Behold, how good and how pleasant it is for brethren to dwell together in unity!

† **Matthew 18:20 (KJV)** For where two or three are gathered together in My name, there am I in the midst of them.

† **Mark 3:24–25 (KJV)** And if a kingdom be divided against itself, that kingdom cannot stand. And if a house be divided against itself, that house cannot stand.

† **Luke 5:5–7 (NIV)** Simon answered, "Master, we've worked hard all night and haven't caught anything. But because you say so, I will let down the nets." When they had done so, they caught such a large number of fish that their nets began to break. So they signaled their partners in the other boat to come and help them, and they came and filled both boats so full that they began to sink.

† **Acts 2:1–2 (KJV)** And when the day of Pentecost was fully come, they were all with one accord in one place. And suddenly there came a sound from heaven as of a rushing mighty wind, and it filled all the house where they were sitting.

† **Acts 2:46 (NIV)** Every day they continued to meet together in the temple courts. They broke bread in their homes and ate together with glad and sincere hearts,

† **Romans 15:5–7 (KJV)** Now the God of patience and consolation grant you to be likeminded one toward another according to Christ Jesus: That ye may with one mind and one mouth glorify God, even the Father of our Lord Jesus Christ. Wherefore receive ye one another, as Christ also received us to the glory of God.

† **1 Corinthians 1:10 (KJV)** Now I beseech you, brethren, by the name of our Lord Jesus Christ, that ye all speak the same thing, and that there be no divisions among you; but that ye be perfectly joined together in the same mind and in the same judgment.

† **2 Corinthians 6:14–15 (AMPC)** Do not be unequally yoked with unbelievers [do not make mismated alliances with them or come under a different yoke with them, inconsistent with your faith]. For what partnership have right living *and* right standing with God with iniquity *and* lawlessness? Or how can light have fellowship with darkness? What harmony can there be between Christ and Belial [the devil]? Or what has a believer in common with an unbeliever?

† **Ephesians 4:13 (KJV)** Till we all come in the unity of the faith, and of the knowledge of the Son of God, unto a perfect man, unto the measure of the stature of the fulness of Christ:

† **Ephesians 4:11–16 (KJV)** ¹¹ And he gave some, apostles; and some, prophets; and some, evangelists; and some, pastors and teachers; ¹² For the perfecting of the saints, for the work of the ministry, for the

edifying of the body of Christ: ¹³ Till we all come in the unity of the faith, and of the knowledge of the Son of God, unto a perfect man, unto the measure of the stature of the fulness of Christ: ¹⁴ That we henceforth be no more children, tossed to and fro, and carried about with every wind of doctrine, by the sleight of men, and cunning craftiness, whereby they lie in wait to deceive; ¹⁵ But speaking the truth in love, may grow up into him in all things, which is the head, even Christ: ¹⁶ From whom the whole body fitly joined together and compacted by that which every joint supplieth, according to the effectual working in the measure of every part, maketh increase of the body unto the edifying of itself in love.

† **2 Peter 1:1–3 (KJV)** ¹ Simon Peter, a servant and an apostle of Jesus Christ, to them that have obtained like precious faith with us through the righteousness of God and our Saviour Jesus Christ: ² Grace and peace be multiplied unto you through the knowledge of God, and of Jesus our Lord, ³ According as his divine power hath given unto us all things that pertain unto life and godliness, through the knowledge of him that hath called us to glory and virtue:

Victorious

G*iving Is God* book has compiled God's Word and discovered that we don't have to live a defeated life, because we have the victory through Christ (See Philippians 4:13 here). **Let us live victorious through Christ !!!**

† **Exodus 7:10–12 (AMPC)** So Moses and Aaron went to Pharaoh and did as the Lord had commanded; Aaron threw down his rod before Pharaoh and his servants, and it became a serpent. Then Pharaoh called for the wise men [skilled in magic and divination] and the sorcerers (wizards and jugglers). And they also, these magicians of Egypt, did similar things with their enchantments and secret arts. For they cast down every man his rod and they became serpents; but Aaron's rod swallowed up their rods.

† **Isaiah 41:10, 13 (AMPC)** Fear not [there is nothing to fear], for I am with you; do not look around you in terror and be dismayed, for I am your God. I will strengthen and harden you to difficulties, yes, I will help you; yes, I will hold you up and retain you with My [victorious] right hand of rightness and justice. For I the Lord your God hold your right hand; I am the Lord, Who says to you, Fear not; I will help you!

† **Jeremiah 1:19 (KJV)** And they shall fight against thee; but they shall not prevail against thee; for I am with thee, saith the Lord, to deliver thee.

† **Joel 3:10 (AMPC)** Beat your plowshares into swords, and your pruning hooks into spears; let the weak say, I am strong [a warrior]!

† **Luke 10:17–19 (AMPC)** The seventy returned with joy, saying, Lord, even the demons are subject to us in Your name! And He said to them, I saw Satan falling like a lightning [flash] from heaven. Behold! I have given you authority and power to trample upon serpents and scorpions, and [physical and mental strength and ability] over all the power that the enemy [possesses]; and nothing shall in any way harm you.

† **Romans 8:37 (AMPC)** Yet amid all these things we are more than conquerors *and* gain a surpassing victory through Him Who loved us.

† **2 Corinthians 2:14 (AMPC)** But thanks be to God, Who in Christ always leads us in triumph [as trophies of Christ's victory] and through us spreads and makes evident the fragrance of the knowledge of God everywhere,

† **Philippians 4:13 (KJV)** I can do all things through Christ which strengtheneth me.

† **Colossians 2:13–15 (KJV)** ^{13} And you, being dead in your sins and the uncircumcision of your flesh, hath he quickened together with him, having forgiven you all

trespasses; ¹⁴ Blotting out the handwriting of ordinances that was against us, which was contrary to us, and took it out of the way, nailing it to his cross; ¹⁵ And having spoiled principalities and powers, he made a shew of them openly, triumphing over them in it.

† **1 John 2:12-14 (KJV)** I write unto you, little children, because your sins are forgiven you for his name's sake. I write unto you, fathers, because ye have known him that is from the beginning. I write unto you, young men, because ye have overcome the wicked one. I write unto you, little children, because ye have known the Father. I have written unto you, fathers, because ye have known him that is from the beginning. I have written unto you, young men, because ye are strong, and the word of God abideth in you, and ye have overcome the wicked one.

† **1 John 5:4 (KJV)** For whatsoever is born of God overcometh the world: and this is the victory that overcometh the world, even our faith.

† **Revelation 2:7 (KJV)** "He that hath an ear, let him hear what the Spirit saith unto the churches; To him that overcometh will I give to eat of the tree of life, which is in the midst of the paradise of God,"

† **Revelation 2:7 (AMPC)** He who is able to hear, let him listen to and give heed to what the Spirit says to the assemblies (churches). To him who overcomes (is victorious), I will grant to eat [of the fruit] of the tree

of life, which is in the paradise of God.

† **Revelation 12:10 (AMPC)** Then I heard a strong (loud) voice in heaven, saying, Now it has come—the salvation and the power and the kingdom (the dominion, the reign) of our God, and the power (the sovereignty, the authority) of His Christ (the Messiah); for the accuser of our brethren, he who keeps bringing before our God charges against them day and night, has been cast out!

† **Revelation 15:2 (KJV)** And I saw as it were a sea of glass mingled with fire: and them that had gotten the victory over the beast, and over his image, and over his mark, and over the number of his name, stand on the sea of glass, having the harps of God.

Voice

God is giving of Himself through His Word to us. Do you hear His voice? We can hear God's voice through His Word; the Word of God is the Bible. God gives us different ways of receiving His voice; we can discern what He is saying to us. We can receive revelation knowledge as we meditate on His word. We receive everything of God by faith, so it is important to believe with your heart (spirit) and confess it with your mouth. We give voice to His word by saying it, and it manifests in our lives. We don't hear God through a violent storm, for that is fear and confusion, which is from the devil. We can hear God clearer, when we are calm. He has a still small voice.

The key is to stay calm.

We all may have heard that we are human sponges. We absorb whatever we see, hear, say, or do. By absorbing a certain thing, such as a behavior, we are transforming into that thing. It will continue to make us its best, whether it is good or bad; life or death is its purpose.

This is why it is so important to be aware of what we see, hear, and say, so that we won't do the things we don't want to do. What we observe begins to absorb into our heart (spirit). Let us continue to renew our minds with the Word of God, which is the only way to allow God to help us.

Most importantly know that Jesus is the Word and He is God. (See John 1:1 right here.)

† **Genesis 1:3, 6, 9, 11, 14, 20, 24, 26, 29 (KJV)** ³ And God said, Let there be light: and there was light. ⁶ And God said, Let there be a firmament in the midst of the waters, and let it divide the waters from the waters. ⁹ And God said, Let the waters under the heaven be gathered together unto one place, and let the dry land appear: and it was so. And ¹¹ God said, Let the earth bring forth grass, the herb yielding seed, and the fruit tree yielding fruit after his kind, whose seed is in itself, upon the earth: and it was so. ¹⁴ And God said, Let there be lights in the firmament of the heaven to divide the day from the night; and let them be for signs, and for seasons, and for days, and years: ²⁰ And God said, Let the waters bring forth abundantly the moving creature that hath life, and fowl that may fly above the earth in the open firmament of heaven. ²⁴ And God said, Let the earth bring forth the living creature after his kind, cattle, and creeping thing, and beast of the earth after his kind: and it was so. And ²⁶ God said, Let us make man in our image, after our likeness: and let them have dominion over the fish of the sea, and over the fowl of the air, and over the cattle, and over all the earth, and over every creeping

thing that creepeth upon the earth. ²⁹ And God said, Behold, I have given you every herb bearing seed, which is upon the face of all the earth, and every tree, in the which is the fruit of a tree yielding seed; to you it shall be for meat.

† **Deuteronomy 30:14 (NASB)** But the word is very near you, in your mouth and in your heart, that you may observe it.

† **2 Samuel 23:2 (KJV)** The Spirit of the LORD spake by me, and his word was in my tongue.

† **1 Kings 19:11–12 (KJV)** And he said, Go forth, and stand upon the mount before the Lord. And, behold, the Lord passed by, and a great and strong wind rent the mountains, and brake in pieces the rocks before the Lord; but the Lord was not in the wind: and after the wind an earthquake; but the Lord was not in the earthquake: And after the earthquake a fire; but the Lord was not in the fire: and after the fire a still small voice.

† **Job 6:24–25 (KJV)** Teach me, and I will hold my tongue: and cause me to understand wherein I have erred. How forcible are right words! but what doth your arguing reprove?

† **Ezekiel 36:36 (NKJV)** Then the nations which are left all around you shall know that I, the LORD, have rebuilt the ruined places *and* planted what was desolate. I, the LORD, have spoken *it,* and I will do *it.*"

† **Daniel 10:12 (KJV)** Then said he unto me, Fear not, Daniel: for from the first day that thou didst set thine heart to understand, and to chasten thyself before thy God, thy words were heard, and I am come for thy words.

† **Psalm 5:3 (KJV)** My voice shalt thou hear in the morning, O Lord; in the morning will I direct my prayer unto thee, and will look up.

† **Psalm 119:171–173 (NKJV)** My lips shall utter praise, For You teach me Your statutes. My tongue shall speak of Your word, For all Your commandments are righteousness. Let Your hand become my help, For I have chosen Your precepts.

† **Proverbs 6:2 (KJV)** Thou art snared with the words of thy mouth, thou art taken with the words of thy mouth.

† **Proverbs 14:25 (KJV)** A true witness delivereth souls: but a deceitful witness speaketh lies.

† **Proverbs 18:21 (KJV)** Death and life are in the power of the tongue: and they that love it shall eat the fruit thereof.

† **Proverbs 21:23 (AMPC)** He who guards his mouth and his tongue keeps himself from troubles.

† **Isaiah 48:3 (AMPC)** I have declared from the beginning the former things [which happened in times past to Israel]; they went forth from My mouth and I made them known; then suddenly I did them, and they

came to pass [says the Lord].

† **Jeremiah 23:28-29 (AMPC)** ²⁸ The prophet who has a dream, let him tell his dream; but he who has My word, let him speak My word faithfully. What has straw in common with wheat [for nourishment]? says the Lord. ²⁹ Is not My word like fire [that consumes all that cannot endure the test]? says the Lord, and like a hammer that breaks in pieces the rock [of most stubborn resistance]?

† **Jeremiah 33:3 (KJV)** Call unto Me, and I will answer thee, and show thee great and mighty things, which thou knowest not.

† **Matthew 12:34 (KJV)** O generation of vipers, how can ye, being evil, speak good things? for out of the abundance of the heart the mouth speaketh.

† **Matthew 12:36-38 (NKJV)** But I say to you that for every idle word men may speak, they will give account of it in the day of judgment. For by your words you will be justified, and by your words you will be condemned."

† **Mark 4:14 (KJV)** The sower soweth the word.

† **Mark 13:10–11 (KJV)** And the gospel must first be published among all nations. But when they shall lead you, and deliver you up, take no thought beforehand what ye shall speak, neither do ye premeditate: but whatsoever shall be given you in that hour, that speak ye: for it is not ye that speak, but the Holy Ghost.

† **John 1:1 (AMPC)** In the beginning [before all time] was the Word (Christ), and the Word was with God, and the Word was God Himself.

† **John 10:5 (KJV)** And a stranger will they not follow, but will flee from him: for they know not the voice of strangers.

† **John 10:26–28 (KJV)** But ye believe not, because ye are not of My sheep, as I said unto you. My sheep hear My voice, and I know them, and they follow Me: And I give unto them eternal life; and they shall never perish, neither shall any man pluck them out of My hand.

† **Romans 7:19–21 (NIV)** [19] For I do not do the good I want to do, but the evil I do not want to do—this I keep on doing. [20] Now if I do what I do not want to do, it is no longer I who do it, but it is sin living in me that does it. [21] So I find this law at work: Although I want to do good, evil is right there with me

† **1 Corinthians 2:4 (KJV)** And my speech and my preaching was not with enticing words of man's wisdom, but in demonstration of the Spirit and of power:

† **Ephesians 6:18–20 (KJV)** Praying always with all prayer and supplication in the Spirit, and watching thereunto with all perseverance and supplication for all saints; And for me, that utterance may be given unto me, that I may open my mouth boldly, to make known

the mystery of the gospel, For which I am an ambassador in bonds: that therein I may speak boldly, as I ought to speak.

† **Philippians 1:27 (KJV)** Only let your conversation be as it becometh the gospel of Christ: that whether I come and see you, or else be absent, I may hear of your affairs, that ye stand fast in one spirit, with one mind striving together for the faith of the gospel;

† **Philippians 3:20 (KJV)** For our conversation is in Heaven; from whence also we look for the Saviour, the Lord Jesus Christ:

† **Colossians 4:4–6 (KJV)** That I may make it manifest, as I ought to speak. Walk in wisdom toward them that are without, redeeming the time. Let your speech be always with grace, seasoned with salt, that ye may know how ye ought to answer every man.

† **Hebrews 4:6–8 (AMPC)** Seeing then that the promise remains over [from past times] for some to enter that rest, and that those who formerly were given the good news about it and the opportunity, failed to appropriate it and did not enter because of disobedience, Again He sets a definite day, [a new] Today, [and gives another opportunity of securing that rest] saying through David after so long a time in the words already quoted, Today, if you would hear His voice and when you hear it, do not harden your hearts. [This mention of a rest was not a reference to their entering into Canaan.] For if Joshua had given them rest, He [God] would not

speak afterward about another day.

† **1 Peter 3:9–11 (KJV)** [9] Not rendering evil for evil, or railing for railing: but contrariwise blessing; knowing that ye are thereunto called, that ye should inherit a blessing. [10] For he that will love life, and see good days, let him refrain his tongue from evil, and his lips that they speak no guile: [11] Let him eschew evil, and do good; let him seek peace, and ensue it.

† **James 3:7-10 (AMPC)** For every kind of beast and bird, of reptile and sea animal, can be tamed and has been tamed by human genius (nature). But the human tongue can be tamed by no man. It is a restless (undisciplined, irreconcilable) evil, full of deadly poison. With it we bless the Lord and Father, and with it we curse men who were made in God's likeness! Out of the same mouth come forth blessing and cursing. These things, my brethren, ought not to be so.

Wealth

I confess and claim that wealth and riches are in my house! Do you? Why not? I have no desire to be in lack another day in my life—not that I desired it at anytime, but I know now that my thinking and my speech had caused the circumstances to come in my life. Now that God has opened my eyes, because someone prayed for me, I can see that I am truly one of His sons. I am the righteousness of God in Christ. I have more than enough to live off and more than enough to give. I, like my Father takes pleasure in giving and I will according to His way of doing things.

† **Deuteronomy 6:10–11 (KJV)** And it shall be, when the Lord thy God shall have brought thee into the land which He sware unto thy fathers, to Abraham, to Isaac, and to Jacob, to give thee great and goodly cities, which thou buildedst not, And houses full of all good things, which thou filledst not, and wells digged, which thou diggedst not, vineyards and olive trees, which thou plantedst not; when thou shalt have eaten and be full;

† **Psalm 52:6-8 (AMPC)** The [uncompromisingly] righteous also shall see [it] and be in reverent fear *and* awe, but about you they will [scoffingly] laugh, saying, See, this is the man who made not God his

strength (his stronghold and high tower) but trusted in *and* confidently relied on the abundance of his riches, seeking refuge *and* security for himself through his wickedness. But I am like a green olive tree in the house of God; I trust in *and* confidently rely on the loving-kindness *and* the mercy of God forever and ever.

† **Psalm 66:12 (KJV)** Thou hast caused men to ride over our heads; we went through fire and through water: but thou broughtest us out into a wealthy place.

† **Psalm 112:3 (KJV)** Wealth and riches shall be in his house: and his righteousness endureth for ever.

† **Psalm 118:25 (KJV)** Save now, I beseech thee, O Lord: O Lord, I beseech thee, send now prosperity.

† **Psalm 122:6-7 (NKJV)** Pray for the peace of Jerusalem: "May they prosper who love you. Peace be within your walls, Prosperity within your palaces."

† **Proverbs 8:12 (KJV)** I wisdom dwell with prudence, and find out knowledge of witty inventions.

† **Proverbs 13:22 (KJV)** A good man leaveth an inheritance to his children's children: and the wealth of the sinner is laid up for the just.

† **Proverbs 18:16 (KJV)** A man's gift maketh room for him, and bringeth him before great men.

† **Isaiah 48:17 (KJV)** Thus saith the Lord, thy Redeemer, the Holy One of Israel; I am theLord thy God which teacheth thee to profit, which leadeth thee

by the way that thou shouldest go.

† **Zechariah 1:17 (NIV)** "Proclaim further: This is what the LORD Almighty says: 'My towns will again overflow with prosperity, and the LORD will again comfort Zion and choose Jerusalem.'"

Wisdom / Wise

To have the wisdom of God is to be wise in the things of God. The Holy Spirit is our teacher who teaches us all things, and to learn from Him, we have to receive through Jesus Christ, for He is the only way. **Be Wise.**

† **1 Kings 3:4-5 (KJV)** And the king went to Gibeon to sacrifice there; for that was the great high place: a thousand burnt offerings did Solomon offer upon that altar. In Gibeon the LORD appeared to Solomon in a dream by night: and God said, Ask what I shall give thee.

† **1 Kings 3:7-14 (AMPC)** ⁷ Now, O Lord my God, You have made Your servant king instead of David my father, and I am but a lad [in wisdom and experience]; I know not how to go out (begin) or come in (finish). ⁸ Your servant is in the midst of Your people whom You have chosen, a great people who cannot be counted for multitude. ⁹ So give Your servant an understanding mind *and* a hearing heart to judge Your people, that I may discern between good and bad. For who is able to judge *and* rule this Your great people? ¹⁰ It pleased the Lord that Solomon had asked this. ¹¹ God said to him, Because you have asked this and have not asked for long life or for riches, nor for the

lives of your enemies, but have asked for yourself understanding to recognize what is just and right, ¹² Behold, I have done as you asked. I have given you a wise, discerning mind, so that no one before you was your equal, nor shall any arise after you equal to you. ¹³ I have also given you what you have not asked, both riches and honor, so that there shall not be any among the kings equal to you all your days. ¹⁴ And if you will go My way, keep My statutes and My commandments as your father David did, then I will lengthen your days.

† **Job 32:6-10 (MSG)** [God's Spirit Makes Wisdom Possible] This is what Elihu, son of Barakel the Buzite, said: "I'm a young man, and you are all old and experienced. That's why I kept quiet and held back from joining the discussion. I kept thinking, 'Experience will tell. The longer you live, the wiser you become.' But I see I was wrong—it's God's Spirit in a person, the breath of the Almighty One, that makes wise human insight possible. The experts have no corner on wisdom; getting old doesn't guarantee good sense. So I've decided to speak up. Listen well! I'm going to tell you exactly what I think.

† **Daniel 1:17 (KJV)** As for these four children, God gave them knowledge and skill in all learning and wisdom: and Daniel had understanding in all visions and dreams.

† **Daniel 1:20 (KJV)** And in all matters of wisdom and

understanding, that the king enquired of them, he found them ten times better than all the magicians and astrologers that were in all his realm.

† **Daniel 1:17-20 (MSG)** God gave these four young men knowledge and skill in both books and life. In addition, Daniel was gifted in understanding all sorts of visions and dreams. At the end of the time set by the king for their training, the head of the royal staff brought them in to Nebuchadnezzar. When the king interviewed them, he found them far superior to all the other young men. None were a match for Daniel, Hananiah, Mishael, and Azariah. And so they took their place in the king's service. Whenever the king consulted them on anything, on books or on life, he found them ten times better than all the magicians and enchanters in his kingdom put together.

† **Psalm 34:10-12 (KJV)** The young lions lack [food] and grow hungry, But they who seek the LORD will not lack any good thing. Come, you children, listen to me; I will teach you to fear the LORD [with awe-inspired reverence and worship Him with obedience]. Who is the man who desires life And loves many days, that he may see good?

† **Proverbs 1:5 (KJV)** A wise man will hear, and will increase learning; and a man of understanding shall attain unto wise counsels:

† **Proverbs 1:20-31 (AMPC)** [20] Wisdom cries aloud in the street, she raises her voice in the markets; [21] She

cries at the head of the noisy intersections [in the chief gathering places]; at the entrance of the city gates she speaks: ²² How long, O simple ones [open to evil], will you love being simple? And the scoffers delight in scoffing and [self-confident] fools hate knowledge? ²³ If you will turn (repent) *and* give heed to my reproof, behold, I [Wisdom] will pour out my spirit upon you, I will make my words known to you. ²⁴ Because I have called and you have refused [to answer], have stretched out my hand and no man has heeded it, ²⁵ And you treated as nothing all my counsel and would accept none of my reproof, ²⁶ I also will laugh at your calamity; I will mock when the thing comes that shall cause you terror *and* panic—²⁷ When your panic comes as a storm *and* desolation and your calamity comes on as a whirlwind, when distress and anguish come upon you. ²⁸ Then will they call upon me [Wisdom] but I will not answer; they will seek me early *and* diligently but they will not find me. ²⁹ Because they hated knowledge and did not choose the reverent *and* worshipful fear of the Lord, ³⁰ Would accept none of my counsel, and despised all my reproof, ³¹ Therefore shall they eat of the fruit of their own way and be satiated with their own devices.

† **Proverbs 3:7 (KJV)** Be not wise in thine own eyes: fear the Lord, and depart from evil.

† **Proverbs 3:18 (KJV)** She is a tree of life to them that lay hold upon her: and happy is every one that

retaineth her.

† **Proverbs 4:7 (KJV)** Wisdom is the principal thing; therefore get wisdom: and with all thy getting get understanding.

† **Proverbs 8:11-17 (KJV)** ^{11} For wisdom is better than rubies; and all the things that may be desired are not to be compared to it. ^{12} I wisdom dwell with prudence, and find out knowledge of witty inventions. ^{13} The fear of the LORD is to hate evil: pride, and arrogancy, and the evil way, and the froward mouth, do I hate. ^{14} Counsel is mine, and sound wisdom: I am understanding; I have strength. ^{15} By me kings reign, and princes decree justice. ^{16} By me princes rule, and nobles, even all the judges of the earth. ^{17} I love them that love me; and those that seek me early shall find me.

† **Proverbs 9:9 (KJV)** Give instruction to a wise man, and he will be yet wiser: teach a just man, and he will increase in learning.

† **Proverbs 9:10 (KJV)** The fear of the Lord is the beginning of wisdom: and the knowledge of the holy is understanding.

† **Proverbs 3:13-20 (KJV)** Happy is the man that findeth wisdom, and the man that getteth understanding. For the merchandise of it is better than the merchandise of silver, and the gain thereof than fine gold. She is more precious than rubies: and all the

things thou canst desire are not to be compared unto her. Length of days is in her right hand; and in her left hand riches and honour. Her ways are ways of pleasantness, and all her paths are peace. She is a tree of life to them that lay hold upon her: and happy is every one that retaineth her. The LORD by wisdom hath founded the earth; by understanding hath he established the heavens. By his knowledge the depths are broken up, and the clouds drop down the dew.

† **Proverbs 14:24 (KJV)** The crown of the wise is their riches: but the foolishness of fools is folly.

† **Mark 3:27 (KJV)** No man can enter into a strong man's house, and spoil his goods, except he will first bind the strong man; and then he will spoil his house.

† **Luke 2:52 (KJV)** And Jesus increased in wisdom and stature, and in favour with God and man.

† **1 Corinthians 1:27 (KJV)** But God hath chosen the foolish things of the world to confound the wise; and God hath chosen the weak things of the world to confound the things which are mighty;

† **Ephesians 1:16–18 (AMPC)** ¹⁶ I do not cease to give thanks for you, making mention of you in my prayers. ¹⁷ [For I always pray to] the God of our Lord Jesus Christ, the Father of glory, that He may grant you a spirit of wisdom and revelation [of insight into mysteries and secrets] in the [deep and intimate] knowledge of Him, ¹⁸ By having the eyes of your heart

flooded with light, so that you can know *and* understand the hope to which He has called you, and how rich is His glorious inheritance in the saints (His set-apart ones),

† **Ephesians 3:9-12 (NIV)** ⁹ and to make plain to everyone the administration of this mystery, which for ages past was kept hidden in God, who created all things. ¹⁰ His intent was that now, through the church, the manifold wisdom of God should be made known to the rulers and authorities in the heavenly realms, ¹¹ according to his eternal purpose that he accomplished in Christ Jesus our Lord. ¹² In him and through faith in him we may approach God with freedom and confidence.

† **1 Thessalonians 5:19 (KJV)** Quench not the Spirit.

† **James 1:5 (NIV)** If any of you lacks wisdom, you should ask God, who gives generously to all without finding fault, and it will be given to you.

† **James 1:5–6 (KJV)** If any of you lack wisdom, let him ask of God, that giveth to all men liberally, and upbraideth not; and it shall be given him. But let him ask in faith, nothing wavering. For he that wavereth is like a wave of the sea driven with the wind and tossed.

† **James 3:13–18 (AMPC)** ¹³ Who is there among you who is wise and intelligent? Then let him by his noble living show forth his [good] works with the [unobtrusive] humility [which is the proper attribute]

of true wisdom. ¹⁴ But if you have bitter jealousy (envy) and contention (rivalry, selfish ambition) in your hearts, do not pride yourselves on it and thus be in defiance of *and* false to the Truth. ¹⁵ This [superficial] wisdom is not such as comes down from above, but is earthly, unspiritual (animal), even devilish (demoniacal). ¹⁶ For wherever there is jealousy (envy) and contention (rivalry and selfish ambition), there will also be confusion (unrest, disharmony, rebellion) and all sorts of evil *and* vile practices. ¹⁷ But the wisdom from above is first of all pure (undefiled); then it is peace-loving, courteous (considerate, gentle). [It is willing to] yield to reason, full of compassion and good fruits; it is wholehearted *and* straightforward, impartial *and* unfeigned (free from doubts, wavering, and insincerity). ¹⁸ And the harvest of righteousness (of conformity to God's will in thought and deed) is [the fruit of the seed] sown in peace by those who work for *and* make peace [in themselves and in others, that peace which means concord, agreement, and harmony between individuals, with undisturbedness, in a peaceful mind free from fears and agitating passions and moral conflicts].

† **Revelation 2:7 (NIV)** Whoever has ears, let them hear what the Spirit says to the churches. To the one who is victorious, I will give the right to eat from the tree of life, which is in the paradise of God.

† **Revelation 5:11-13 (KJV)** And I beheld, and I heard the voice of many angels round about the throne and the beasts and the elders: and the number of them was ten thousand times ten thousand, and thousands of thousands; Saying with a loud voice, Worthy is the Lamb that was slain to receive power, and riches, and wisdom, and strength, and honour, and glory, and blessing. And every creature which is in heaven, and on the earth, and under the earth, and such as are in the sea, and all that are in them, heard I saying, Blessing, and honour, and glory, and power, be unto him that sitteth upon the throne, and unto the Lamb for ever and ever.

† **Revelation 7:11-14 (KJV)** And all the angels stood round about the throne, and about the elders and the four beasts, and fell before the throne on their faces, and worshipped God, Saying, Amen: Blessing, and glory, and wisdom, and thanksgiving, and honour, and power, and might, be unto our God for ever and ever. Amen. And one of the elders answered, saying unto me, What are these which are arrayed in white robes? and whence came they? And I said unto him, Sir, thou knowest. And he said to me, These are they which came out of great tribulation, and have washed their robes, and made them white in the blood of the Lamb.

Work(s)

The works that we do or can do is from the Father, who is in Heaven, for He does the work. Yes, we can do things in our own strength, but why labor in vain, works that doesn't please God? Let us go to the Father in prayer to receive His will in what we should do for the advancement of the Kingdom of God. Listen to His voice and act on it.

Jesus said, we will do Greater works !!!

† **Psalm 73:28 (NKJV)** But *it is* good for me to draw near to God; I have put my trust in the Lord GOD, That I may declare all Your works.

† **Psalm 127:1 (KJV)** Except the Lord build the house, they labour in vain that build it: except the Lord keep the city, the watchman waketh but in vain.

† **Psalm 139:13–14 (NIV)** For You created my inmost being; You knit me together in my mother's womb. I praise You because I am fearfully and wonderfully made; Your works are wonderful, I know that full well.

† **Ecclesiastes 2:10–11 (KJV)** And whatsoever mine eyes desired I kept not from them, I withheld not my heart from any joy; for my heart rejoiced in all my labour: and this was my portion of all my labour. Then

I looked on all the works that my hands had wrought, and on the labour that I had laboured to do: and, behold, all was vanity and vexation of spirit, and there was no profit under the sun.

† **Habakkuk 1:5 (NKJV)** "Look among the nations and watch—Be utterly astounded! For *I will* work a work in your days *Which* you would not believe, though it were told *you.*

† **John 5:19-20 (NASB)** Therefore Jesus answered and was saying to them, "Truly, truly, I say to you, the Son can do nothing of Himself, unless *it is* something He sees the Father doing; for whatever the Father does, these things the Son also does in like manner. For the Father loves the Son, and shows Him all things that He Himself is doing; and *the Father* will show Him greater works than these, so that you will marvel.

† **John 14:12 (KJV)** Verily, verily, I say unto you, He that believeth on me, the works that I do shall he do also; and greater works than these shall he do; because I go unto my Father.

† **2 Corinthians 9:8 (KJV)** And God is able to make all grace abound toward you; that ye, always having all sufficiency in all things, may abound to every good work:

† **Galatians 2:16 (AMPC)** Yet we know that a man is justified or reckoned righteous and in right standing with God not by works of the Law, but [only] through

faith and [absolute] reliance on and adherence to and trust in Jesus Christ (the Messiah, the Anointed One). [Therefore] even we [ourselves] have believed on Christ Jesus, in order to be justified by faith in Christ and not by works of the Law [for we cannot be justified by any observance of the ritual of the Law given by Moses], because by keeping legal rituals and by works no human being can ever be justified (declared righteous and put in right standing with God).

† **Ephesians 2:10 (KJV)** For we are his workmanship, created in Christ Jesus unto good works, which God hath before ordained that we should walk in them.

† **Philippians 1:6 (AMPC)** And I am convinced *and* sure of this very thing, that He Who began a good work in you will continue until the day of Jesus Christ [right up to the time of His return], developing [that good work] *and* perfecting *and* bringing it to full completion in you.

† **Philippians 2:13 (AMPC)** [Not in your own strength] for it is God Who is all the while effectually at work in you [energizing and creating in you the power and desire], both to will and to work for His good pleasure and satisfaction and delight.

† **1 Timothy 6:18 (KJV)** That they do good, that they be rich in good works, ready to distribute, willing to communicate;

Yielding Good Fruit

When God made man, He Blessed him. We were blessed also, because we were the seed inside of Adam. God provided food for us, every herb having in itself, seed(s) to make, to produce, and to yield more. God made sure we didn't run out. Likewise, God made us in His image and after His likeness. He gave us the ability to reproduce and yield good fruit of ourselves by reproducing mankind through childbirth. God also gave us the ability to co-create what we need. First we speak it then we take the actions. We shall create multitude of businesses and jobs so that the earth is back the way God created it.

Let us get to yielding an abundant of good fruit !!!

† **Genesis 1:11–12 (KJV)** And God said, Let the earth bring forth grass, the herb yielding seed, and the fruit tree yielding fruit after his kind, whose seed is in itself, upon the earth: and it was so. And the earth brought forth grass, and herb yielding seed after his kind, and the tree yielding fruit, whose seed was in itself, after his kind: and God saw that it was good.

† **Genesis 1:29 (KJV)** And God said, Behold, I have given you every herb bearing seed, which is upon the face of all the earth, and every tree, in the which is the

fruit of a tree yielding seed; to you it shall be for meat.

† **Genesis 17:6 (KJV)** And I will make thee exceeding fruitful, and I will make nations of thee, and kings shall come out of thee.

† **Job 14:8-9 (KJV)** Though the root thereof wax old in the earth, and the stock thereof die in the ground; Yet through the scent of water it will bud, and bring forth boughs like a plant.

† **Job 14:8-9 (NIV)** Its roots may grow old in the ground and its stump die in the soil, yet at the scent of water it will bud and put forth shoots like a plant.

† **Psalm 67:5–7 (AMPC)** Let the peoples praise You [turn away from their idols] and give thanks to You, O God; let all the peoples praise and give thanks to You! The earth has yielded its harvest [in evidence of God's approval]; God, even our own God, will bless us. God will bless us, and all the ends of the earth shall reverently fear Him.

† **Proverbs 18:20 (KJV)** A man's belly shall be satisfied with the fruit of his mouth; and with the increase of his lips shall he be filled.

† **Ezekiel 36:33-36 (KJV)** 33 Thus saith the Lord GOD; In the day that I shall have cleansed you from all your iniquities I will also cause you to dwell in the cities, and the wastes shall be builded. 34 And the desolate land shall be tilled, whereas it lay desolate in the sight of all that passed by. 35 And they shall say, This land

that was desolate is become like the garden of Eden; and the waste and desolate and ruined cities are become fenced, and are inhabited. ³⁶ Then the heathen that are left round about you shall know that I the LORD build the ruined places, and plant that that was desolate: I the LORD have spoken it, and I will do it.

† **John 15:16 (KJV)** Ye have not chosen Me, but I have chosen you, and ordained you, that ye should go and bring forth fruit, and that your fruit should remain: that whatsoever ye shall ask of the Father in My name, He may give it you.

† **Romans 6:17–19 (AMPC)** But thank God, though you were once slaves of sin, you have become obedient with all your heart to the standard of teaching in which you were instructed and to which you were committed. And having been set free from sin, you have become the servants of righteousness (of conformity to the divine will in thought, purpose, and action). I am speaking in familiar human terms because of your natural limitations. For as you yielded your bodily members [and faculties] as servants to impurity and ever increasing lawlessness, so now yield your bodily members [and faculties] once for all as servants to righteousness (right being and doing) [which leads] to sanctification.

† **Philippians 1: 11 (AMPC)** May you abound in *and* be filled with the fruits of righteousness (of right standing with God and right doing) which come

through Jesus Christ (the Anointed One), to the honor and praise of God [that His glory may be both manifested and recognized].

† **Colossians 1:9-10 (KJV)** For this cause we also, since the day we heard it, do not cease to pray for you, and to desire that ye might be filled with the knowledge of his will in all wisdom and spiritual understanding; That ye might walk worthy of the Lord unto all pleasing, being fruitful in every good work, and increasing in the knowledge of God;

† **Colossians 1:10 (AMPC)** That you may walk (live and conduct yourselves) in a manner worthy of the Lord, fully pleasing to Him and desiring to please Him in all things, bearing fruit in every good work and steadily growing and increasing in and by the knowledge of God [with fuller, deeper, and clearer insight, acquaintance, and recognition].

CONNECT WITH US !!!

www.kingdomofGodflag.com/

www.facebook.com/TRINITYFlag

www.twitter.com/IAcknowledgeHim

www.linkedin.com/in/Claudette-Gunter/

www.ingramcontent.com/pod-product-compliance
Lightning Source LLC
Chambersburg PA
CBHW022054150426
43195CB00008B/134